Decentralisation and Community Participation:
Local Development and Municipal Politics in Cameroon

Numvi Gwaibi

Langaa

Langaa Research & Publishing CIG
Mankon, Bamenda

Publisher:
Langaa RPCIG
Langaa Research & Publishing Common Initiative Group
P.O. Box 902 Mankon
Bamenda
North West Region
Cameroon
Langaagrp@gmail.com
www.langaa-rpcig.net

Distributed in and outside N. America by African Books Collective
orders@africanbookscollective.com
www.africanbookscollective.com

ISBN: 9956-763-91-8

© Numvi Gwaibi 2016

Table of Contents

Chapter IV: Self-Reliance in Anglophone
Cameroon: The Bali Community

Chapter V: Land Tenure and
Inter-Community Politics:

Chapter VI: 'Wrath from the Gods:'
Traditional Institutions and Electoral
Politics in Bali.. 145

Chapter VII: In The Name of Investiture:
CPDM Party Discipline in Mbankomo........................ 179

Acknowledgements

I want to thank the Almighty God for the inspiration, the wisdom, and the strength that guided and enabled me to complete this study. This study is the fruit of hard work, dedication and devotion to achieving a higher level of academic excellence. My research with the Human Economy Programme at the University of Pretoria was funded in collaboration with the Andrew J. Mellon Foundation, and the Social Science Research Council's Next Generation Social Science in Africa Fellowship. Much of the writing up process was carried out at the superb facilities of the Old College House at the University of Pretoria. Special thanks to my supervisor Professor John Sharp for leading me down a challenging but ultimately fruitful path to academic success. To Professor Keith Hart, your incisive comments and wise counsel were crucial in the process of obtaining the ticket into this prestigious trade union. I also wish to thank everyone I encountered during my fieldwork in Cameroon specifically in Mbankomo and Bali, for lack of space I cannot mention all of you however, Mr Pefok, Mr Essomba and Mr Daniel your inputs was crucial in ensuring the success of this project. This study is dedicated to my family for supporting me throughout this process. I am eternally grateful to my late mother Mami NUNYONGA GRACE who despite the pain and suffering of ill-health and until the point of death never failed to remind me of the importance of my study and the need to stay focused despite the very traumatic effects of her malady. Mami, your courage and steadfastness in the face of the most unbearable pain and your determination to overcome the illnesses that afflicted you is a powerful source of inspiration to us as we face the gruelling challenges of life without your physical presence...

List of Acronyms and Abbreviations

AFD	Agence Française de Développement
AfDB	African Development Bank
AIP	Annual Investment Plans
AusAID	Australian Agency for International Development
B.C.W.C	Bali Community Water Committee
CAMWATER	Cameroon Water Utilities Corporation
CAR	Central African Republic
CARE	Cooperation for American Relief Everywhere
C.B.O	Community Based Organisations
C.C	Central Committee
C.D.D	Community Development Department
C.D.P	Council Development Plans
CELLUCAM	Cellulose du Cameroun
CFA	Communauté Financière Africaine
CIACC	Cameroon Industrial and Civic Contractors
CNU	Cameroon National Union
CPDD	Cercle des Promoteurs du Développement Durable
CPDM	Cameroon Peoples Democratic Movement
CPM	Communist Party of India-Marxist
CRTV	Cameroon Radio Television
CWE	China Water and Electricity Corporation
CYL	Cameroon Youth League
CYSD	Centre Youth and Social Organisation
DFID	Department of International Development
DO	Divisional Officer
EEC	European Economic Community
ELECAM	Elections Cameroon
EU	European Union
FEICOM	Fonds Spécial d'Equipement et d'Intervention Intercommunale
FMO	Forces des Maintiens de l'Ordre
GBSS	Government Bilingual Secondary School
GDP	Gross Domestic Product
GIZ	German Organisation for International Cooperation
IDP	Internally Displaced Persons

IFI	International Financial Institutions
IMF	International Monetary Fund
JICA	Japan International Cooperation Agency
KFW	German Development Bank
KIA	Kom Improvement Association
KNC	Kamerun National Congress
KNDP	Kamerun National Democratic Party
KPP	Kamerun People's Party
LNG	Liquefied Natural Gas
L.P.A	Lagos Plan of Action
L.S.O	Local Support Organization
MINATD	Ministry of Territorial Administration and Decentralisation
MRC	Mouvement pour la Renaissance du Cameroun
N.A	Native Authorities
NCNC	National Council of Nigeria and the Cameroons
NGO	Non-Governmental Organisations
NOWELA	Northwest Elite Association
NUDP	National Union for Democracy and Progress
OAU	Organisation of African Unity
OBAC	Odisha Budget and Accountability Centre
ODI	Overseas Development Institute
PADDL	Programme d'Appui à la Décentralisation et au Développement Local
P.C.D	Plan Communal de Développement
PDP	Peoples Democratic Party
PNDP	Programme National de Développement Participatif
P.P	Popular Participation
PT	Partido dos Trabalhadores
PTA	Parent's Teachers Association
P.V.C	Polyvinyl Chloride
P.W.D	Public Works Department
SAP	Structural Adjustments Program
SATA-HELVETAS	Swiss Association for Technical Assistance
SCAPO	Southern Cameroons Peoples Organisation
SCDP	Société Camerounaise des Dépôts Pétrolière.
SCNC	Southern Cameroons National Council

SDF	Social Democratic Front
SDO	Senior Divisional Officer
SG	Secretary General
SIBADEF	Sustainable Integrated Balanced Development Foundation
SNEC	Société National des Eau du Cameroun
SNV	Netherlands Development Organisation
SOCAME	Société Camerounaise des Engrais
SODEBLE	Société pour le Développement de la culture du Blé
SONEL	Société National d'Electricité
SWELA	South West Elite Association
SWOT	Strength, Weaknesses, Opportunities and Threats
UC	Union Camerounaise
UCCC	United Councils and Cities of Cameroon
UDC	Union Démocratique du Cameroun
UN	United Nations
UNDP	United Nations Development Programme
UPC	Union des Populations du Cameroun
VAT	Value Added Tax
YCPDM	Youths of the Cameroon Peoples Democratic Movement

Foreword

John Sharp
Emeritus Professor of Anthropology and South Africa Director, the
Human Economy Research Programme, University of Pretoria

Numvi Gwaibi's work on political decentralisation in Cameroon stands out for three reasons.

The first is the fact that it brings the methods of inquiry and the insights of two disciplines together to address the topic. Numvi's early postgraduate training was in political science, but he has also brought the relevant literature from social anthropology and its characteristic research method of participant observation to bear on his study. The result is an account of the processes of so-called political decentralisation that tacks successfully back and forth between macro- and micro-levels – the Cameroon state and the lives of ordinary Cameroonians in different parts of the country. At the macro-level his argument is similar to the one put forward by political scientists who have examined the process of decentralisation in Cameroon and other African states in the 1990s and 2000s. Like them, he shows that these states adopted a policy aimed, ostensibly, at bringing government closer to the people under the impetus of the demands for 'good governance' that were made by international agencies – particularly the Bretton Woods institutions – in this period. But, as he shows in some detail, in Cameroon's case the policy and the manner in which it was implemented were hedged about with so many conditions and qualifications that the substance of governance has remained as far from the grasp of ordinary citizens as it was before the notion that good governance required decentralisation became fashionable. In short, as Numvi demonstrates convincingly, Cameroon's policy of decentralisation has not achieved its advertised goal, and there are strong grounds for supposing that the state's political elite never intended it to do so.

The second reason his work stands out is that he anchors the findings from his field research in Cameroon in a detailed account of the history of the regions under discussion. This makes it possible for his analysis to go well beyond the conclusion that political decentralisation in Cameroon has been a sham. Whether or not the state pursued the policy with serious intent, its implementation involved a number of practical interventions at levels of society below that of the central state. For instance councils that were ostensibly charged with decision-making, administrative, and fiscal responsibilities were introduced at regional, district and village levels throughout the country. Although these councils may have been hobbled by the small print in the legislation that set them in motion, they did introduce a new dimension to political contestation at levels other than that of the state as a whole. Numvi explores the unintended consequences of these practical interventions in welcome detail, drawing not only on the findings of his ethnographic field research in different locations in present Cameroon, but also on his understanding of the long-term history of political dynamics in these areas. His argument here is that regions, districts and villages have long-standing forms of political organisation and contest that merit understanding in their own right, and that, from this perspective, the significance of central-government interventions such as decentralisation lies in the manner in which they interact with these local dynamics. Decentralisation may not have worked, or been intended to work, in text-book fashion, but it had the effect of strengthening the hand of some participants in more localised political arenas and weakening that of others.

The third strength of this book is that it involves comparative analysis. Numvi conducted field research in two locations in Cameroon – one in the Francophone part of the country, near the capital Yaounde, and the other in Anglophone North-West Region, in the chiefdom of Bali. His field research recorded the divergent responses to the implementation of the decentralisation policy in these areas. His grasp of regional history in Cameroon, going back to the start of the colonial period and the differences between the policies pursued by the two colonial powers after the First World War, makes it possible for him to give a convincing explanation of the difference in the responses to decentralisation in the two locations.

Numvi Gwaibi's book is sure to be of considerable interest to social anthropologists and political scientists who work in Cameroon and other African states.

Chapter I

Introduction and Methods

1.1 Contextualising Decentralisation and Community Participation in Cameroon

Decentralisation was inscribed in the constitution of Cameroon in 1996 and was presented as a panacea for the developmental challenges facing the country. These changes were intended to herald a major overhaul of the system of governance in the direction of devolution of power and decision-making by the state. It was envisaged that power to take decisions in a significant number of areas was to be devolved to the level of municipal councils. According to the United Councils and Cities of Cameroon (UCCC), there are 373 municipal councils spread throughout the country, some in rural areas and others in urban centres.

The new system of governance was implemented in 2004 following promulgation of the law on the orientation of decentralisation,[1] and the law on the rules applicable to councils.[2] These laws detailed powers and responsibilities accorded to municipalities, Mayors, councillors and representatives of the state.[3] These statutes were preceded by the creation[4] and reorganisation[5] of the *Programme National de Développement Participatif* (PNDP) by the Prime Minister. The role of this organisation was to collate submissions from below, decide on priorities and allocate funds necessary for councils to implement development plans. At the core of these policies was the notion of community participation in local development. Community participation was projected by donors and the government as the best means of promoting politically engaged and informed citizenries, active civil society and sustainable development.

---

[1] Law N° 2004/017 of 22 July 2004.
[2] Law N° 2004/018 of 22 July 2004.
[3] These include Senior Divisional Officers, Regional Governors, and the Minister of Territorial Administration and Decentralisation.
[4] Decree N° 002/PM of 09 January 2004.
[5] Decree N°299/Cab/PM of the Prime Minister, Head of Government on 07 October 2009.

However, community development through 'self-help' was not a new phenomenon, not least in Anglophone Cameroon (Page, 2003).

Within the framework of the policies of decentralisation and community participation therefore, elected municipal councils which had existed for many years were turned from bodies with minimal responsibilities such as performing civil ceremonies into fully fledged agents of local development. In practice, councils, in partnership with non-governmental organisations (NGO), and or community based organisations (CBO), drew up Council Development Plans (CDPs) following consultations with local residents of the areas over which they had jurisdiction. On the other hand, Mayors were empowered to select development projects from CDPs and implement them on a yearly basis. Development projects were financed by the state in conjunction with subsidiaries, notably the PNDP and the *Fonds Spécial d'Equipement et d'Intervention Intercommunale* (FEICOM).[6] The whole scheme was presented as a major step towards participatory democracy as well as open and accountable governance on the part of a government that by the turn of the century had been in power for 30 years and was facing growing popular opposition to its hitherto autocratic rule.

Widespread popular movements against the political regime in Cameroon began in the 1990s during the 'second wind of change' that swept across Africa. At the time, the ruling elite was faced with mounting unpopularity caused by economic mismanagement, corruption, and political inertia. The general feeling was that change on the economic and the political fronts was imperative. For many Cameroonians, constitutional reform was seen as the best way out of the political impasse that gripped the country. However, the elite feared that succumbing to popular demands for change was tantamount to political suicide, as was the case elsewhere on the continent. These elites, some of whom had been shuttling around the state apparatus since independence, responded with half-baked economic reforms and politicisation of democratic reform. These manoeuvres enabled them to thwart popular demands for change and they have remained in power to the present.

---

[6]FEICOM was created in 1974, and rendered operational in 1977. Just like the PNDP, its mission was to provide technical and financial support to councils on local development. source: <http://feicom.cm/www/index.php/le-feicom/presentation-generale>

After fiercely rejecting calls for a national conference, the government organised a Tripartite Conference and *'Grand Débat.'* This took place between 1992 and 1993, involving delegates from Anglophone and Francophone Cameroon. The bone of contention at the constitutional talks centred on the return to the status quo ante i.e. the two-state federation that was dissolved in 1972, the position held by Anglophone delegates. On the other hand, Francophones advocated for a loose decentralisation within the unitary structure (Eyoh, 1998).

In late 1992 discussions reached deadlock. However, in April 1993 the government made public a draft constitution which purportedly emanated from the constitutional forum. This action was vehemently denounced by the Anglophone members of the committee, but it was quickly endorsed by government supporters and adopted into Law No. 96-06 of 18 January 1996 to amend the Constitution of 2 June 1972 (Takougang & Krieger, 1998). This constitution presented decentralisation as a genuine opportunity for grassroots autonomy, and municipal councils as credible forums for community participation in local development. However, some viewed it as a façade of meaningless cosmetic changes tantamount to adapting the structures of an authoritarian regime to a democratic environment.

1.2 Objective of the Study

Contemporary political development in Cameroon is often described as impressive, enigmatic fascinating etc. For those belonging to the ruling party and its affiliates, what obtains in the country is a form of *démocratie avancée;* which in reality is a smokescreen to mask the personality cult around the president and his office. Likewise, for the opposition and many others it is the stuff of nightmare. Nevertheless, the issue at stake is how did the ruling elite in Cameroon successfully turn a volatile political situation around and remain in power to the present? Over the years, many scenarios have been advanced to explain this situation; these include privatisation transactions in favour of political allies (Page, 2002); mobilisation of the military to supress the opposition (Mentan, 1998); a weak and divided opposition and the co-optation of its leaders (Konings & Nyamnjoh, 2003); ethnic diversity and complexity (Gabriel, 1999); playing the tribal card (Mentan, 2011); use of 'motions of support' to buttress the system and monopolise

3

governance (Mbuagbo & Akoko, 2004); proliferation of opposition political parties, numbering 291 at the last count;[7] electoral engineering and vote-rigging (Geschiere, 2009); manipulation of the constitution-making process (Takougang & Krieger, 1998); and the unflinching support of France (Renou 2002 and Keese 2007). On the other hand, the government often describes Cameroonians as peace-loving people, in tune with its democratic ideals (Page, 2002).

These analyses of what I term the Cameroon enigma have largely focused on macro-level economic, social, and political developments, as well as on skillful political craftsmanship by the governing elite. These constitute outstanding scholarly endeavours and will be highlighted to varying degrees in the ensuing chapters. For the purposes of this research, I adopted a holistic approach involving macro- and micro-level analysis to examine the constitutional changes that occurred in Cameroon in 1996, and how these reforms have played out on the ground since 2004. First, I employed ethnographic case studies of actual events that occurred during fieldwork in Mbankomo, and Bali. These local municipalities are located in Francophone and Anglophone Cameroon respectively. Secondly, in line with the "umbrella concept of 'the human economy' which refers to an emphasis both on what people do for themselves and on the need to find ways forward that must involve all of humanity" (Hart, et al., 2010, p. 2), I situated events in their local contexts and histories and demonstrated how they are linked to national discourses and political processes.

Going by the experience of local governance in Anglophone Cameroon prior to reunification therefore, I contend that it is too simplistic to argue that implementation of these policies has brought about real devolution of power and increased popular participation in political decision-making. On the other hand, were the yardstick to be placed on what obtained during the monolithic era, then it is also a simplification to contend as some have done that these policies are no more than a façade of meaningless cosmetic changes. Nevertheless, this should not preclude acknowledging that policy-makers in Cameroon need to take concrete steps to ensure that decentralisation and community participation becomes a genuine enterprise worthy of the

---

[7]Source: Ministry of Territorial Administration and Decentralisation (MINATD). <http://minatd.cm/index.php/en/en/annuaires/partis-politiques?view=partis> accessed 1 February 2015.

aspirations of many Cameroonians for credible and autonomous local institutions.

1.3 Problem Statement

The history of Cameroon was marked by very colourful episodes. First it was a German protectorate, a League of Nations Mandate and later a United Nations Trust Territory administered by Great Britain and France. The two colonial powers exported various forms of governance into the territories they occupied. In principle, what obtained in French Cameroon was a highly centralised form of governance in which decisions regarding the entire territory were taken by the authorities in Yaoundé. On the other hand the British governed Southern Cameroons under a system known as indirect rule in which traditional and local authorities in some parts of the territory had greater scope of autonomy in running local affairs (Njoh, 2011).

Following reunification in 1961, the country operated under a Federal system of government whereby the English and French sections were known as West and East Cameroon respectively (Forje, 2008). However, the federal structure was dissolved in 1972 and in 1974 the first major decentralisation reform was implemented.[8] The 1974 law on the organisation of councils stipulated in Article 1 (1) that a council shall be a decentralised public authority, having the status of a corporate body, and shall manage local affairs on behalf of the state with the aim of promoting economic, social and cultural development of the people. Article 13 outlined the number of councillors per municipality based on population size; for example, an area of 0-10,000 inhabitants was represented by 15 councillors, 10,000-20,000 inhabitants 20 councillors etc. The 1974 law therefore constituted the basis after reunification for the establishment of municipal councils in Cameroon. Curiously, many of its provisions notably the role of the 'representatives of the state' are quite similar to the 2004 laws on the orientation of decentralisation and the rules applicable to councils.

The 2004 laws[9] were preceded by *Law No. 96-06 of 18 January 1996*, amending the *Constitution of 2 June 1972*. In principle, this statute

---

[8] Law N° 74/23 of 5 December 1974.
[9] Law N° 2004/017 of 22 July 2004 on the orientation of decentralisation and Law N° 2004/018 of 22 July 2004 on the rules applicable to councils.

reshaped the national political landscape and introduced new institutions, notably the senate (Article 20), a constitutional council (Article 46), and regional and local authorities (Article 55). However, the senate became operational in 2013 amid controversy over the legitimacy of members of the Electoral College required to elect senators, and the Constitutional Council and Regional Assemblies are still pending. In what was clearly a move designed to stall the momentum of reform, Article 56 (6), states: "The rules and regulations governing councils shall be defined by law." However, it was not until 2004 that policies regulating council management were promulgated. Cynics viewed the time it took for these laws to be drafted with utmost contempt. However, supporters of the regime argue that "benefits ought to be given little by little, so that the flavour of them may last longer" (Machiavelli, 1515, p. 42).

Others dismissed the content of the 2004 laws as mere cosmetic changes with no real autonomy for elected Mayors. Accordingly, the whole scheme (some say scam) was designed to reinforce central control and bind municipal authorities through the intermediaries of 'representatives of the state' to the central administration in Yaoundé. According to (Fombad, 2012, p. 8): "Not only does he [President Biya] have the right to decide when if at all the regional and local authorities will be created, he also has the power to determine their powers and can dissolve them and dismiss their officials when he deems it proper."

1.4 Research Question

Why did the government of Cameroon adopt constitutional reform in 1996? How have policies of decentralisation and community participation implemented in 2004 impacted local development and municipal politics?

1.4.1 Working questions

The economic crisis that affected Cameroon in the 1980s and 1990s witnessed the intervention of the IMF and World Bank, the imposition of structural adjustment programmes and a prescription of 'governance' reform. Economic reforms prescribed liberalisation, privatisation etc. and political reform promoted devolution or decentralisation.

What were the circumstances in Cameroon that brought about economic crisis in the 1980s and political upheaval in the 1990s? How did these engender constitutional reform in 1996?

The adoption of decentralisation in 1996 was presented as a major step towards participatory democracy and open and accountable governance by an elite that had been shuttling around the state apparatus since independence and was facing growing popular resentment to its autocratic rule.

Why did the governing elite in Cameroon resist popular demands for change and how did they turn around a volatile political situation to remain in power to the present?

During colonial times, community development through self-help was the motto in the Southern Cameroons. However, community development was side-lined during political monopoly (1966-1990) in favour of modernisation. Under political pluralism (1990 onwards) decentralisation and community participation became a development mantra.

What is the legacy of community development in Cameroon and to what extent does decentralisation promote active community participation in local development?

Decentralisation in principle transformed municipal councils from bodies with minimal responsibilities into engines of local development.

What is the level of autonomy accorded local authorities, and to what extent do municipal councils constitute arenas for development in Cameroon?

1.5 Literature Review

In the aftermath of the Second World War, modernisation was the dominant discourse in development circles. At its core was centralisation or big government in almost every arena of policy-making. (Pellini, 2007). At independence, developing countries pursued centralisation as a nation-building strategy, but decades later, development challenges still persist (Higgott, 2000). Belief in big solutions and a conviction that one program would be fitting for all world regions side-lined local particularities (Escobar, 1995). This was due to the view that local authorities, identities and associations as traditional features or colonial constructions would dissolve with modernisation and post-colonial state-building. Likewise, globalisation was also posited as a homogenising force capable of subduing states and people everywhere to the global market. However, local politics has proven to be quite resilient in the face of modernisation and globalisation, and issues related to governance and poverty persist (Harriss, et al., 2004).

The challenges of poverty in developing countries mean that local distributional consequences of policy actions are crucial to igniting and/or resolving crisis. The negative implications of economic policy are particularly marked, especially when such policies are insensitive to local distributional implications and eschew delicate mechanisms of social cohesion (Mkandawire & Soludo, 1999). The structural adjustment reform policies in sub-Saharan Africa are widely argued to have failed because of inadequate consideration for local particularities (Mkandawire, 1997). Like structural adjustment in the 1980s, decentralisation was another policy programme actively encouraged by donors in developing countries in the 1990s. Structural adjustment may have been accepted without conviction and speed (Rodrik, 2006), but decentralisation has struck a chord with the leadership of many developing countries.

Decentralisation can be defined as any act in which central government formally transfers powers to actors and institutions at lower levels in a politico-administrative and territorial hierarchy (Crawford 2004; Eyoh and Stren 2007; Manor 1999). Decentralisation consists of two broad elements: deconcentration and devolution (Crook & Manor, 1998); others include delegation (UNDP 1993 & Grindle 2007). In practice, however, all three forms are often combined, even though the

8

rhetoric is generally at odds with the practice (Grindle 2007 and Ferguson 1994). According to Conyers (2000, 9): "Most decentralization efforts have both explicit and implicit objectives. Those objectives likely to appeal to the general public, such as local empowerment and administrative efficiency, are generally explicitly stated, while less popular ones, such as increasing central control and passing the buck, are unlikely to be voiced."

Inasmuch as external pressure to decentralise is often presented as a genuine opportunity for grassroots autonomy, it is also the case that, where such pressures are not to the liking of recipient governments, the process risks becoming "a kind of theatrical performance for donors in which the image is produced but the power distributions do not change" (Ribot & Oyono, 2005, p. 211). This therefore feeds into the argument that experiments with local government often end up in a shambles (Mawhood, 1983).

Although discourses on decentralisation are as old as the nation-state, the core question about decentralisation is not whether the technical form of governance has undergone any change, but what decentralisation has meant for ordinary people in their everyday lives (Kaiser 2006 and Harriss, et al., 2004). Decentralisation has generated significant debate among policy makers, researchers, and academics about its relevance for development policy. Within this debate two camps have emerged; one for whom it is a way of empowering communities and another for whom it is simply recentralisation. In the midst of this controversy however, a penchant for devolved governance has not waned.

Proponents of decentralisation within donor circles have high expectations of the positive role devolution can play in enhancing local democracy. It is presumed that representative political systems at the grassroots level will generate greater legitimacy for local political leaders and incentivise them to mobilize local developmental resources hitherto stifled by rigid control exercised by centralized bureaucracies (Bierschenk, 2004). This position is in tune with findings from studies conducted by a number of international bodies including amongst others the German Organisation for International Cooperation (GIZ) (Diprose & Ukiwo, 2008), the Australian Agency for International Development (AusAID, 2001), the UNDP (1993), and the World Bank (2000).

The role of the World Bank (hereafter referred to as the Bank) in the development arena is particularly marked. Its stance on the role of the state in development has shifted over the years (Hann & Hart, 2011). The state was sometimes thought of as predatory and at other times as politically rational and economically irrational (Stein, 2008). From the 1980s the core belief amongst Bank ideologues was that the realities of underdevelopment could be tackled by economic science, which was viewed as if it were one of the natural sciences (Escobar, 1995). At the time, the development agenda pursued an intensive drive to free up global markets (Hann & Hart, 2011). Confident in their beliefs, neoliberal ideologues deemed critiques of possible market defects as strangely old-fashioned and contrary to contemporary culture (Sen, 1999).

Since the 1980s, the Bank has placed a lot of emphasis on decentralisation as a solution to developmental challenges (Mkandawire & Soludo, 1999). In 2004, the government of Cameroon, with financial support from the Bank and other donors, created the PNDP. The aim of the PNDP was to 'assist government to set up and execute a decentralised financing mechanism to ensure participatory community development' (PNDP, 2009). At its inception, the organisation was financed through the following formula: the government of Cameroon (69.5%), the Bank (20%), the KFW[10] (9.2%), beneficiary councils (1.2%) (PNDP, 2009). The PNDP is represented throughout the country and presents itself as the key partner in assisting councils towards realisation of development projects within municipalities.

Promotion of decentralisation by the Bank and other stakeholders was described as a 'market-surrogate strategy' designed to transform state bureaucracies by making them more responsive to their clientele and to enable them to achieve closer connection between inputs and outputs (Stein, 2008). However empirical evidence suggests that the market approach to decentralisation, especially in sub-Saharan Africa, most often contradicts the very optimistic prognosis of its proponents. According to Rodrik (2006, p. 340), "the market-oriented reforms of the 1990s proved ill-suited to deal with the growing public health emergency in which the continent became embroiled."

---

[10] German Development Bank.

Despite setbacks, donor emphasis shifted from an earlier focus on the nature and performance of a country's subnational government systems to examining the motivations behind decentralisation, the role of key stakeholders and the question of how it has shaped the process (Eaton, et al., 2010). However, what is often wanting is the impact of decentralisation on the day-to-day activities of ordinary peoples and local communities. This study attempts to fill this gap by using case studies in two municipalities in Cameroon i.e. Bali and Mbankomo. My research follows the lead of other critical studies addressing issues about governance and development such as the failed attempts of numerous donor agencies to produce any meaningful economic progress in Lesotho (Ferguson, 1994), the propagation of western development discourses as the only path to prosperity for developing countries (Escobar, 1995), employing development models that overlook the input of affected communites (Munro & Hart, 2000), and passing rules and responsibilities down the politico-administrative line without the necessary financial resources (Bryden, 2010).

The historiography of the politics of development in Africa could be represented in the form of a dichotomy between state and community. Within this framework, the state is often identified with its colonial past, membership of the global comity of nations, and centralised forms of government. Community for its part is often associated with the social setting prior to colonisation, social embeddedness and forms of reciprocity and a bottom-up approach to development (Hyden, 2006). Further, the term 'local development' is often employed to contrast centralised decision-making and self-reliant or community development (Bryden, 2010). Oversimplification of the state–community dichotomy overlooks myriad complexities that characterise rapport between the 'summit' and 'grassroots', leaving the middle ground unexplored (Hyden, 2006). However, several concepts have been developed to bridge the gap, involving use of themes such as 'social capital' (Harriss 2012); 'third sector' (Alexander 2010) and 'civil society' (White 1996).

According to Cooper (2008, p. 184), "the line between state and 'not-state' is not so clear, and much of the literature assumes a single type of state juxtaposed against a particular vision of civil society, both based on idealized extrapolations of European forms." As a result, the application of civil society to the African context is rather embryonic

11

due to the somewhat blurred lines between civil society and other traditional forms of associations (Luckham & White 1996 and Hyden 2006), leading White, (1996, p. 183) to conclude that "[t]he advance of civil society which does not necessarily contain democratic ideals, does not in itself ensure democratisation of the political system." In Cameroon, a host of NGOs, and civil society organisations are engaged in decentralisation; but their work is fraught with numerous hurdles, not least their lack of capacity and funding (Cheka, 2007).

Meanwhile, traditional forms of association and community grouping, often headed by powerful chiefs, have for several decades played crucial roles in local development, particularly in the North West Region of Anglophone Cameroon (Cheka, 2008). As noted earlier, this area was governed by the British through a system known as indirect rule under which local communities were grouped together into Native Authorities which served as incubators for self-reliant development. According to Page (2003, p. 486) the idea of self-help, was to "induce in the people a desire for progress and the will to achieve it by their own efforts." Generally, community development in the global South established strong roots in certain areas owing mostly to their colonial experience (Taylor, 2010). It was therefore around the 1950s that community development through self-help was formalised into the governance structures of the Southern Cameroons.

In the 1960s and 70s, there was a flurry of state-sponsored community activities aimed at tackling poverty within the welfare state system in the global North. In recent times, governments in developing countries with strong donor support have adopted the rhetoric of participatory democracy. However, the reality remains that central bureaucracies and experts located far from the impact of their decisions retain key levers of power and control over development activities (Munro & Hart, 2000). In Cameroon, decentralisation and community participation were promoted as panaceas for developmental challenges. However, myriad shortcomings in the process led many to cast doubt on the state's commitment to implement these policies practically and also on the feasibility of real grassroots autonomy (Fombad 2012; Mbuagbo 2012; Njoh 2011; Cheka 2007 & 2008; Mentan, 1998).

1.6 Research Methods

The purpose of my research was to explore how decentralisation has played out on the ground in Cameroon following its implementation in 2004. Based on a solid academic foundation in political science and international relations, my initial approach was to analyse political developments, specifically the interaction between local municipalities, the state and donor organisations on the one hand, and the motivations for decentralisation, the role of state officials and how these actors shape the process on the other. Based on this dichotomy therefore, the outcome would not be much different from similar studies conducted elsewhere. However, a key component which I consider to be at the heart of decentralisation policy specifically the everyday experiences of ordinary people on the ground would be wanting.

Knowledge of anthropology therefore enabled me to plug this gap. In fact, it opened up other avenues and broadened the appeal of my research to include traditional institutions and local socio-cultural features. It further widened the scope of the study to include other disciplines, notably history, economics and public policy. The ethnographic component of my study was conducted in two local municipalities, Mbankomo in Francophone Cameroon and Bali in Anglophone Cameroon. The choice of these locations was based on their proximity to two politically significant urban settlements, Bamenda and Yaoundé. Fieldwork in these locations enabled me to reach ordinary people and to record their experiences through episodes which occurred while I was present.

Mbankomo subdivision (hereafter referred to as Mbankomo) is situated in the Mefou and Akono Division in the Central Region; it is roughly 22km from Yaoundé the political capital of Cameroon, often referred to as the 'seat of state institutions;' it also doubles as the headquarters of the Central Region. On the other hand, Bali subdivision (hereafter referred to as Bali) is located in Mezam Division in the North West Region; it is roughly 16 km from Bamenda, the hotbed of uprising against the regime of President Paul Biya in the 1990s, and also the seat of the main opposition Social Democratic Front (SDF) party. Interestingly the two leading political parties in Cameroon i.e. the Cameroon Peoples Democratic Movement (CPDM) and the SDF were both founded in Bamenda in 1985 and 1990 respectively. My fieldwork was also marked by two major political events; the pioneer senatorial elections which took place on 14th April 2013, and the municipal and legislative elections of 30th September 2013.

1.6.1 Preliminaries

Following approval of my proposal by the Faculty of Humanities research committee in February 2013, I immediately began poring through literature on anthropological research methods. Coming from an international relations and political science background, this was my first encounter with anthropology. Upon arriving in Cameroon in April, I continued the process up to a point where I felt confident enough to engage in ethnographic data collection. This enabled me to engage in fieldwork with great zeal.

According to (Whitehead, 2004, pp. 17-18): "The primary aim of ethnography is to understand the socio‑ cultural contexts, processes, and meanings of a cultural system from the perspective of the members of that system." This therefore involves continual observation, asking questions, making inferences until "those questions have been answered with the greatest emic validity possible." The ethnographic method I employed for this research was Participant Observation. According to Bernard (2006, p. 342): "Participant observation involves getting close to people and making them feel comfortable enough with your presence so that you can observe and record information about their lives." Being the foundation of cultural anthropology, participant observation fieldwork requires both scientific and humanistic approaches, as well as other aspects that fall under social anthropology, including qualitative and quantitative research methods (Crowley-Henry, 2009).

According to Nurani (2008, p. 443): "The cycle in ethnographic research begins with data collection. The next stage is analysing data. Data collection can be carried out through observation and interviewing. Other complementary methods of data collection are reviewing other sources." Suryani (2008) has outlined several characteristics of ethnography, these include creating a social relationship with participants, playing an active role in the research and ensuring that research is not carried out under controlled circumstances. Unlike the "classical ethnographers who primarily studied local communities in the field setting 24 hours per day, 7 days per week, [contemporary] ethnographers work in settings other than simply local communities, where 24-7 immersion is not possible, and unnecessary" (Whitehead, 2005, pp. 3-4). Likewise, the length of time spent in a community depends on the "nature of the research topic and the amount of detail required" (Palmer, 2001, p. 302).

During fieldwork in Cameroon, I combined participant observation with a number of research techniques including note-taking, documentary analysis, some archival research and a review of the relevant historical, socio-cultural, economic and political literature on Cameroon. This enabled me to merge political history and local investigation, and to glide from macro-historical surveys, political economy and public policy to local ethnography and back. Another crucial research method I employed was interviews (in-depth, informal, and unstructured). According to (Bernard, 2006, p. 211): "Informal interviewing is the method of choice at the beginning of participant observation fieldwork, when you're settling in." Informal interviews can also be employed to strengthen contacts with informants and also to tease out new ideas that would not have been explored in a structured interview or observed personally. In light of Bernard's (2006) observation, I always made sure to memorise key events, remembering conversations and gossip overheard in the course of the day. I often jotted key points, highlighted pointers and endeavoured to type out my notes at the end of the day or a few days later, so as not to lose crucial details. This enabled me to develop questions for prospective informants. I also employed situational analysis to document key local events and how they impact or are impacted upon by national issues (Gluckman, 1940).

In my original research plan, I proposed to conduct fieldwork in three areas; the North West, the Centre and the Adamawa Regions. The North West Region in Anglophone Cameroon is my home area and Bamenda its capital is the town where I grew up. Though relatively young at the time, I had first-hand experience of the tumultuous political events in Cameroon. In the 1990s, Bamenda was the hotbed of opposition politics and bastion of the main opposition SDF party. My assumption was that being an opposition stronghold, municipal councils were deprived of development funds as a way of ensuring they fail, so that the opposition could be blamed for incompetence. Although I did not find any clear evidence of this, I was however informed by the former SDF Mayor of Bali Council that during the period when the party was running the council (1996-2007), his team often came under sustained pressure from elites at home and abroad to give up the council to the governing CPDM party, so that development projects would flow to Bali. The CPDM which took over Bali Council in 2007 refuted allegations of coercion, but acknowledged that government would not be happy giving 'things' to an area that does not support it.

My second research site was a local municipality in the Southern part of Cameroon specifically around Yaoundé the political capital. My assumption was that being situated close to the heartbeat of the country, a local municipality in this area will be relatively better-off compared with one located in an area with strong opposition support. In the 1990s, at the peak of civil disobedience campaigns organised by the opposition dubbed 'Operation Ghost Towns' or *villes mortes*, President Paul Biya described the tenacity of the capital in the face of sustained onslaught by the opposition to choke the economy and force him to concede to a national conference in these terms; *"Tant que Yaoundé respire, le Cameroun vie"*/as long as Yaoundé breathes Cameroon is alive. I was therefore curious to contrast how a local municipality in this area fared compared to one in the North West.

My third research site was in Northern Cameroon. In 2010, I took a semester abroad from my Masters studies to conduct a research internship with the PNDP in Ngaoundere in the Adamawa Region. My aim was to experience the practical phases of decentralisation and to gain first-hand knowledge of community participation in drafting a Council Development Plan. My objective was to assess how the process had evolved from the experimental phases to actual CDP's and also the extent of community participation. I abandoned the Adamawa project due to limited funds and the short time at my disposal. With hindsight, it was a wise move because by focusing on the North West and Centre Regions I was able to get rich and in-depth data.

1.6.2 Bali

Upon arriving in Cameroon in April 2013, I sought and obtained authorisation from the SDO of Mezam Division to conduct research in Bali and Bamenda. I considered Bali as home ground before plunging into the unknown by commencing fieldwork in Mbankomo. As noted earlier, Bali is situated in Mezam Division and Bamenda is the chief town of the latter and also capital of the North West Region. Unlike

Mbankomo, where it took me a while to settle-in and build trust with locals before actual data collection, ethnography in Bali was pretty straightforward. This was due in part because Bali is my home village (my parents were born there), and when I was growing up I usually visited my grandparents during summer holidays. Located 16 km from Bamenda and traversed by the Lagos to Mombasa line of the Trans-Africa Highway Network, Bali was easily accessible. While in Mbankomo, I was kept abreast with events about the senatorial and municipal/legislative elections in Bali by a close friend based there. It was via his news feeds that I learnt about the *Fon*[11] of Bali's foiled attempt to run for the senatorial elections (he was subsequently appointed senator by President Paul Biya), and also gained partial insights into the controversy over the role of *Voma* during the municipal/legislative elections.

Bali is situated in a hostile social environment, and the historical relationship between the dominant community (Bali Nyonga) and neighbouring villages was fraught with land conflicts, some dating back over a century. Land was therefore a very delicate issue there and sensitivity over it meant that obtaining information was often tricky. Likewise, information gleaned from interviews, oral and written sources was analysed with great care, a high sense of objectivity and a greater degree of balance. Because Bali is a short distance from Bamenda, I deemed "24/7 immersion unnecessary" (Whitehead 2005, pp. 3-4). My almost daily commute using public transport enabled me somewhat to conduct ethnography on the move. For example, it was during one such trip from Bali to Bamenda that I overheard a couple of farmers discussing the potential negative effects of heavy rainstorms on crops and its likely disruption of the farming season. The causes of this were

---

[11] In the North West Region of Cameroon, *Fon* is an indigenous common denominator for a traditional ruler (Awasom, 2003). However, the situation is a bit complicated in Bali subdivision because the area is made up of three major communities i.e. Bali Nyonga, Bawock and Bossa. Bawock is relatively new in the area, having settled there in the early 1900s. Moreover, they are of Bamiléké origin, with a distinctive culture that is quite dissimilar in many respects to that of Bali and other communities in the area. Many in Bali therefore argue that the traditional ruler of Bawock village does not deserve to be called *Fon*. In fact, he is sometimes purposefully referred to as chief (equating him to the level of other sub-chiefs and quarter heads), others go further, calling him by name to spite him because of his alleged 'trouble making' and 'insubordination' to the *Fon* of Bali. For the purpose of consistency in this study I will refer to him as chief.

blamed on inappropriate use by the traditional authorities of the ancestral cult or *Voma* for campaign purposes.

Aside from campaigns for the Municipal/Legislative elections, there was the official installation ceremony of the newly elected Mayor and his team. This ceremony was presided over by the SDO of Mezam who also doubles as the 'representative of the state' and overseer of the activities of local municipalities in Mezam Division. Prior to this, there was another very significant public event for the CPDM party. This took place on 6 November 2013 marking the 31th anniversary celebrations of the accession to power of the head of state Paul Biya. Unlike during the monolithic era when such events was marked by a public holiday, it was not the case on this occasion. However, like elsewhere in the country the event was attended/presided over by senior state officials, giving it the hallmarks of an unofficially sanctioned public holiday. In Bali the coterie of state officials included the junior cabinet minister from Bali, civil servants of various ranks, local administrative, municipal and security officials and also a cadre from Bossa village.

Meanwhile, this was one occasion that brought together all branches (men, women and youths) of the CPDM party. The speeches delivered on that occasion sounded a lot like dirges for the SDF party in Bali. It was also an opportunity for intercommunity rivalries, notably between Bali Nyonga and Bawock, to be temporarily swept under the rug in a show of unity in honour of the party chairman. The event was also attended by the *Fon* of Bali who was appointed Senator by the head of state in 2013; but the Chief of Bawock and an alternate Senator was nowhere to be found.

Following the 30th September municipal elections in Bali, there was a lot of jostling within the CPDM for the position of Mayor amongst elected councillors and other influential local political actors. There were allegations of money changing hands, influence peddling, intimidation and coercion; as a result, the person who headed the CPDM list into the elections and Mayor designate ended up becoming 1st deputy instead. Further, it was widely rumoured that the man who eventually emerged as Mayor was 'advised' by the *Fon* and other influential elite members to pull out of the race in favour of a younger and more energetic candidate. The then Mayoral aspirant was described as sickly and unfit to steer the affairs of the Council for a full term. He persisted in his quest to become

Mayor and eventually triumphed during the largely ceremonial s/election that was held in the Bali Multipurpose Hall.

This ceremony took place in the presence of some party militants and the above-mentioned elites who were visibly resigned to the fact that the Mayor-elect had succeeded in forcing his way into office despite their objections. On the day he was publicly declared Mayor after emerging victorious from what was clearly a bruising internecine fight, he confidently described himself as 'a man of action and few words.' This occasion was not without drama because an elected councillor who was gunning for one of the four posts of deputy Mayor fainted and was rushed to hospital when he realised his aspirations were doomed.

Following the s/election came the swearing in ceremony of the Mayor and his four deputies at the Bali Court of First Instance or Magistrates Court. The ceremony also witnessed the swearing in of a sanitary officer and civil status secretaries. After administering the oaths, the president of the court took a moment to advise the municipal officials on the following issues. First, he warned of very harsh penalties for municipal executives found guilty of producing fake civil status certificates (especially birth and marriage certificates), because of its negative impact on the image of the country in general and the council in particular. Second, he urged the sanitary official to ensure proper hygiene and sanitation in Bali town. He reminisced about the glorious epoch of sanitary inspectors who went round inspecting family compounds and toilets to ensure hygienic rules were respected on the pain of hefty fines for defaulters. He also expressed surprise that there was only one sanitary official in a big town like Bali and requested the Mayor to recruit additional manpower. Third, he requested the Mayor to urgently look into the water crisis in Bali now that water management was under the authority of the council. He drew the attention of municipal officials to the severity of the water crisis by noting that the court premises did not have potable water.

Bali owns an autonomous potable water supply system that was constructed in 1957. This water project experienced numerous challenges in recent times the most pressing being the issue of unpaid water bills. Before I left Bali in February 2014, a long list of debtors had been compiled and were threatened with legal action if they did not pay outstanding water bills by the expiration of a deadline. I also visited the main water catchment, treatment and pumping sites at Gola and Koblap.

The former is powered by electrical engines and water is treated with chemicals before being pumped for public consumption. High electricity bills and the cost of chemicals, when coupled with the cost of maintaining water pumping machines and other expenditures, makes it a very expensive venture.

On the other hand, the design of the Koblap site was quite innovative and was aimed at cutting costs while providing the population with high quality drinking water. The idea was to use biological treatment also known as slow sand filtration to purify water from five springs before pumping it to the main storage tank in Jamjam. However this failed because of structural problems in the design of the canalisation pipes for transporting water from the high catchment downhill and up into the storage tanks. Because the pipes were smaller relative to the volume of water that was pumped through them, it witnessed frequent breakdowns. Failure at Koblap meant the community relied on the expensive water source at Gola. I also held meetings and interviewed members of the water management committee as well as council officials who were now in charge of the water supply following its controversial transfer from the community to the council in May 2013.

Land disputes with neighbouring communities were a constant feature in conversations I held with informants and other contacts in Bali. It was during one such encounter that I was directed to the sub-prefecture as a potential source of precious historical information on land conflicts in the area. In the course of rummaging through the disused shelves harbouring archival material at the sub-prefecture, I stumbled across files about the land disputes. Some of the documents were of no use due to repeated exposure to the elements. However, I was able to glean useful information from files that were in a good state. My objective during this exercise was to collect information on the controversial decree N° 77-525 of 23 December 1977 which carved out large expanses of land from Bali and handed it to neighbouring communities. However, the Divisional Officer (DO) would not allow me make copies for fear that I could write something that would stoke up further troubles in the area.

Curiously, he learned about the existence of such files only when I requested permission to access them. Fortunately, other informants had copies of this decree and related documents which greatly facilitated my assessment and analysis of the land conflicts in Bali. Informants from Bali Nyonga enthusiastically provided me with data because, as they often said, I am one of them and will certainly put it to good use by contributing to dispel widespread and long-held myths about people from Bali Nyonga being very aggressive, easily prone to violence and land grabbing. Regarding the dispute with Bawock community, the information provided to me confirmed by way of historical and empirical facts that the latter's claims to land in Bali subdivision were largely unfounded and misguided. On the other hand, many people in Bawock often portrayed themselves as 'innocent' victims of Bali Nyonga expansionist aggression aimed at chasing them from the area.

1.6.3 Mbankomo

As noted earlier, I began fieldwork in Mbankomo in the Centre Region and prior to my arrival I didn't know much about the place. Following conversations with friends living in Yaoundé, during which I teased out possible locations, and also personal research on the websites of the Ministry of Territorial Administration and Decentralisation (MINATD), FEICOM and the PNDP, I resolved that Mbankomo would be suitable. I was quite intrigued by the staunch support for the CPDM in every election there since the 1990s, and also the sheer number of government ministers notably Secretary General of the presidency (a key cabinet post), that this subdivision had produced over the years. One of my contacts had a relative who, after hearing about my wish to conduct research in the area, offered to host me. Further, I settled for Mbankomo because it is located roughly 22 km from Yaoundé and is traversed by the economically strategic highway linking Cameroon's economic and political capitals and a lifeline for landlocked Central African Republic (CAR) and Chad.

I arrived in Mbankomo town on 6th May 2013, and settled in at my host Mr Ahmadou's residence. The next day I headed out to Ngoumou (roughly 16 km away) the chief town of the Mefou and Akono Division to seek authorisation to conduct fieldwork from the Senior Divisional Officer (SDO) or *Préfet*. After obtaining this authorisation, I spent time moving around to familiarise myself with my new environment. I took solitary walks around Mbankomo centre to identify key locations such as hospitals, markets, the council, the sub-prefecture, the local police and gendarmerie stations amongst others. Interestingly, most of these places were situated within walking distance from each other. For example, the Council and the sub-prefecture were a stone's throw from each other and separated by the esplanade of the municipal grandstand where public ceremonies such as the installation of the Divisional Officer or *sous-préfet* took place.

After wandering around for a few days, I headed to Mbankomo Council where I met the Secretary General (SG) to discuss my research activities and to obtain a copy of the CDP. Curiously, he claimed not to be in possession of the document and advised me to seek one from the Centre Regional Delegation of the PNDP in Yaoundé. Before leaving his office we agreed to meet at a later date, but he insisted that I must call him a day or two before to arrange an appointment. I held a number of meetings with him during which I sought information about how the council was managed and clarification of issues I encountered in the field, and tried but failed to get him to book me an appointment with the Mayor. I must add that meeting him sometimes was quite daunting because I would make an appointment to turn up and he was either not available or had another meeting and sometimes asked me to return the next day. This circus sometimes lasted for a week. Apparently, gossip went round Mbankomo that my sudden appearance at the council when I presented my letter of introduction from the University of Pretoria and also the authorisation to conduct research from the *Préfet* did very little to convince the SG that I was not a special agent sent to investigate corrupt practices in the council. This partly explains why he avoided meeting me on occasion. As a result I ambushed him when I needed pertinent information by turning up at the council unannounced.

My stay in Mbankomo, also coincided with the installation of my host as head of the Anglophone[12] community in the town. Prior to this event, there were several preparatory meetings at his residence. On one such occasion, after learning that my research was linked to the council, he introduced me to a municipal councillor and a civil servant resident in the area. Both men belonged to what I dubbed the 'hygiene team', charged with enforcing the weekly clean-up activities. The second contact, whom I call Mr Abesolo, proved to be a key informant and also a crucial hub of gossip about local events. He linked me up with another

---

[12] Anglophone in this context refers to people from the North West and South West Regions of Cameroon.

municipal councillor whom I call councillor Zele, and who also proved to be useful.

Councillor Zele was an influential member of the outgoing Mayor's team. In the run-up to the 2013 municipal elections, the list to which they belonged was disqualified under controversial circumstances. I held several meetings with Abesolo and Zele on different issues related to the activities of the council. Because both supported different factions in the investiture saga, I shuttled between them, bouncing off information received from one against the other. This sometimes entailed several long sessions during which I allowed myself to be lectured on local issues. In the process I gleaned crucial insights about the area.

I attended the installation of the *sous-préfet*, and later accompanied him on the last leg of his tour of all villages in the subdivision. I attended a meeting held at Mbankomo council hall to select CPDM candidates for the municipal elections, and also the last council meeting of the year to adopt the Mayor's administrative account, which incidentally was the final official gathering of the outgoing councillors prior to the 2013 municipal elections. While pursuing these events, I regularly followed-up developments in other parts of the country through radio, TV and newspapers. Most of the newspapers I read were online versions of national weeklies or dailies such as Cameroon Tribune, Le Messager, Le Jour, and Cameroon Postline amongst others. I found articles from these and other newspapers on a web-hub, Cameroon-info.net. Some articles and reports were crucial for filling gaps in my data.

Mbankomo also served as a hub from where I made several trips to Yaoundé to glean information from government departments, notably the Ministry of Territorial Administration and Decentralisation, and government agencies working on decentralisation such as FEICOM and the PNDP. I also met representatives of international organisations such as the World Bank, the African Development Bank (AfDB), the United Nations Development Programme (UNDP), the European Union (EU), the French Development Agency (AFD), the German Organisation for International Cooperation (GIZ), the German Development Bank (KFW), the Japan International Cooperation Agency (JICA), and the Netherlands Development Organisation (SNV). These organisations support decentralisation in Cameroon to varying degrees, including funding, training and capacity building. For example the GIZ subsidiary or *Programme d'Appui à la Décentralisation et au Développement Local,*

(PADDL), provides training programmes for Mayors, municipal councillors, and other council staff. It also produces manuals, pamphlets and reference guides to educate municipal actors about decentralisation.

1.7 Chapter Outline

France implemented a highly centralised form of governance under which major decisions about the colony was taken by the central authorities in Yaoundé. This policy shaped the mind-set of the leadership that emerged in French Cameroon after independence. Following reunification Cameroon operated a federal system of government until 1972 when the federation was dissolved. Chapter two demonstrates how the two sections of Cameroon were created, the legacy of colonial rule, and its impact on the form of state that emerged following independence and reunification in 1961. It also demonstrates how the relatively greater degree of grassroots autonomy in English speaking Cameroon was gradually eroded under the one party system instituted by President Ahmadou Ahidjo and legated to his successor Paul Biya, and how this set the stage for a tense relationship between Anglophones and Francophones in later years.

Chapter three starts with the initially peaceful transfer of power from Ahidjo to Biya, and the sharp deterioration in the relationship between the two men, followed by a failed putsch in 1984 allegedly orchestrated by Ahidjo. It also examines the economic crisis that affected Cameroon in the 1980s and the austerity measures that were imposed on Cameroon by the Bretton Woods institutions. It demonstrates how the government selectively implemented 'shock treatment' and used privatisation as an outlet for patronage to political allies and ethnic kin. The chapter further explores how the economic hardship brought about by austerity, specifically salary/benefits cuts and retrenchment of state employees, engendered corruption, tribalism and nepotism. Decay in the system of governance created resentment and degenerated into political ferment.

Political turmoil was manifested by demands for the legalisation of political parties, electoral reform and the convening of a 'sovereign' national conference to discuss constitutional reform. Some Anglophones also demanded a return to the two-state federation that was dissolved by Ahidjo in 1972. The government defiantly rejected these demands and organised a Tripartite Conference instead. This chapter demonstrates how the government of Cameroon thwarted popular demands for change, manipulated the constitutional debate, produced a document that failed to meet the aspirations of many Cameroonians and successfully maintained itself in power to the present.

Chapter four examines the migrations that brought Bali Nyonga to its present location, the conflicts that ensued with the Widekum or Meta communities they met in place and how compensation money from one such conflict was channelled into a community development project. It also documents the creation of the Bali Community Water Project which poignantly demonstrates how a local community in Anglophone Cameroon under the leadership of Galega II developed and successfully managed an autonomous scheme for decades. This project was constructed in 1957 and in 1984 the community sought assistance from government to expand the project. The government revamped the water project, but upon completion surreptitiously turned it over to the state-run National Water Corporation or *Société National des Eau du Cameroun* (SNEC). SNEC managed the water scheme as a for-profit venture in stark contrast to its founding goal as a self-help scheme. In 1994, the population of Bali violently expelled SNEC and repossessed the water installations. This action led to open but non-violent confrontation, pitting the population of Bali against local state officials. The latter's reaction was a combination of coercion, intimidation, disinformation and eventual surrender. This chapter therefore explores community development from an historical perspective, but with contemporary overtones.

Chapter five examines the 1974 Land Ordinance which was described as an attempt to harmonise customary practices with western precepts of rational land management. It also analyses a presidential decree issued in 1977 which carved out large expanses of land from Bali and awarded them to neighbouring areas. The 1974 law was controversial because it abolished all customary land rights in Cameroon, but tolerated customary land-use practices. This contradiction was often cited as the principal cause of violent land conflicts in North West Cameroon. The 1977 decree was presented as the final solution to historical land conflicts in Bali subdivision; but its practical implementation was also controversial because it exacerbated land disputes. This chapter therefore demonstrates how a decision by the authorities of Bali Council to conduct a survey to document the developmental potential of the area rapidly degenerated into land and boundary disputes, notably between the Bali Nyonga and Bawock communities.

Chapter six is the first of two chapters that focus on the municipal elections held in Cameroon in 2013. This chapter examines the electoral battle for control of Bali Council between the governing CPDM and main opposition SDF parties. After emerging victorious in the first multiparty municipal elections in Cameroon in 1996, the SDF party controlled Bali Council until 2007 when its list of candidates was disqualified by electoral authorities under controversial circumstances. The 2013 municipal elections therefore presented both parties with an opportunity to contest the polls on a somewhat equal footing. The CPDM accused the SDF of importing witchdoctors from Nigeria and Pygmies from the East Region of Cameroon to cast magical spells on the population and enable it to secure victory. The SDF countered with accusations that the CPDM employed the services of a sacred ancestral cult to intimidate people to vote for it. This chapter therefore assesses the methods adopted by the two main political parties in Cameroon to retain and or regain Bali Council which was at the centre of an electoral showdown that failed to happen in 2007.

Chapter seven pursues the 2013 electoral train by examining how the CPDM party sought to enforce party discipline in Mbankomo, which is an area where the party was described by a local chief as a religion. Following the announcement of elections, the chairman of the CPDM and head of state called upon grassroots militants to come up with consensus lists for the polls. This was followed by another circular letter by the Secretary General of the party dispatching special teams throughout the country to coordinate the selection of candidates. Other political parties, notably the SDF, conducted primaries, although this was not without controversy. The incumbent Mayor of Mbankomo was seeking another mandate, and hoped his party would endorse his candidature; but some elite members dubbed *hommes politiques* had other ideas. They colluded with the above-mentioned party envoys and thwarted the outgoing Mayor's ambitions for re-election. This chapter therefore demonstrates how the governing CPDM party in Cameroon enforces party discipline amongst grassroots militants irrespective of the fact that the area in question had been a bastion of support for its decades-long rule.

Chapter eight examines decentralisation and community participation as projected by the government of Cameroon and contrasts it with case studies from elsewhere in the Global South; specific examples are drawn from Colombia, Brazil, Bolivia, India, and Uganda. The chapter demonstrates that community participation in Cameroon was limited to NGOs and CBOs collecting data from local people and drafting Council Development Plans (CDP). Unlike elsewhere, local people had practically no say in the implementation of development projects. Prior to their practical phases, CDPs are deliberated upon by elected municipal councils and approval is subject to the assent of the 'representative of state'. The chapter also assesses the internal workings of municipal councils, as seen through two meetings: the examination of the Mayor's administrative account in Mbankomo and the budget session at Bali Council. The chapter therefore argues that the functions of municipal councils in Cameroon are a marked improvement on what obtained during the monolithic era; but, when compared with other cases in the Global South, the shortcomings are obvious.

Chapter nine highlights and amplifies key arguments developed throughout the study. The main conclusion is that decentralisation in Cameroon, like many complex issues, is difficult to pin down: on the one hand, some contend that the constitutional changes of 1996 followed by the policy decisions of 2004 merely represented the adaptation of the structures of an authoritarian regime to a democratic environment -- thus, unlike in the past municipal councils are no longer limited to issuing birth, marriage, and death certificates but in principle have powers to carry out local development activities. On the other hand, prior to reunification, local institutions in the Southern Cameroons had a greater degree of local autonomy than what obtained in Francophone Cameroon. At the time, the stifling role of the 'representative of the state' did not exist and municipal officials (elected or otherwise) worked closely with grassroots communities to promote local development. Moreover, grassroots autonomy in Anglophone Cameroon was such that local people practiced what was known as 'self-reliance' and depended on themselves first before looking up to the state for subventions/assistance to carryout developmental activities. These factors have brought many to lament the fact that contemporary political developments in Cameroon have not brought about real devolution of power and community participation in local development.

Chapter II

Cameroon:
From Mandate to Independence & Reunification

Their antipathy to democracy was already evident when they inherited the colonial state, instead of democratising it and when disingenuously insisting that development requires unity, they disallowed all opposition and dissent (Ake, 1996, p. 12).

2.1 Introduction

Cameroon has enjoyed a relative measure of political stability that is unprecedented in the Central African sub-Region (Delancy, 1989). A key reason for this was the form of state adopted at independence. A unitary approach to the nation-state was the predominant choice of African leaders in the decades following independence. According to Bayart (2009, p. 175); "independent Africa chose simply to step into the shoes of departing European powers." The unitary state was therefore a continuation of the colonial state's nation-building agenda which was aimed at fusing disparate ethnic and regional groupings into a single entity. Centralisation was also presented in some quarters as the best means to hold the state together and prevent chaos. However, as laid bare in the opening quote of this chapter 'national unity' was often a subterfuge for political monopoly. The unitary state agenda was therefore modelled on modernisation which was the dominant discourses in development circles around the 1960s.

In Africa, modernisation was aimed at achieving rapid economic development which partly mirrored the situation in the Soviet Union. This was manifested by institutionalisation of five-year development plans which largely focused on developing the primary sector of agriculture, mineral and other natural resource exploitation along with import substituting industrialisation (Pellini, 2007, p. 26). At the political level, there was a concerted drive towards one-party systems as the sole vehicle for expressing political diversity (Anyang-Nyong'o, 1995). With hindsight, it is generally agreed that this approach to statehood "fostered authoritarianism at the expense of constitutionalism" (Konings & Nyamnjoh, 2003, p. 1).

Following reunification, Cameroon followed a slightly different path from other sub-Saharan states and briefly dabbled with a measure of federalism. However, because French policies of assimilation and association was deeply ingrained in Francophone Cameroon (Geschiere, 2009), it didn't take long after reunification in 1961 for measures designed to centralise the state to be disseminated into Anglophone Cameroon.

Unlike most African states, Cameroon's history was quite colourful. 'Kamerun' was a German protectorate from 1884-1919, then a League of Nations Mandate following the defeat of Germany in the First World War and later a United Nations Trust Territory, administered by Britain which controlled one-fifth of the territory and France four-fifths respectively (Anyangwe 2013 and Chiabi 2011). Following reunification, the country operated a Federal system whereby the French-speaking part was known as East Cameroon and the English-speaking area as West Cameroon (Forje 2008 and Jua 2005). The colonial powers implemented different systems of governance in their respective territories. Britain governed the Southern Cameroons under what was known as 'indirect rule' whereby native authorities had greater scope for autonomy in running local affairs. On the other hand, the system of governance that obtained in French Cameroon was a combination of assimilation and association whereby all decisions regarding the entire territory were taken by the central authorities in Yaoundé (Njoh 2011).

Despite the special status of both territories, as spelt out under the terms of the agreement which formalised the transition from League of Nations Mandate to UN Trusteeship, neither colonial power implemented any special administrative measures in their respective territories. Rather, Britain worked towards integrating the Southern Cameroons into Nigeria. France did not administer French Cameroon any differently from its West or Equatorial African possessions and sought to absorb the territory into the *metropole* (Le Vine, 1964). As a result French Cameroon was admitted into the French Union and participated in the Union Assembly whose fundamental legislative and administrative powers rested with key organs of the French State such as the *Assemblée Nationale* and the *Conseil de la République,* (Johnson, 1970).

Meanwhile, contrary to the widely held view that indirect rule was the sole preserve of the British and direct rule of the French, the situation in Cameroon was not very straightforward because both policies were implemented to varying degrees in each part of the country. This was due mainly to the fact that some areas in both Cameroons were ruled by powerful traditional chiefs, and as a result, colonial authorities found it expedient to use them to enhance their rule. However, in places where chiefs were weak or non-existent they were simply created and imposed on the population (Njoh 2006).

Geschiere (2009, 1997, 1993, 1992), has documented the nature of the segmentary societies of the Southern forest regions of Cameroon which arguably facilitated the imposition of direct rule by France. However, this was not true of the entire French section of Cameroon, nor was it the case that British Cameroon was made up entirely of powerful traditional chieftaincies. In relation to the areas that were controlled by the French, some, notably the Western Bamilike highlands and other parts of Northern Cameroon, were ruled by powerful traditional chiefs. Some of the chiefdoms in these areas remained unperturbed throughout the colonial period (Johnson 1970).

As noted earlier, Germany's colonial footprint in Kamerun was relatively short-lived and rapidly dissipated following its defeat in the First World War. On the other hand, British and French colonialism (notably the latter) had far-reaching repercussions on the form of state that emerged following reunification in 1961 (Argenti, 2007). The Federal Republic in the immediate post-independence period consisted of the two systems operating parallel modes of administration (Elong, 2013). This was partly because the Anglophone minority and the Francophone majority were somewhat nostalgic about their inherited models, causing a dilemma which was subsequently tackled by what was described as "well-calculated manoeuvrings and aggressive policies of national integration vigorously pursued by the Francophone-dominated government, first under Ahidjo and later under Biya" (Njoh, 2003, p. 25).

The dismantling of the federation under the regime of Cameroon's first president Ahmadou Ahidjo was often passed-off as a cost-cutting measure designed to streamline red tape that clogged the Federal bureaucracy, making it too expensive to manage. In order to understand how Cameroon became a federal and later a unitary state after independence, I must delve into its colonial past and unearth the policies that fundamentally shaped the historiography of both entities and eventually the political systems inherited at independence. The political situation in British and French Cameroon, and the build-up to independence and reunification therefore constitute key themes that will be developed throughout this chapter, but first I begin with a historical overview of French colonial policies.

2.2 French Colonial Policy in Africa

One of the most decisive features of the colonial system was the presence of Africans serving as economic, political, and cultural agents of the European colonialists (Rodney, 1982, p. 142).

Unlike Britain France never envisaged self-government for its overseas territories. From the outset it conceived of a scenario where the *metropole* and the colonies would merge into a single political and economic unit (Le Vine 1964). Under the policy of assimilation therefore, French citizenship was conferred on all inhabitants of its colonies regardless of colour. This policy was a direct outcome of Article 109 of the French Constitution of 1848 which stated that colonies are French territory in the same way as the *metropole,* and enjoyed the same position in private and public law (Mandani, 1996, p. 82). A practical fallout of this law was granting citizenship and the right to vote to inhabitants of French trading posts along the coast of Senegal (Le Vine 1964).

The French authorities therefore instituted a policy of 'direct administration' in their African colonies. Under this policy citizens of the Four Communes[13] of Senegal were drafted into the local administration (Suret-Canale 1971 and Crowder 1964). According to (Rodney, 1982, p. 142) these Africans and Mulattos "played a key role in extending European activity from the coast into the hinterland, as soon as Europeans thought of taking over political power." Within a decade of its implementation however, the rationale of direct administration was called into question.

---

[13] Saint-Louis, Dakar, Gorée, and Rufisque.

The futility of the policy of assimilation as in the Four Communes experiment, particularly trying to turn Africans into Frenchmen was a key reason why it was abandoned in favour of the policy of association (Chiabi 2011 and Njoh 2006). According to Mamdani (1996, p. 83); "the older ideal of assimilation was shed as quickly as the newer notion of association was embraced." In practice however, assimilation was never entirely abandoned; as one time Governor General of French Overseas Territories Robert Delavignette remarked, the two formulas were often combined, the only difference being that the dosage varied with the practitioner's dexterity and the temperature of events (Johnson, 1970).

2.2.1 Assimilation to Association

In 1922, Colonial Minister Albert Sarraut endorsed the doctrinal ideals of conservative theorist Jules Harmand[14] who proposed direct administration of French colonies. The aim was to preserve and improve the institutions of the conquered people while ensuring respect for their past. However, Crowder (1964) contends that *la politique d'association* was certainly not the 'Lugardian' idea about the relationship between the colonial power and African people advocated by Jules Harmand. Instead he argues, the "French were not prepared to undertake the massive work of social transformation which alone could make it a reality" (Crowder p. 202 - 203). Whatever the case, there was a change of policy which in no small way constituted the genesis of the policy of association throughout the French colonial empire. A key tenet of this policy was the *politique de protectorat* or the policy of differentiation; this was exemplified by 'administrative separatism' which applied differing policies and standards to inhabitants of French colonies based on the level of advancement towards French social ideals (Le Vine 1964).

As French colonialism expanded into the hinterlands, there was a greater need for other actors to assist in local administration. As Robert Delavignette remarked, the African village is still a living entity where there has always been one chief who, despite appearances, still 'retains the ancient, intrinsically African authority' (Johnson 1970). He also admitted that the French administration would have been helpless were

---

[14] He wrote the book titled; *Domination et Colonisation*, which according to Crowder (1964) greatly influenced/inspired the change from a policy of assimilation to one of association.

there no chiefs capable of liaising between the administration and the communities and vice-versa (Mandani, 1996, 82).

The penchant for chiefs as 'auxiliaries of the administration' in certain instances necessitated creating artificial chiefs; it was also deemed expedient to use those found in place (Geschiere 1993). Despite their usefulness, African chiefs were put in an entirely subordinate position vis-à-vis colonial administrators. Robert Delavignette succinctly puts it thus:

> *[t]he man who really personified the Cercle was the Commandant.... He was the Chief of a clearly defined country called Damaragam (Zinder in Niger), and chief in everything that concerned that country. Yet this was the Damaragam once ruled over by the powerful Sultans of Zinder, who are now reduced to little more than exotic showpieces of traditional Africa (Freedom and Authority in West Africa (London, p. 95), cited in Crowder (1964, p. 201).*

In Cameroon the political officer or Commandant was the Commissioner of the Republic who was directly responsible to the Minister of Colonies in Paris. Appellation notwithstanding, the Commissioners like Governors elsewhere wielded administrative and military powers that enabled them to appoint regional administrators, district officers and advisory boards. Collaboration between the colonial administration and the indigenous elite was based on political institutions whose policies were dictated from the higher echelons of the administration. Meanwhile, the institutions that incarnated French indirect rule in Cameroon included the *indigénat*,[15] the *Conseils de Notables*, and traditional chieftaincies (Le Vine 1964).

The *Conseils de Notables* was an appointed organ of the colonial administration tasked with examining problems related to farming, animal husbandry and the improvement of human capital. The administration kept a close watch over the activities of these councils so as to ensure that they did not exceed their prescribed mandates. At their inception, membership consisted of between 10-20 people drawn from superior, cantonal and regional chiefs as well as representatives of the major ethnic groups in a particular area. Eligible members had to be over 30 years of age, live in the area, possess land, and have visible and

---

[15] This was a set of laws which created an inferior legal status for natives of French Colonies from 1887 to 1947.

acceptable sources of income and a clean criminal record. The council had to be consulted on matters concerning labour levies and public works; but acceptance of their recommendations was at the discretion of the colonial administrator. The council also had no autonomous sources of funding and was at the mercy of officials (Le Vine 1964).

Until this point the *Conseils de Notables* were the only local political institutions open to ordinary people. However, in 1949 a decree was issued expanding the composition of the councils from thirty to forty members. It also broadened the base of membership to include representatives of traditional associations, local cooperatives, trade unions and members of the newly created Territorial Assembly.[16] The next section therefore examines the roles of chiefs in the French colonial administrative structure.

2.2.2 Traditional Chiefs as 'Administrative Auxiliaries' in French Cameroon

In *The Wretched of the Earth* (1963), Fanon described the colonial world as being divided into two spheres, distinguished on the one hand by barracks and on the other by police stations. Armed personnel therefore constituted the official mediators between the European and the African, and the language often employed was that of 'pure force' (Fanon, 1963, p. 38). Therefore, violence was often the marker of the division between the French colonial authorities and African chiefdoms. In the pre-colonial West African state of Futa Jallon for example, French policy towards traditional authorities was often marked by 'progressive suppression of chiefs and the parcelling out of authority' (Crowder, 1964). Similarly, when the African kingdoms of Segou and Sikasso and the state created by Samory refused to submit to French expansion, they were violently supressed (Mamdani, 1996). On the other hand, force was not necessary in every circumstance; other subtle power tactics was often employed. In the French territory of Dahomey (present-day Benin), the most important traditional chief of Yorubaland, also known as the *Alaketu of Ketu*, was seen waiting outside the sub-prefecture and when the official's attention was drawn to his plight he dismissed it,

---

[16] The territorial assembly was a direct outcome of constitutional reforms that were carried out following the Brazzaville conference of 1944. Members of these Assemblies were guaranteed a seat in the councils of larger administrative units or regions.

saying *qu'est ce qu'il va se faire engueuler?* What is he going to yell at? -- and kept him waiting (Crowder 1964).

Meanwhile, in 1923 the French decided to curtail the authority of the Sultan of Ngaoundere in Northern Cameroon ostensibly because he was badly counselled, refused to cooperate fully with them and had misused funds. The Sultan was summarily dismissed and replaced with a local notable who exercised his powers in conjunction with the *Conseils des Notables*. A similar situation occurred in the Bamoum kingdom, where the Sultan was deported in 1931 because of a dispute about suzerain rights over sub-chiefs (Le Vine, 1964).

Whereas these examples illustrate cases of outright usurpation and humiliation of established traditional chiefs, the case of the paramount chief[17] of the Ewondos, Charles Atangana, was quite intriguing. During German rule, he served as an interpreter and instructor of Beti at government schools in Hamburg and Berlin. He was rewarded with the title of chief of the Ewondos. During the First World War he served as a Second Lieutenant in the German army, but, following the defeat of Germany, he was interned at Rio Muni (present-day Equatorial Guinea), along with remnants of the German forces. He was later allowed to return by the French and reinstated to his former position with extended authority over the Bane tribe, a kin group of the Ewondo (Le Vine, 1964, p. 96).

As if creating, imposing, deporting and humiliating chiefs was not enough to satisfy their egos, the French proceeded in 1922 to classify them hierarchically according to importance. For example there were first, second and third degree chiefs; the first degree chiefs consisted of Lamibe (plural for Lamido), Sultans and *chefs supérieurs* or paramount chiefs who were presumed to be successors of antiquated feudal institutions. The second degree chiefs or *chefs de groupements* and cantons were a German invention that died after their exit but was reinstituted by the French for 'administrative convenience.' Those who fell under this category were regarded as assistants to the first degree chiefs. Finally the third degree chiefs were small village chiefs and *chefs de quartier*

---

[17] It should be noted that there was no such title among the segmentary groups of the forest region of Cameroon. Each village was autonomous and the Ewondos never had a paramount chief. However, the Germans created this position (it was maintained by the French) to serve their own interests.

(neighbourhood heads), usually designated with the popular approval of inhabitants of neighbourhoods in big towns (Le Vine, 1964, p. 97).

The *chefs de quartier* were responsible for the management of affairs in their jurisdictions, under the watchful eyes of the sub-divisional or regional administrators. A key function of chiefs was tax collection from which they received stipends[18] amounting to a percentage of the amount of tax collected. The manner of collecting taxes also varied according to the rank of the chiefs. Whereas the lower echelon chiefs directly collected taxes themselves, the higher chiefs had collecting agents or used the lower level chiefs for such purposes.

Following independence, President Ahidjo issued a decree[19] that continued the colonial policy of classifying chiefs. This not only organised chiefs into a hierarchy (Page, 2003), but further entrenched them as auxiliaries of the administration[20] (Awasom 2003; Fisiy and Goheen 1998). Their 'non-political' functions bestowed upon chiefs privileges that enabled them to serve as intermediaries between the government and the people, to help in the execution of government directives, and also to serve as tax collectors for the state (Jua, 2011).

The pace of institutional evolution in French Cameroon did not only affect traditional chieftaincies. The Brazzaville conference of 1944 recommended greater administrative freedoms for individual French territories, modelled on a form of federal structure between the *metropole* and the colonies. It also opened up overseas participation in metropolitan institutions, notably the Assembly of the French Union (Johnson, 1970). This conference came at a time when France was under Nazi occupation and run by the Vichy regime of Marshall Petain. It was

---

[18] This practice continued after independence. However, the economic crisis that affected Cameroon in the 1980s and 1990s caused the indefinite suspension of state stipends to chiefs. This was compounded by changes in the mode of tax collection from poll tax to value added tax (VAT). Chiefs therefore lost a vital source of income in the form of the regular stipends received from tax collection. However, following Decree N° 2013/332 of 13 September 2013, traditional chiefs were awarded monthly salaries. Accordingly, first class chiefs are entitled to CFA 200,000 francs, second class CFA 100,000 francs, and third class CFA 50,000 francs. This presidential decision, which came on the eve of municipal/legislative elections in 2013, was seen by some observers as bending chiefs to political purposes.

[19] Decree N°. 77/245 of 5 July 1977

[20] According to Decree No. 77/245 of July 1977, all traditional chiefs were transformed into auxiliaries of the administration and subordinated to government appointed SDO's. This statutory provision effectively enshrined the pre-eminence of the SDOs over chiefs (Awasom, 2003).

therefore around this time that the first municipal institutions appeared in French Cameroon. Known as *communes mixtes urbaines*, they were first experimented upon in Douala and Yaoundé. These communes were headed by an Administrator-Mayor assisted by a municipal commission; unsurprisingly the Mayors and councillors were appointed by the High Commissioner.

By 1948 a veritable patchwork of local administrative institutions had sprung up over the territory. In addition to the Territorial Assembly, the territory was carved into 17 Regions administered by professional French administrators known as *Chefs de Région,* assisted by the *Conseils des Notables* (Le Vine, 1964). In sum, the constitutional and institutional reforms that proceeded from the Brazzaville conference provided French Cameroon with a platform for future political action. I now proceed to examine what obtained in the British section of Cameroon.

2.3 The British Mandate in Cameroon

The principal motivation behind British colonialism was to expand trade, secure trade routes at sea and land, and to expand the 'power and prestige of Great Britain.' British colonialists' limited moral commitment to radically altering the traditional status-quo of indigenous societies was attributed to the fact that Britain was in favour of the colonies becoming 'self-sufficient' and able to 'pay their own way' (Johnson, 1970). Further, the underlying thrust of British colonial policy in Africa was the system of indirect rule which is usually associated with Frederick Lugard, one time High Commissioner of the Protectorate of Northern Nigeria and Uganda. According to Scott (1998, p. 77), indirect rule "required only a minimal state apparatus but rested on local elites and communities." The choice of whether to apply direct or indirect rule in the colonies therefore depended on a number of variables including local exigencies, the presence of powerful yet malleable traditional political institutions, and the availability of adequate manpower and resources (Geschiere 1993; Mandani 1996 and Bayart 2009).

According to Le Vine (1964, p. 196); "the system had been tailored to fit the needs of British administration in situations where explicit traditional political systems were available to cushion the impact of western institutions on traditional ones." Like most British territories the Southern Cameroons[21] was governed through Native Authorities whose structure did not significantly differ from the political systems that existed prior to the arrival of Europeans (Vubo & Ngwa, 2001, p. 169). Further, Britain governed Southern Cameroons as part of Eastern Nigeria, and pushed for the territory to be integrated into the Nigerian Federation (Elong 2013 and Fombad 2012). The reluctance of Britain to groom the Southern Cameroons for independent statehood meant the territory did not have a house of assembly until the 1950s and prior to 1951 was represented in the Eastern House of Assembly by two traditional chiefs and heads of native authorities i.e. Galega II of Bali, and Manga Williams of Victoria (Vubo & Ngwa, 2001).

2.3.1 Native Authorities in the Southern Cameroons

Mamdani (1996, p. 52), describes the Native Authority system as a "decentralised arm of the colonial state" that dispensed customary law to those living within the territory of the tribe. The Native Authority system presumed a king at the centre of every polity and consequently modelled itself on patriarchy and authoritarianism. Native Authorities operated on the premise that villages within the same geographical or cultural spheres were brought together to conduct local administration, as well as economic and social development activities (Chiabi 2011 and Diduk 1989). According to Nyamdi (1988), the system involved the natives in what was essentially a colonial administration designed to reduce the alienation that might have resulted from an outright British Administration.

In contrast to what obtained in *Iboland*, where the British created and imposed chieftaincy rule on the population, most areas in the Southern Cameroons, particularly in the Bamenda grassfields,[22] had established

---

[21] The British section of Cameroon was made up of two non-contiguous territories (Northern and Southern Cameroons) both territories were initially administered from the neighbouring colony of Nigeria. However at independence only the Northern part remained with Nigeria, the Southern section voted to join the Republic of Cameroon.

[22] The term grassfields is derived from the savannah vegetation that covers the Western highlands of Cameroon (Fonchingong & Tanga, 2007). The western highlands or grassfields of Cameroon range from 5 to 7 degrees north of the Equator along the Cameroon-Nigerian border (Warnier 1993, p. 304).Grassfields is the name given to the highlands of the North West Region of Cameroon. It lies immediately north of the tropical forest zone and ranges in altitude between 2000 and 6000 ft above sea level. The Bamenda plateau lies within the south-western part of the area, and is

traditional authorities (Vubo and Ngwa 2001). The Native Authorities were divided into three broad categories including a council of elders in areas where authoritative leadership could not be imposed, district heads appointed by the British and the well-grounded hereditary *Fons* (or chiefs) in the Grassfields (DeLancey, et al., 2010). Because the Native Authority system was intrinsically tribal, the sheer number of tribes in Southern Cameroons required the creation of numerous native authorities to cater for the needs of each and every one of them.

From the onset of British administration in the Southern Cameroons in 1916, traditional authorities were co-opted in the administration of the territory so as to encourage local self-government (Crowder 1964 and Awasom 2003). This was partly a direct outcome of the colonial administration's policy of actively discouraging the formation of a class of 'Europeanised Africans' through the administrative service, because it was thought to be an "alien superstructure [fit only for] "colonial officials from the upper classes [who] at home could be chiefs in their own country" (Mamdani, 1996, p. 77).

Around 1926 British officials approved the creation of a number of native authorities based on the findings of assessment and intelligence reports. The aim of creating these administrative units according to colonial officials was to avoid earlier mistakes in Eastern Nigeria where, because of difficulties in locating chiefs or sound traditional authority structures, they appointed a number of 'synthetic warrant chiefs', most of whom were not to the liking of the population and resulted in a period of rioting and political unrest (Crowder 1964 and Le Vine 1964). Meanwhile, in the 1930s, the preponderance of chiefs in Southern Cameroon politics became increasingly challenged by the educated elite[23] who, according to Chem-Langhee, (1983, 660) "British colonialism had produced but ignored in the development of native administration."

---

defined by a series of escarpments which dip down into the lowland forest zone of the Upper Cross River Valley to the south-west and the Mentchum Valley to the north (Rowlands, 1979, pp. 3-4).

[23] Interestingly some of these educated elite were sons of chiefs e.g. E.M.L Endeley, J.N Foncha and others were from royal families.

2.4 Political Developments in the Southern Cameroons

Multi-party politics first came on the African scene in the period after the Second World War. It was introduced as part of the colonial reform that sought to stabilise and contain a situation made fluid by widespread popular struggles (Mamdani 1995, 51).

Because the British governed the Southern Cameroons as part of Eastern Nigeria, they did not pay much attention to the educational and infrastructural needs of what was a fringe part of its Nigerian colony. Consequently, most Southern Cameroonians who wanted to obtain higher education went abroad, principally to Nigeria but also to Europe and North America. As a result there was a significant Southern Cameroonian diaspora in Lagos and Enugu (Elong, 2013). Around the 1930s some diaspora elite members became actively involved in the political ferment that was brewing in Eastern Nigeria. This activism culminated in the formation of the first Southern Cameroons political organisation known as the Cameroon Youth League (CYL) in Lagos in 1939.

The Southern Cameroonian elite, including Dr E.M.L Endeley, and N.N Mbile, played an active role in the formation of Dr Nnamdi Azikiwe's National Council of Nigeria and the Cameroons (NCNC). Upon returning home, Endeley sought to replicate such activism and was instrumental in reviving dormant community groups such as the Bakweri Improvement Union and the Bakweri Land Committee[24] (Le Vine 1964 and Johnson 1970). Most of these associations were found in urban areas and were quite vocal about local issues. Other associations outstepped narrow tribal confines and highlighted broader issues such as Britain's failure to promote the economic development of the territory. These associations were subsequently to form the backbone of political organisations such as the Kamerun National Congress (KNC), and the Kamerun People's Party (KPP).

2.4.1 Educated Elite vs. 'illiterate' Traditional Chiefs

In the 1940s, British political officers in the Southern Cameroons began identifying problems inherent in the Native Authority system,

---

[24] This association was concerned with the recovery of Bakweri lands alienated during the German colonial period and used for large-scale agricultural plantations.

particularly the increase in population that was not matched by proportionate increases in the number of administrative structures. For example, in the Bamenda division, the Senior Divisional Officer proposed that the division be carved up into four administrative sub-units. It was also around this time that the colonial office issued a dispatch from London urging local administrators to implement electoral reform (Le Vine 1964). The idea was to move away from the traditional format of appointive Native Authorities to elected forms of local government. This dispatch was followed by consultations conducted by local administrators who by 1948 reached the conclusion that the Native Administration system in the territory was in dire need of reform (Chem-Langhee 1983).

Among the early outcomes of these reforms was the creation of the Cameroons Provincial Council in Victoria in 1949 which, to the chagrin of some members of the educated elite, was packed with traditional chiefs. This left some eager to engage in local politics to constitute themselves into voluntary associations such as the Kom Improvement Association (KIA) (Nkwi, 1997). The KIA famously petitioned the UN, complaining about the incompetence of some traditional chiefs, especially the uneducated ones. It also wondered how the territory would develop with such a calibre of people at the helm. The KIA also charged Britain with gross neglect, particularly in its failure to develop the Southern Cameroons economically, socially, and educationally. British intransigence towards the KIA's demands further radicalised them to the point that they not only demanded a complete abdication of 'illiterate' traditional authorities from Native Administration but, failing that, the complete abolition of the Native Administration system (Chem-Langhee 1983).

Britain reluctantly yielded to pressures for reform and in 1949 introduced a number of changes into the administrative setup of the territory. As a result, the Bamenda Division was transformed into Bamenda Province and the Victoria, Kumba and Mamfe Divisions into the Cameroons Province. The result of these changes was that many Native Administrative areas, particularly those in close geographical proximity and sharing common ethnological connections, were amalgamated into larger administrative sub-units. Each federation consisted of a council, treasury, central court and appeal court, (Kaberry 2004; Chem-Langhee 1983; Johnson 1970 and Kaberry 1962). The

Native Authority Federations and the Cameroons Provincial Council meeting in Victoria served as arenas for discussing issues pertaining to the management of the federated administrative units, as well as forums for debates about issues relevant to the entire colony. Although both institutions were dominated by chiefs, it nevertheless witnessed the entry of the educated elite, thereby providing a platform for them to contribute towards the development of the territory.

In 1951 general elections were held for the Eastern House of Assembly in Nigeria. The results of this vote constituted a remarkable turnaround in the fortunes of the educated elite because all thirteen people selected to represent the Southern Cameroons in the above legislature came from this class. In contrast to some traditional rulers and their followers whose main focus in the Native Authority was limited to issues within the narrow confines of ethnic and tribal boundaries, the interest of the educated elite revolved around broader political issues such as autonomy, separation, secession, reunification etc. Prominent among them were J. N. Foncha, E. M. L. Endeley, S. T. Muna, and N. N. Mbile. Most of them would in later years play key roles in the independence and reunification of Cameroon (Chem-Langhee, 1983).

2.5 The path to Independence in the Southern Cameroons

The Southern Cameroons gained independence in 1961, following a UN-organised Plebiscite (DeLancey, et al., 2010). In the lead-up to this event Britain did not relent in its efforts to integrate the territory into Nigeria. At a UN Trusteeship Committee meeting the British representative declared that the best course for the Southern Cameroons was for the "people to prepare themselves to participate in training towards self-government within Nigeria" (Le Vine, 1964, p. 200). Initially British sentiment took tangible form through the participation of Nigeria-based Southern Cameroonians in the formation of the NCNC, notably Endeley and Mbile. However, the formation of the Cameroon Youth League by these same Lagos-based Southern Cameroonians signalled a shift in position.

The path to independence for the Southern Cameroons was not smooth sailing, principally because of fundamental differences between the two main political parties over the future direction of the territory.

The issue over which the governing Kamerun National Democratic Party (KNDP), led by Foncha, and the opposition KPP led by Endeley fought during the UN-sponsored referendum boiled down to the question of whether to join the Republic of Cameroun or the Federation of Nigeria.

In the years leading up to the UN-sponsored plebiscite, Endeley's position on the issue of reunification was quite ambiguous. As a member of the Southern Cameroons Legislature in 1956, in what was seen as a move to demonstrate his party's commitment to the reunification of Cameroon, he pushed for the elimination or relaxation of restrictions on naturalisation requirements for French Cameroonians[25] residing in the territory. However, in 1957 he made a complete volte-face during the London Constitutional Conference, where he made plain his inclination towards integration with Nigeria. Upon returning home, he was reported to have pressured the Southern Cameroons Parliament to disfranchise the French Cameroonians living in the territory. This shift in Endeley's position on the issue of reunification occasioned a major split in his party including the defection of S.T Muna to the KNDP. It also cost him the crucial backing of traditional chiefs, notably those from the Bamenda Division (Johnson, 1970).

Despite the loss of key allies over the issue of integration with Nigeria, Endeley managed to cobble up an alliance with the KPP party led by N.N Mbile with whom they now found common ground after an earlier split in 1953 when Mbile left the KNC to form the KPP. In 1958 Endeley, as leader of the majority party in the Southern Cameroons legislature, proposed constitutional changes that introduced a ministerial system, enabling him to become the first premier of the Southern Cameroons. These changes also enlarged the legislature from twenty-one to twenty-six seats and looked to full regional self-government after elections in 1959 (Le Vine, 1964). In the general elections held in January 1959, Foncha and the KNDP party won fourteen out of twenty-six seats in the legislature, replacing Endeley as Prime Minister of the Southern Cameroons. Interestingly, the main slogan during the KNDP campaign was secession from Nigeria (Johnson, 1970).

---

[25] There were many French Cameroonians in the British territory whose presence not only stimulated and facilitated cooperation between the political leaderships of the two territories, but also greatly influenced political debate and courted controversy during the period leading up to the UN plebiscite.

Foncha interpreted his victory as a mandate to disengage from Nigeria, and almost immediately travelled in the company of Endeley to the UN in New York to plead their respective causes before the General Assembly. Whereas Foncha and Endeley agreed on the need for a plebiscite, they differed widely on the question to be put to voters. In Foncha's view reunification could only come after separation and upon agreement with the government of French Cameroon. On the other hand, Endeley insisted on a clear-cut choice between continued association with Nigeria as a fully autonomous member of the Nigerian federation and reunification with an independent French Cameroon (Le Vine, 1964). Faced with divergent views from the leadership of the Southern Cameroons, the United Nations (UN) General Assembly decided that a separate plebiscite would be held in Northern and Southern Cameroons. It also requested both men to return home and find a compromise on the plebiscite question.

Back home, an all-party conference was held in Mamfe from 10 to 11 August 1959. The conference deliberations was inconclusive because both parties stuck to their guns. Interestingly, the one choice which both political leaders did not openly espouse but which was strongly held by other stakeholders within the Southern Cameroons was that of independence. In fact, P.M Kale strongly argued for the termination of the trusteeship agreement, even if it left Southern Cameroonians on their own. Likewise, the *Fon* of Bali was much more forthcoming on the issue, arguing that French Cameroons was on fire due to the civil war raging there and Nigeria was water in which the Southern Cameroons could easily drown if it opted to go there. Galega II, like most chiefs, supported the idea of 'secession without reunification' (Johnson 1970 & Konings and Nyamnjoh 2003).

After failing to reach agreement during the Mamfe conference, both leaders returned to the UN where they came under sustained pressure from the General Assembly. For a moment it appeared that both leaders agreed to rally round P.M Kale's suggestion to ask for an independent nation. However, they were pressured by delegates from African countries to back down for fear that the creation of a new state would further balkanise the continent (Johnson, 1970). Following long and intractable negotiations at the General Assembly, both parties finally agreed to a plebiscite vote that contained two options, integration with Nigeria or reunification with French Cameroon.

This compromise was enshrined in General Assembly Resolution 1352, dated 14 March 1959, which called on the plebiscite to be held in Northern and Southern Cameroons on or before March 1961.[26] As to eligibility to vote in the plebiscite, it was agreed that only persons born in Southern Cameroons or who had one parent born there would be allowed to vote (Le Vine, 1964). While the Southern Cameroonians were preparing for a referendum on independence, French Cameroon was granted independence in January 1, 1960 under the leadership of Ahmadou Ahidjo who, after some initial scepticism, became a key proponent of a merger between Anglophone and Francophone Cameroon. As will be seen later, it was during Ahidjo's autocratic rule that the Federation born out of the political merger of both Cameroons was dissolved.

2.6 Ahmadou Ahidjo and Political Activities in East Cameroon

Ahmadou Ahidjo was Prime Minister (1958), then President (1960) of Francophone Cameroon before becoming the first President of the Federal Republic of Cameroon in 1961 and from 1972 president of the United Republic of Cameroon. He was a Muslim from the Fulani people in Northern Cameroon (Eyongetah & Brian, 1974). Compared to his Northern heartland, Ahidjo did not initially command support in the Southern part of the country and was often dismissed as 'merely a French stooge', particularly because of the crucial support he received from the French High Commissioner Jean Ramadier in the events leading up to his accession to power (Ndedi 2008, and Le Vine 1964). However, his detractors underestimated him because a couple of years later "Ahidjo was to display an unexpected political craftsmanship that would enable him to strengthen his originally weak position and eventually to construct a system of personal rule" (Konings and Nyamnjoh 2003, p. 4).

Upon assuming power, Ahidjo's most pressing challenge came in the form of an ongoing armed rebellion from the *Union des Populations du Cameroun* (UPC), a nationalist movement/party founded in 1948 and later proscribed by the French in 1955 because it demanded immediate

---

[26] On March 13 1959 the General Assembly unanimously endorsed a draft resolution proposing January 1, 1960 as the date of independence for French Cameroon (Le Vine, 179).

independence and reunification of the former German Kamerun (Austen and Derrick 1999; Le Vine 1964). The UPC was often vilified by the colonial authorities as communist agitators bent on taking French Cameroon into the Soviet bloc. In response to UPC activities, the colonial authorities meted out the full force of the counterinsurgency apparatus that "the French military had perfected in Indochina and Algeria, which included rounding up entire communities into detention camps, torture, beheadings and arson" (Argenti, 2007, p. 167).

Known locally as the *maquis* or *maquizards*, the UPC insurgency was the first armed uprising that caused widespread violence in Cameroon. The organisation conducted a guerrilla-style hit and run campaign mainly in the Southern part of the country around the Littoral and Bamilike areas, (Konings & Nyamnjoh, 2003). Following its proscription in French Cameroon, the organisation made inroads into the Southern Cameroons by nominally allying with the KNDP, before it was subsequently banned by the British authorities in 1957. Familiarity with the terrain enabled it to use the forests of the Southern Cameroons as rear bases from which to conduct forays into French Cameroon (Le Vine, 1964).

Following an intensification of violence in French Cameroon in 1959, Ahidjo requested and obtained *pleins pouvoirs* or emergency powers (not without protest from the opposition) which he used eventually to crush the UPC by the 1970s with the backing of the French military (Takougang and Krieger 1998; Le Vine 1964). With the UPC insurgency on the wane, Ahidjo turned his attention to consolidating his hold on the national polity. Accordingly, he employed nation-building rhetoric as an ideological smokescreen for concentration of powers in the office of the president and in his person. Centralisation, coalition-building and outright repression were the major strategies employed to attain these objectives (Konings & Nyamnjoh, 2003).

In April 1960, Ahidjo organised the first post-independence elections, for the 100 member Legislative Assembly during which the *Union Camerounaise* (UC) won 51 seats. Not surprisingly the majority of people who voted for the UC were from the Northern part of the country. The UC's initial attempts to penetrate the South proved futile; this, according to Takougang and Krieger (1998), was the main reason that drove Ahidjo to pursue a single party agenda by employing the carrot and stick method to ensure his UC party gained a foothold in the South, and also to co-opt the 'counter-elites' into its ranks (Bayart, 2009).

Ahidjo dished out political carrots during the formation of his first cabinet by allocating only six posts to his own party. The rest were distributed to the other parties in the following manner: three to the *Front Populaire pour l'Unite et la Paix* led by a former leader of one of the guerrilla wings of the UPC, two to the *Democrates Camerounais,* two to the *Parti Progressistes* and one to an independent member of the assembly (Takougang & Krieger, 1998). Such overtures to the opposition could be seen in the first instance as a very successful attempt by Ahidjo to compensate those that were willing to form a coalition with him, and secondly to shore up his scant support in the South by co-opting mainly Southern-based politicians into his cabinet. It is important to note that Ahidjo was not a political novice; he was at one point an MP in the French Fourth Republic, where he is said to have "enjoyed discussing canton elections in France, [and] was as a result a past master in the subtle art of ethnic politics" (Bayart, 2009, p. 150).

The effects of his actions were instantaneous. The *Mouvement d 'Action Nationale du Cameroun* of Charles Assale, which was part of the *Groupe des Progressistes* within the Assembly, dissolved and fused with the UC. In April 1961, the *Front Populaire Pour l'Unite et la Paix* disintegrated, following the announcement by its leader that it was joining the UC. Other opposition parties that were not given cabinet positions but expressed an inclination towards joining Ahidjo's government were given posts in the administration. Ahidjo then proceeded to use the stick to get recalcitrant parties in line. In January 1962 a faction of the UPC attempted to hold a congress in Yaoundé, but it was violently dispersed. Later, when a coalition of opposition leaders published an open letter then a manifesto accusing Ahidjo of attempting to create a de-facto one-party state which they feared could subsequently lead to what was termed 'fascist-type dictatorship', all four leaders were arrested, prosecuted, fined and sent to jail on charges of 'sedition and subversionary activities' (Le Vine, 1964, p. 222). With the imprisonment of key opposition figures, it now dawned on Ahidjo's political opponents that they either had to dissolve their parties and join the UC or face his wrath.

As a marker of his successful penetration of the South, Ahidjo organised the Fourth Congress of his UC party in the southern city of

Ebolowa in July 1962 where he publicly boasted about the UC being "the only political party in East Cameroon with a truly national character" (Takougang & Krieger, 1998, p. 44). This according to Le Vine (1964, p. 223-4), was ample proof that "East Cameroun has for all practical purposes ceased to have a party system." Ahidjo's declaration at the Ebolowa conference therefore marked the apogee of the UC's drive to move the country towards a one-party state, a movement that was trending elsewhere on the continent (Johnson, 1970). Having successfully created a de-facto one-party state in East Cameroon, Ahidjo keenly watched events in the Southern Cameroon, where the UN was about to organise a plebiscite to determine whether the territory would join Nigeria or French Cameroon. Prior to this, Ahidjo and Foncha met several times to discuss future arrangements under which both Cameroons might achieve reunification if the results of the plebiscite went in that direction (Le Vine 1964).

2.7 Plebiscite and Reunification in the Southern Cameroons

The sequence of events leading up to the plebiscite that was held simultaneously on 11 February, 1960 in British Northern and Southern Cameroons, like most election campaigns, was quite contentious. As noted earlier, the key issue in the debate was whether to integrate into the Federation of Nigeria or reunite with French Cameroon. The can of worms that politicians had to grapple with during the campaign included: (a) Deep-seated antipathy amongst Southern Cameroonians towards Nigerians, notably the Ibos (b) General attachment to 'British ways' (c). Feeling of community with certain French Cameroonians (d) General antipathy towards 'French ways' and (e) Fear of terrorists (and the military) from French Cameroon (Johnson, 1970).

Whereas the opposition KNC's campaign message focused on points (b, d & e) which were very much in line with its pro-Nigeria stance, the governing KNDP focused on points (a, b, c, & d), to neutralise point (e). In order to drive home its message, the KNDP placed emphasis on the name (Kamerun) as proof that the Southern Cameroons should join the Republic of Cameroon and not Nigeria. Hence to argue that we are 'Cameroonians not Nigerians' proved quite difficult for the opposition to counter effectively. Likewise, anybody who attempted such was branded a sell-out or traitor to the *Kamerun*[27] nation (my emphasis). The term Kamerun was used throughout the campaign to emphasise that restoration of the former German entity was sought (Chiabi 2011 and Johnson 1970). Interestingly the argument that Cameroon was one was employed by Francophones and some pro-regime Anglophones to counter calls for secession by groups such as the Southern Cameroons National Council (SCNC), and the Southern Cameroons Peoples Organisation (SCAPO).

In the end, the Southern Cameroonians who voted for reunification with the Republic of Cameroon won the plebiscite by 233,571 votes against 97,741 in favour of integration with Nigeria. Interestingly, the number of people who voted for reunification with the Republic of Cameroon was much higher in the North West (3.5 to 1) than in the South West (3 to 2). This disparity not only portrayed the divergent positions during the campaigns but also reflected the ethno-regional backgrounds of the leadership of the two main political parties, Prime Minister Foncha of the KNDP (North-Westerner) and leader of the opposition Endeley KNC (South-Westerner). This division is often cited as constituting the origins of the cleavage among the contemporary Anglophone elite (Konings & Nyamnjoh, 2003).

Initially, Ahidjo's attitude towards reunification with the Southern Cameroons was ambiguous. In his opening speech to the French Cameroon Legislative Assembly in 1958 he committed himself to the reunification of Cameroons only if it was the wish of the Southern Cameroonians. He added that the prospects for reunification could however not delay the onward march to independence of French Cameroon. Paradoxically, as the plebiscite date approached, Ahidjo became much more inclined towards a possible union with British Northern Cameroons. This was because the area had close geographical, ethnic, religious and cultural affinities to his region of origin in Northern Cameroon. It was argued that such a union, were it to happen, would have gone a long way towards boosting his political fortunes by significantly widening his political base. This is why he cried foul over the result and vainly sought to get it cancelled (Le Vine, 1964).

---

[27]The three main parties; KNC, KPP and KNDP, all used the letter K, unlike in French Cameroon where political parties mostly used the letter C, e.g. *Union Camerounaise* and *Démocrates Camerounaise*.

Ahidjo's lukewarm attitude towards reunification, was the principal reason for his initial hesitation to commit himself fully to Foncha's overtures to enter into negotiations about the establishment of a federal state. Nevertheless, he occasionally voiced an opinion on the issue and, whenever he did so it was to reassure Southern Cameroonians that the reunification process would be held in a serene atmosphere with equal representation of both parties. He went further to say that the process would be gradual and would in no way constitute the annexation of the Southern Cameroons by the Republic of Cameroon (Le Vine, 1964). However, when they eventually got down to the business of negotiating the details of reunification, differences in the views of both men on the proposed federation were not only strong, but the asymmetrical power relation between them was quite evident.

Foncha's ideas about the proposed federation tilted towards decentralisation and deconcentration of power, similar to what obtained in the Southern Cameroons. This was starkly at odds with Ahidjo's thoughts which had been shaped by the 'centralised and assimilative' mode of governance inherited from French colonialism. Ahidjo's inclination was very much in line with the spirit of the times. As noted earlier, modernisation and nation-building placed heavy emphasis on a strong unitary state as the main conduit for promoting economic development, and for Ahidjo this could only be accomplished by having undisputed control of the state apparatus. Both parties nevertheless agreed in principle to a centralised form of federation as a preliminary arrangement, with the expectation of future negotiations on concrete arrangements. Many scholars have argued that the term 'preliminary arrangements' agreed upon in Fumban, was merely a smokescreen that Ahidjo never intended to honour (Konings and Nyamnjoh 2003; Bayart 2009; Fombad 2012; Forje 2008 and Njoh 2011).

2.8 The Fumban Constitutional Conference

The formalisation of the post-plebiscite negotiations between Ahidjo and Foncha, during which details of the federation was fleshed out, took place in the town of Fumban in the West Region of Cameroon. The aim of the Fumban conference was to resolve all outstanding differences between the two leaders and to draft a federal constitution (Le Vine, 1964). The issues to be ironed out during this conference included federal jurisdiction, state autonomy, and the nature of institutions, among others (DeLancey, et al., 2010).

Prior to this conference, the Fourth Committee of the UN General Assembly proposed to appoint three administrative and constitutional experts to assist both parties during the negotiation process. Considering the issues at stake such a proposal should have been welcomed to help bridge the divergent views of Ahidjo and Foncha on the federation question. However, the offer was turned down, allegedly by Ahidjo with the tacit support of Foncha, on the grounds that both parties were already engaged in constitutional negotiations, hence expert advice was deemed 'unnecessary interference in a strictly Cameroonian affair.' As events in later years were to prove, "Foncha's naive complicity in this matter proved to be fatal to the Southern Cameroonians" (Konings & Nyamnjoh, 2003, p. 40).

Meanwhile, the British stance on the issue gravely weakened the bargaining position of the Southern Cameroonians. Britain's apparent indifference over the fate of the Southern Cameroons was a direct outcome of plebiscite result favouring reunification with French Cameroon. Whereas East Cameroon came into the negotiations at Fumban with significant diplomatic and technical support from France (Takougang & Krieger, 1998), West Cameroonians were left to themselves as Britain "in a spirit of abandonment, appeared not to care whether the new constitution sufficiently protected the Anglophone minority or would survive the post-reunification era" (Konings & Nyamnjoh, 2003, p. 41).

Further, Johnson (1970) notes that records of the constitutional debates reveal little knowledge on the part of the Southern Cameroons delegates about the disparity between their expectations of federation i.e. a decentralised federation, and the highly centralised federation favoured by Ahidjo. Likewise their arguments were replete with contradictions and a lack of comprehension over issues such as centralisation of power. He adds "most of the items on Ahidjo's list of federal powers that did not appear on their own were accepted with little debate [or in cases of debate] concentrated solely on the need to align wording of the eastern proposals with no debate of the underlying issues" (Johnson, 1970, p. 189).

Notwithstanding this, there were also two very contentious issues during the Fumban negotiations to do with the nature of Presidential powers and the length of the transition period. In a bid to lengthen the time available for states to exercise executive powers, the West Cameroon delegation proposed a transition period of 18 months during which they envisaged a transitory structure composed of equal membership from both sides and a decision-making body made up of the two PMs and fourteen members from both legislatures. Ahidjo not only dismissed the 18th month transition period, suggesting six instead, but proposed that the interim assembly be elected by the two legislatures based on proportional representation.

The agreement reached at Fumban failed to accommodate the desires of West Cameroonians, particularly in relation to the composition of the federal government decision-making body. Some cosmetic changes left the legislature not far from what it was prior to the negotiations. For example, the Southern Cameroons House of Assembly was renamed West Cameroon Legislative Assembly, the House of Chiefs remained unchanged and the Ministerial system headed by a Prime minister and cabinet stayed the same. East Cameroon also retained its legislature with only a name change from National Assembly to East Cameroon Legislative Assembly. But for the introduction of the position of Secretary of State, its ministerial system remained unchanged.

Regarding the issue of presidential powers, the Fumban constitution bestowed the latter with unmitigated powers, i.e. a federal president with powers to appoint and dismiss a Prime Minister and cabinet members. It also empowered him to intervene in state affairs in emergency situations, suspend or dissolve state legislatures and rule by decree (Elong, 2013). In sum, the constitution that took the force of law on 1st October 1961 effectively "create[d] a hybrid President who combines the attributes of a British-style Governor-General, a Fifth Republic[28] President and an American chief executive" (Le Vine, 1964, p. 228).

---

[28] The Fifth Republic constitution here refers specifically to what obtained in France, which according to Le Vine (1964) was drafted in the context of the constitutional crisis of 1958 that brought General De Gaulle to power, and which was not in any way analogous to the context of writing the Cameroon constitution.

2.9 Conclusion

Ahidjo's proposals during the Fumban conference poignantly demonstrated the disparities in political values between himself and the leadership of West Cameroon. The outcome of the constitutional talks was starkly at odds with the expectations of the West Cameroon delegation who came to the conference expecting to maintain their relative autonomy inherited from British colonialism, and to uphold this inheritance in a federation of two equal partners (Chiabi 2011 and Konings 2011). This starkly contrasted with Ahidjo's thinking which was long shaped by the highly centralised and assimilative administrative legacy of French colonialism (Elong 2013; Jua and Konings 2004). The capitulation of Foncha and his colleagues in the face of Ahidjo's intransigent insistence on presidential powers as an influential segment of the state-level executive and legislative process had far reaching implications, specifically because it forfeited a crucial element of the Southern Cameroon's sovereignty and autonomy.

It is clear that the Federal system of territorial administration that came into existence following the reunification of East and West Cameroon on 1st October 1961, sounded the death-knell to any degree of grassroots autonomy in the Federal Republic in general and West Cameroon in particular (Elong 2013; Konings and Nyamnjoh 2003; Takougang and Krieger 1998; Rubin 1971; Johnson 1970; and Le Vine 1964). The concentration of powers in the hands of the president also meant he was able to act without restraint. By appropriating all decision-making powers from the states and concentrating them at the centre and by appointing civil administrators to serve as conveyor belts, the Federal authorities were in a position to monitor and supervise political life at all levels in both states. This was accentuated by the fact that the federal constitution, like most political texts in Cameroon, was notoriously vague on definition and content, leaving specific issues to decrees of application that emanated exclusively from the President. With such wide-ranging powers, Ahidjo did not hesitate to begin systematically dissolving the federation.

His first action was the slow but steady dismantling of the multiparty system on both sides of the national divide. Just like his peers on the continent, Ahidjo strongly believed that effective management of ethnic diversity required a united political organisation. It was in this light that he agreed with Foncha to limit the activities of the UC and the KNDP to one side of the country each (Konings and Nyamnjoh 2003; Eyongetah and Brian 1974). This was followed in 1966 by the dissolution of all political parties and the formation of the Cameroon National Union (CNU) party.

Having achieved this feat, Ahidjo on 20 October 1966, issued decree N° 61-DF-15, reorganising the country into six administrative structures with East Cameroon divided into five administrative regions, and West Cameroon left as a single unit (Elong 2013; Takougang and Krieger 1998). These administrative structures were headed by Federal Inspectors of Administration, who were answerable to the President rather than the Prime Ministers of the respective states (Eyongetah & Brian, 1974).

Finally, the Federal government also took control over all the important sources of revenue, including customs duties and foreign aid, leaving no autonomous financial provision for the federated states (Chem-Langhee, 1983). This decision was crucial for West Cameroon specifically because by regulating fiscal authority and tightly controlling financial disbursements to the federated states, the central government greatly disempowered the state governments (Page, 2003). Having politically and economically emasculated the federal states, Ahidjo proceeded to his ultimate goal of a unitary state not without passing through a referendum that was held on 20 May 1972. The referendum result was a 99.99% YES to a United Republic of Cameroon.

Chapter III

Political Transition and Economic Crisis: 'Wind of Change' But No Change

Economic relations are, ipso facto, political relations, which explain why economic stagnation inevitably leads to political stagnation (Mentan 1998, p. 49).

Change in the nature of African political systems since 1989 has not come about because authoritarian leaders suddenly decided to mend their ways and introduce measures producing accountability. Change has been forced upon those leaders by their being subjected to a wide range of pressures (Wiseman 1996, p. 35)

3.1 Introduction

On 6 November 1982 Cameroon's first head of state stepped down and voluntarily handed over the reins of power to his constitutional successor Paul Biya (Bayart 2009; Mbembe 2001; Akoko 2004; Konings and Nyamnjoh 2003). According to Delancy (1989, p. 65), "not only have voluntary surrenders of power been rare in modern African politics, but there had been no hints within Cameroon that President Ahidjo was contemplating giving up any of his powers." This feat by Ahidjo was quite unprecedented and followed a similar act two years earlier by Senegalese President Leopold Senghor (Takougang & Krieger, 1998).

Despite leaving the presidency, Ahidjo did not resign as chairman of the Cameroon National Union (CNU) party, from where he hoped to control the levers of the state and his constitutional successor by proxy. According to Delancy (1989, p. 66); "Ahidjo created Biya as a political actor, trained him and groomed him." To buttress this point, he argues that upon returning to Cameroon in 1962 from university in France, Biya was immediately absorbed into the civil service, became a cabinet minister in 1968, served in various capacities at the presidency until 1975 and thereafter was appointed Prime Minister.

A constitutional amendment in 1979 shifted succession at the helm of the state from the president of the National Assembly to the Prime Minister. Accordingly, "Ahidjo had put in place a skilled technocrat, a man with no political following of his own, no base of support other than Ahidjo's patronage" (Delancy 1989, p. 66). This was likely the case in the immediate aftermath of Ahidjo's resignation. However, as he was to find out to his peril not only was Biya no stooge, but his accession to power was an opportunity for the "elites of the central-southern region of the country, [who] allowed a northerner to take power in 1958, [to] recover it with obvious satisfaction in 1982" (Bayart, 2009, pp. 194-5).

Cameroon's new president was not only given the keys to the state on a gold platter, but by various accounts inherited a healthy economy (Amin 2011, Takougang & Krieger, 1998 and Nkwi 1997) At the time Cameroon's economy had a number of advantages including an extensive territory, favourable climate and fertile soils which enabled it to produce food crops for local consumption and cash crops for export. The country also experienced minimal population pressure and a stable, albeit authoritarian government which "maintained a stable economy [and] by the end of the 1970s was amongst the structurally best balanced in Africa" (Rambousek, 1982, p. 167). For example, between 1978 and 1985 Cameroon's Gross Domestic Product (GDP) witnessed an annual growth rate of 10% placing it amongst the countries with the highest per capita income growth in 1986 (Diduk, 1992, p. 205).

The hikes in the price of oil on the world market in the 1970s led to an increase in government revenues, occasioning a positive net effect on the economy. For example, from 1970 to 1985 the economy witnessed an annual growth rate of over 7% (Page, 2002), and an external debt of around US$2.3 billion in 1982 (Takougang & Krieger, 1998). This growth was aided in part by the discovery of oil in the 1970s, and commercial production effectively took off in 1978 and accelerated to its peak in the 1980s. Petroleum therefore became a pivotal element in Cameroon's economy (Delancy, 1989).

The importance of crude oil could be measured by the following figures. In 1977 cash crops contributed 71.9% of state revenue as against 1.4% for oil. However, by 1985 cash crops contributed 21.4% of state revenue against 65.4% for oil (Page, 2002, p. 44). At the time it was fashionable to "sterilise the windfall by allocating it in special development accounts" (Auty, 1988, p. 148). These special accounts, known in Cameroon as *compte hors budget*, were mostly held in foreign banks, and were meant to store oil funds and accumulate profits to be reinvested in the domestic economy (Konings & Nyamnjoh, 2003). In principle, the injection of oil money into the economy was to be aimed at boosting local investment and consumption patterns by the state and the private sector. These investments were to be directed at vital sectors of the economy such as infrastructural development, notably roads, railways, electricity etc. On the other hand, oil windfalls was also used to stabilise prices and control the exchange rate.

Unlike the situation in neighbouring countries such as Gabon and Nigeria, where oil windfalls witnessed 'rapid domestic absorption' into the national economy, the Cameroon government under Ahidjo deliberately downplayed urges for 'rapid absorption' by not publicly disclosing the true figures, thereby avoiding a 'boom mentality' (Delancy, 1989). Ahidjo's frugal management of the economy earned Cameroon the reputation for "sound macroeconomic management and exemplary windfall deployment" (Auty, 1988, p. 149). However, in the 1980s a combination of internal and external circumstances undermined this positive growth trend. This caused a downturn in the economy and subsequently an economic crisis (Amin, 2011). According to Mbembe (2001, p. 49), "the fall in prices of cash and subsistence crops aided by the economic slowdown accelerated at the same time that the erosion of external financial reserves worsened."

This chapter seeks to demonstrate how the economic crisis that affected Cameroon from the mid-1980s to the late-1990s wrought profound changes in the national economy and occasioned tectonic movements on the political landscape. The mutations that occurred in Cameroon during this period were not without external interventions from the International Monetary Fund (IMF) and the World Bank. Like elsewhere in Africa, both institutions imposed one-size-fits-all structural adjustment programmes (SAP) designed to kick-start the Cameroon economy and align it with the prevailing neoliberal trend. On the other hand, donors pushed for governance reform which was thought to be a panacea to the challenges facing Cameroon as it navigated the treacherous 'second wind of change' that swept across the African continent in the 1990s (Southall, 2003).

At the time, it was generally believed that change on the economic and political fronts was imperative. However, unlike in Taiwan and South Korea where economic changes preceded and partly led political changes (Ottaway, 1997), events in Cameroon were not only dictated by external agendas, but other local, mainly political, elements also came into the fray. The outcome was half-baked economic reform and the politicisation of democratic reforms. In terms of the latter, i.e. decentralisation, I argue here that the elite in Cameroon faced mounting unpopularity caused by economic mismanagement, corruption and political inertia. This elite, some of whom had by the 1990s been shuttling around the state apparatus since independence "could no longer justify its stay in power much less its monopoly of power" (Mentan, 1998, p. 43).

The elite feared that succumbing to the people's demands for change would mean political suicide, as was the case with the regimes of Hastings Kamuzu Banda in Malawi, Moussa Traoré in Mali, and Kenneth Kaunda in Zambia, among others (van de Walle 1997 and Wiseman 1996). This chapter therefore argues that lacking legitimacy because of its failed promises of economic improvement and political liberalisation, the ruling elite in Cameroon successfully thwarted opposition demands for a 'sovereign' national conference to discuss constitutional reform and orchestrated what some describe as a façade of meaningless cosmetic changes that enabled them to remain in power to the present.

3.2 The Political Economy of Cameroon from the 1980s to the 1990s

In Cameroon too the liberalisation undertaken by Biya from 1983 onwards gave the impression that a strongly bureaucratic regime was becoming open to the representation of the national business circles (Bayart, 2009, p. 94)

As noted earlier, the relationship between Ahidjo and Biya was quite cordial in the immediate aftermath of the former's resignation in 1982. In January 1983, Ahidjo dismissed four members of the CNU for alleged insubordination to Biya. Later that year both men embarked on tours around the country in a show of unity (Takougang & Krieger, 1998). When French President François Mitterrand visited Cameroon in 1983 both men paid a courtesy visit to Ahidjo in Garoua. Prior to this visit, Biya moved to stamp his authority at the helm of the state by conducting a cabinet reshuffle that witnessed the dismissal of some Ahidjo acolytes (Delancy, 1989). This move was quite significant because it indicated that Biya was gradually asserting his authority, albeit in the government and not the party where Ahidjo was very much in command.

The descent to hell for Ahidjo began in August 1983 when President Biya announced the discovery of a plot against his government that implicated Ahidjo. This announcement marked the unravelling of a chain of events that culminated in a *putsch* in 1984 which was put down by loyal elements in the army. This was followed by summary trials of alleged plotters, including Ahidjo, who at the time was in exile in France. Many co-conspirators were found guilty and some were sentenced to death and executed. Other death sentences were commuted to life imprisonment, including that handed down to Ahidjo (Takougang and Krieger 1998 and Mbembe 2001). According to Bayart (2009, pp. 150-151): "The patrimonialist recuperation of the state which had been attempted by Ahidjo between January and June 1983 in his desire to assure the supremacy of the party over the Presidency of the Republic had failed." The abortive coup in 1984 therefore "provided Biya the opportunity to remove from office a number of ministers, bureaucrats and politicians who were closely associated with the Ahidjo regime or whose loyalties to the new regime were suspect" (Konings & Nyamnjoh, 2003, p. 7).

After successfully neutralising the perceived threat to his rule, Biya set-out to consolidate himself at the helm of the state. It was therefore with renewed vigour that he announced the next scheduled congress of the Cameroon National Union in Bamenda (Delancy, 1989). He used this occasion to announce the dissolution of the CNU and the birth of the Cameroon Peoples Democratic Movement. Biya launched his vision for the country under the banner of a 'New Deal' and later fleshed it out in a book: *Communal Liberalism* (1987). Biya's vision of communal liberalism entailed the emergence of a new political society and national culture, the promotion of economic development, social justice and human dignity. Within this framework, he pressed for continuation of the one-party system with the CPDM serving as a school for democracy until the country would be in a position to face the complexities of political pluralism (Biya, 1987).

In a remarkable departure from what obtained under Ahidjo and the CNU, the CPDM 'democratic canopy' in 1986 allowed a plurality of candidates to vie for positions in the basic organs of the party. Next came open competition for local council elections in 1987, followed by multiple candidates for elections to the National Assembly in 1988 (Mentan, 1998). Added to this was the president's promise of open and accountable governance, zero tolerance for corruption and illicit enrichment and enabling conditions for all citizens "to participate fully and effectively in governance and the economy" (Mbuagbo & Akoko, 2004, p. 256).

These overtures were an attempt by a new president to win popular support. On the other hand, such hyperbole could be viewed as foresighted attempts to head off an impending storm. Biya's rhetoric also had the unintended consequence of rekindling nostalgia among some segments of the single party for the good old days of multiparty competition. For Anglophones, it wetted appetites for a return to open electoral competitions reminiscent of what obtained in the late 1950s and early 1960s before the reunification of Cameroon. According to Mentan (1998, p. 43); "the entire experience did prepare Cameroonians for the real thing which became a categorical imperative in 1990." Prior to the above-mentioned 'categorical imperative', the economic situation in Cameroon took a turn for the worse and, as noted earlier, it had both internal and external dimensions.

In the years following independence, economic development in Africa was largely driven by the state. In Cameroon, Presidents Ahidjo and Biya based economic development on state planning (Delancy, 1989). Economic development under Ahidjo was encapsulated in the term 'planned liberalism.' This placed emphasis on the promotion of agriculture and industry and also the creation of parastatals and other public corporations (Gabriel, 1999). The state therefore assumed a pivotal position in economic development over and above the local private investor class which was dominated by French interests amounting to roughly two-thirds in 1984 (Mentan, 2011, p. 31).

Economic planning by the state also took the form of five year plans. The first three sets of plans (1960–1965; 1966–1971 and 1972-1975) focused on industrial and infrastructural development, as well as on food crop production (Nkwi, 1997). The fourth plan (1976-1981) placed emphasis on the development of agriculture and agro-industries. The fifth plan (1981-1986) came at a time when oil constituted a significant revenue earner for the country and was marked by the intensification of agriculture and rural projects. The sixth plan (1986-1991) was the first to be drafted under Biya and it envisaged the construction of new housing, extension of electricity services to urban and rural areas, promotion of private land ownership, laying the foundations of a social security programme and development of a preventive healthcare system (Delancy, 1989). As elaborated upon subsequently, the onset of the economic crisis in the mid-1980s disrupted the government's ambitious schemes, including the sixth development plan.

State-run parastatals and public corporations constituted a highly lucrative sector of the economy that developed during the Ahidjo period and continued into the Biya era. The preponderance of parastatals could be seen in vital sectors such as industry, agriculture, transport and utilities. However, a number of these entities were poorly conceived, badly managed and became prime sources of corruption that enabled state officials to accumulate wealth by enriching themselves at the public expense (Gabriel, 1999).

A prime example of an ill-conceived agro-industrial project was the rice development corporation or *Société d'expansion et de modernisation de la riziculture de Yagoua (Semry)*. Conceived of as part of President Ahidjo's 'Green Revolution' campaign, Semry was a capital-intensive integrated rice production scheme located in the semi-arid North of Cameroon (Delancy, 1989). This project received the financial backing of the French government, the World Bank and the European Economic Community (EEC). The project was earmarked as a scheme to modernise the country's agricultural sector and ensure food self-sufficiency. It was also aimed at positioning Cameroon as a major producer of rice which, according to van de Walle (1989), was unimportant for local diets and absent from farming practices. However, Semry's operation was undermined by cheap rice imported from Asia. Paradoxically, the majority of rice importers at the time were from the North of the country. This further weakened what was already a futile attempt at local 'development' in their home area. It was also alleged that, when Biya took over as president, he looked the other way while 'fraudulent rice' was imported into the country, further compromising Semry. To confound things even further, Semry was placed under the Ministry of Industrial and Commercial Development rather than the ministry of Agriculture which, according to van de Walle (1989, p. 596), was 'corrupt because of rent-seeking activities.'

Another example of an overly ambitious agro-industrial scheme was the Wheat Development Corporation, or *Société pour le Développement de la culture du Blé* (SODEBLE). Under the fourth Development Plan (1976-81), Cameroonian authorities envisaged the mass production of wheat. It was hoped that local production of wheat would meet the needs of Cameroon and save the country millions of Francs CFA[29] from wheat imports. Oblivious to the fact that Cameroon's climate was not suitable for wheat production and also to the absence of suitable seed varieties at the time, SODEBLE was created and allocated 50,000 hectares for growing wheat with an expected yield of 125,000 metric tons per year. However, by 1983 only 600 hectares were planted and 900 tons produced (Delancy, 1989, p. 120).

In the domain of industrial production, ill-conceived schemes had no better track records than the agro-industrial projects. For example, in 1976 a fertilizer factory, *Société Camerounaise des Engrais* (SOCAME), was established, shut down in 1977 and reopened shortly afterwards before closing again in 1981 due to very high maintenance costs. In 1980 a paper and pulp factory *Cellulose du Cameroun* (CELLUCAM) became operational, but went bankrupt in 1983. According to Delancy (1989, p. 133), CELLUCAM's bankruptcy stemmed from the fact that its products were expected to be "sold at USD$800 per ton with a break-even price of USD$450. But when production began, the selling price for paper was USD$300 per ton." Other ambitious projects, including Liquefied Natural Gas (LNG), Aluminium and Iron and Steel plants among others, were also envisaged (Auty, 1988). However, the onset of economic crisis saw these projects scaled down or scrapped entirely.

3.3 Economic (Mis)-management and Meltdown

> [T]he interventions of the World Bank and the IMF are imposed by the harsh laws of economics and are viewed, not without justification, by most African leaders as an attack upon their sovereignty (Bayart, 2009, p. 27).

The production of oil added another commodity to Cameroon's exports which included cocoa, coffee, banana and rubber. Whereas Ahidjo was widely praised for frugal management of the oil windfall, the same virtue could not be claimed for Biya. According to Auty, (1988, p. 151), "losses incurred by earlier investments together with extra-

---

[29] *Communauté Financière Africaine.*

budgetary spending [to establish] the authority of the new president who came to power in 1982, undermined the official goal of slow windfall absorption." This process accelerated over the ensuing years, rendering the economy highly dependent on oil revenues (ODI, 1995).

Prior to exhaustion of the *compte hors budget,* the economy of Cameroon had been experiencing a gradual downturn. Several factors were advanced to explain this phenomenon. The first was the drought that affected large parts of the African continent in the 1980s (Shaw, 1992). Although the impact on Cameroon was minimal compared to the Horn of Africa, the country nevertheless witnessed a decrease in rainfall which reduced food and export crop yields. For example, cocoa production fell from 68,200 to 57,200 tons in 1981-1983, Arabica coffee exports dropped from 25,000 to 13,500 tons in1982-1983, other exports such as timber, banana, and palm oil equally declined (Delancy 1989 and Page 2002). Meanwhile, the actual exchange rate appreciated by around 54% in 1986-1993 reducing the country's competitiveness (Mentan, 1998).

Other shocks also kicked in, as exemplified by the slump in both the price and number of exploitable sites for crude oil. As a result, Cameroon's revenue from oil exports dropped by 60% in 1985-1986 (Delancy, 1989, p. 145). This was exacerbated by the fact that a large percentage of oil revenues was valued in US dollars which by mid-1995 had dropped by around 40% against the CFA (ODI, 1995). Consequently, GDP dropped from CFA 4.071 to CFA 2.867 billion in1985-1986 and the state budget was reduced from CFA 800 billion to CFA 550 billion (Mentan, 1998, p. 43).The government resorted to external borrowing and dipped even further into overseas reserves. To illustrate how the *compte hors budget* was depleted, Delancy (1989, p. 141) describes how in 1985 the annual budget of Cameroon was 740 billion, then President Biya added another 180 billion to boost development expenditures, medical supplies and equipment.

It is common knowledge that oil revenues in Cameroon from Ahidjo to Biya were 'official state secrets.' Within this rather murky world, accountability by the executive to elected representatives (the majority of them members of the ruling CPDM) was close to nil. No doubt this created fertile grounds for fraudulent practices or, bluntly, outright theft. For example, in its 1990-91 budget the government claimed that oil revenues amounted to CFA 250 billion francs. However, the French

Treasury's Franc Zone report for the same year estimated oil revenues to be around CFA 305 billion (Awung & Atanga, 2011). Considering the level of French involvement in Cameroon, as seen through expressions for its relationship such as *arrière-cours* or private backyard, *domaine-réserve* or private matter, *chasse-gardée* or exclusive hunting grounds, or *pre-carre* or natural preserve etc. (Renou, 2002), it is clear that the above disparity in Cameroon's oil revenues was a disingenuous move by the leadership to conceal oil money for ulterior motives. Further, having access to such sensitive financial information of what is supposedly an independent state demonstrated the depth of French involvement in Cameroon.

We may deduce then that the regime of President Biya continued Ahidjo's practice of deliberately understating the true value of Cameroon's oil wealth. This prompts the question, where did the difference between the above sums of money come from? Some contend that oil funds (and overseas borrowing) were used to prop up the litany of failing parastatals. For example, in 1984-5 government support to parastatals amounted to CFA 150 billion. (ODI, 1995). Others argue that it simply "disappeared because of corruption and political patronage" (Awung & Atanga, 2011, p. 108). It was also said to have been used to prop up the bloated state bureaucracy (Mentan, 2011). In light of the *modus operandi* of the ruling elite in Cameroon, which by and large operated under what could be termed a form of 'neopatrimonial alliance', one can suggest that all these arguments are reasonable.

Neopatrimonialism, as used in this context, refers to "a highly personal and clientelistic type of rule involving the massive redistribution of state resources" (Gabriel, 1999, p. 173). Within such systems, leaders "maintain authority through personal patronage rather than through ideology" (Bratton & van de Walle, 1994, p. 458). It has also been described as an all-encompassing term involving "clientelism, ethnicity, tradition, tribalism, nepotism, or rent-seeking" (Mkandawire, 2013, p. 6). Neopatrimonialism can be seen as the interconnection of two types of domination: "Under patrimonialism, all power relations between ruler and ruled are personal relations... Under neopatrimonialism, the distinction between the private and the public formally exists and is accepted" (Erdmann & Engel, 2006, p. 18); however, the issue is how this distinction is observed in practice. As elaborated upon subsequently, the blurring of the line between public and private in Cameroon during the volatile 1990s meant personal favours, including jobs, contracts licenses etc., were often awarded preferably to tribal clients/kin and select regional clients in exchange for personal loyalty.

Despite the deteriorating economic situation, the government maintained its reliance on the *compte hors budget* and also on crucial support from France to finance investment programmes and support consumer demand. However, by 1986 the account was almost empty (Delancy, 1989). Despite calls from donors for economic reforms, the government insisted that Cameroon would overcome the crisis without external assistance (Page, 2002). This could be explained by the fact that: "For African states, regardless of ideological disposition, resisting the IMF and the World Bank became an essential ingredient in the continuing quest for internal legitimacy" (Nyang'oro, 1992, p. 14).

In line with this logic, a new finance law was adopted by the National Assembly in June 1987. This law contained the government's Economic Stabilisation Plan under which it enumerated a streamlining of government expenditure on water, electricity and fuel, as well as housing and other benefits to civil servants. However, "the Economic Stabilisation Plan failed to achieve the desired results" (Awung & Atanga, 2011, p. 109). Forced to the wall, and faced with the inadequacies of its budgetary adjustments, the government embarked with the IMF on a series of reform packages in September 1988, November 1991 and March 1994, and with the World Bank in 1989 and 1994 (ODI, 1995).

3.4 Economic Crisis, Structural Adjustment and Political Impasse

Structural adjustment lending usually requires containment of the public wage bill and reduction of government employment to meet near-term fiscal targets (Goldsmith 2003, p. 192).

Most African economies began experiencing economic difficulties in the early 1980s. At the time there was some controversy between the advocates of the Lagos Plan of Action (LPA) and the Bretton Woods institutions over the causes of the crisis. The LPA was spearheaded by the then Organisation of African Unity (OAU) and its objective was to seek solutions to the economic crisis plaguing the continent. Inasmuch as both parties sought solutions to the economic crisis, they disagreed on the causes. Whereas the World Bank blamed the crisis on 'internal political and policy aspects,' the LPA blamed external causes, notably shocks from the oil crisis as well as the falling price of primary products in the world market. Disparity over the origins of the crisis can be explained by the fact that on the one hand, "African governments, having committed themselves to a welfare agenda at the time of independence, could not afford to abruptly abandon this commitment" (Young 1982, cited in Nyang'oro 1992, p. 13). On the other hand the World Bank and IMF were committed to a "liberal global political economy whose smooth operation is dependent on group members following certain rules" (Nyang'oro, 1992, p. 13)

Under structural adjustment therefore, "African civil services were perceived as bloated and a drain on the state's scarce resources" (Olowu, 2003, p. 101) and as a result public services had to be streamlined and the private sector revived. Shrinking the public purse meant eliminating ghost workers, downsizing the state, departmental restructuring, streamlining budgets, curbing expenditures, privatisation and dependence on contractors. The paradox in the austerity measures was the development of a 'revolving door' phenomenon whereby many states rehired or redeployed laid-off staff into other departments (Olowu, 2003, p. 110). For example, in Senegal "the number of civil servants continued to increase throughout the adjustment period" (Graham, 1997, p. 85), despite pressures by donors to downsize.

In Cameroon, the 'revolving door' phenomenon was not only an outlet for patronage, but also took on an ethnic dimension. In what was seen as a move to secure and strengthen his Southern power base, President Biya increased the size of the civil service with his 'ethnic faithful.' For example, between 1983 and 1988, the number of public service personnel increased from 120,600 to 180,000, amounting to 70% of state recurrent expenditure (Mentan, 2011). To buttress the overtly ethnic bias of state personnel, it was reported that around August 1991, "thirty-seven of the forty-nine *prefets* or senior divisional officers (administrative heads of divisions), three-quarters of the directors and general managers of parastatal corporations in the country, and twenty-two of the thirty-eight senior administrative personnel in the office of the prime minister were from the president's Beti ethnic group"

(Takougang and Krieger 1998, p. 95). Going by the overtly ethnic dimension of the upper echelons of state administration, it was anybody's guess how the effects of such a tribal logic would be reflected at the lower levels of the administrative pyramid.

It was against this backdrop that on May 16, 1989, the government of Cameroon agreed an SAP loan of US $150 million with the World Bank. The purpose of this loan was to redress the marked decline in the country's GDP and to achieve positive per capita growth by 1995 (The World Bank, 1989). Key tenets of the agreement included restructuring of public finances, restructuring and rehabilitation of public enterprises, stabilisation and liberalisation of the export crop sector, and deregulation of internal commerce. The SAP package also included three stand-by agreements containing specific reforms within the above-mentioned sectors. The stand-by agreement was reviewed in December 1989 and it was revealed that the reform agenda was facing a number of challenges. The first issue that hindered the implementation of this strategy was deterioration in non-oil tax revenues. The second was delays in reforming the parastatal sector, and the third was worsening world market prices for export crops, notably cocoa, coffee and cotton. Ironically, a 40% reduction in the producer prices of these cash crops was deemed a remarkable success (ODI, 1995).

The second stand-by agreement sought to intensify the reforms and the fiscal measures aimed at broadening the tax base. Its implementation was hampered by opposition calls for a civil disobedience campaign dubbed 'operation ghost town or *villes mortes*' which was aimed at bringing the economy to its knees. During this campaign, Cameroonians were urged to stay at home, civil servants to boycott work, and market vendors, commercial enterprises and other businesses to operate only on weekends, while abstaining from paying taxes. These actions were aimed at forcing the government to concede to a number of opposition demands prior to parliamentary elections scheduled for 1992, notably convening a 'sovereign' national conference and electoral reforms (Konings 2006; Konings and Nyamnjoh 2003, Takougang and Krieger 1998). The civil disobedience campaign devastated tax collection which amounted to a paltry 1.5% of GDP (ODI, 1995).

Further, there was no progress in reforms of the parastatal sector, officially due to a dearth of investment for improving efficiency and reducing costs (ODI, 1995). However, it was no secret that parastatals constituted a massive drain on state resources through subsidies enabling them to be juicy outlets of patronage to ethnic kin. For example, created on 13 May 1967, the *Société National des Eaux du Cameroun (SNEC)*, had only one general manager until 2002, when he was sacked and the corporation put under administration (Page, 2002). Reforming such an entity at a time when the regime was navigating treacherous economic waters could only land it on shaky political ground. It would have sounded the death-knell for gratuitous prebendaries and would have also alienated ethnic faithful whose support was badly needed during the treacherous 1990s.

Despite opposition protests, the government went ahead to organise the first multi-party parliamentary elections in 1992. However, the SDF party boycotted the polls following government intransigence over demands for a 'sovereign' national conference and electoral reform (Takougang & Krieger, 1998). The election results gave the CPDM an overwhelming majority in the National Assembly, enabling the government to press on with its economic reform agenda. It proceeded to lower the retirement age, reduced the number of personnel on its payroll and saved CFA 30 billion (ODI, 1995).

Following successful democratic transitions elsewhere on the continent by way of 'sovereign' national conferences and electoral reform, the opposition intensified its demands for such a formula in Cameroon. The expectation was that its popularity with the masses would inevitably secure a successful outcome. However, the opposition failed to anticipate the shrewdness of an unpopular government and its acute awareness that such a venture was tantamount to political suicide. Apprehensive over the fate that befell other autocratic regimes, Biya rejected calls for a 'sovereign' national conference and brought forward presidential elections scheduled for 1993 to October 1992 without reforming the electoral code.

Biya's intransigence in the face of opposition demands was attributed in part to unflinching support from France. For example, French assistance to Cameroon increased from USD $159 million in 1990, to USD $224 million, in 1991, to USD $436 million in 1992. The motivation behind these increases in French aid to "the authoritarian regime of President Paul Biya was to ensure victory, especially since the most popular opponent was John Fru Ndi, an Anglophone politician perceived as hostile to France" (Renou, 2002, p. 17).

Biya's victory in the disputed presidential elections further deepened the political crisis in Cameroon and intensified the civil disobedience campaigns. Opposition protests was often violently dispersed by the 'forces of law and order.' The opposition leader John Fru Ndi proclaimed himself president after losing the contested 1992 presidential elections and was placed under house arrest (Konings and Nyamnjoh 2003; Takougang and Krieger 1998 and Mentan 1998). Political violence was quite intense in major opposition strongholds, notably Bamenda in the North West Province (now Region), which was placed under a state of emergency from October 27 to December 28 1992.

The political crisis made the economy even worse and accentuated a fall in non-petroleum-related taxes, notably agricultural exports between July and December 1992. In response, the government proceeded to cut civil servants' salaries and benefits. For example, there was a 30% pay cut followed by another 50% cut in 1993, on top of a previous 7% pay cut in 1991. Out-station allowances were also slashed by 50% in 1991, followed by the cancellation of free housing (Page, 2002). Reforms of the civil service enabled the government to unearth around 4000 unfilled positions or 'ghost workers', enabling the state to plug more gaps in the hollow bureaucracy (ODI, 1995).

The third stand-by agreement came in the wake of the devaluation of the CFA currency. The CFA franc was devalued in 1994 from CFA 50 to 100 per French Franc (Renou, 2002). This was accompanied by 'sweeping reforms of trade, tariff, and transit policies' including the scrapping of export levies on raw materials, price subsidies on export cash crops and the liberalisation of commercial activities (Gabriel, 1999 and Mentan, 1998). By making Cameroon's exports cheaper on the world market, devaluation boosted exports of raw materials and primary products and led to an economic revival of tradable goods, marking an overall improvement in the economic level (ODI, 1995).

Despite these measures taken by the government to revive the economy, the Overseas Development Institute (ODI) concluded that Cameroon's adjustment process was by and large a failure for the following reasons:

1. Underestimation for too long of the exchange rate question, which deprived adopted policies of an essential instrument of control for which other budgetary measures were unable to compensate.

2. Inadequate governance, whether for lack of a minimum of political consensus or of full realisation by the economic authorities of the importance of the measures to be taken, or lack of the necessary co-ordination of the admittedly complex steps of the programme

While the ODI report largely blamed the failures of the SAP on shortcomings of fiscal and budgetary measures implemented at the time, it also cited 'inadequate governance' as contributing to the failures (ODI, 1995). The combination of 'governance' and economic deficiencies was therefore not unrelated to these failures.

3.5.1 From 'Non-political' Mission to Political Conditionalities

Discussion about governance during the 'second phase' of external intervention in the economic crisis was because donors, especially the World Bank until 1989, largely saw their mission in the developing world as 'non-political' (Wiseman, 1996, p. 73). However, from the 1990s donor discourses about political conditionalities became much more forceful (Shaw, 1992). This came in the wake of a study by the Bank about the impact of the economic crisis on African countries. From that point governance became a pivotal theme in donor conditionalities (Nyang'oro & Shaw, 1992). According to the Bank, "a root cause of weak economic performance in the past has been the failure of public institutions" (The World Bank, 1989, p. xii). This failure was mostly attributed to the self-serving interest of public officials and the lack of 'countervailing powers.' Governance therefore denoted a patchwork of characteristics, including government accountability, freedom of speech, media, political association, as well as conscious management of government structures with the view to enhancing the legitimacy of public institutions and morality of public officials (Wiseman, 1996).

Ambiguity over 'governance' reform was in sharp contrast to the speed with which economic conditionalities were imposed. The result was that African leaders could get away with anything under the guise of governance reform. On closer examination however, the masses did not require the World Bank or anyone else to impose political conditionalities, because many people were severely affected by the economic crisis and its socio-economic impact which was blamed on inept leadership. Hence, "in retrospect, the inadequate attempt by the World Bank to address the issue of political reforms did not really matter after 1989" (Nyang'oro, 1992, p. 22).

In sum, Mentan (1998, 50), was surely correct when arguing that "Structural Adjustment measures left the public materially impoverished and politically apathetic." However, political apathy in Cameroon did not reflect lack of popular will for change. Rather, it was the culmination of a long drawn-out process that began with President Biya's brief flirtation with democratic ideals in the early days of his rule, albeit within the confines of political monopoly. He later reneged on democratisation on the grounds that Cameroon was not mature enough for plurality.

This episode revealed that Biya's 'democratic' overtures brought back memories of the vibrant political landscape that obtained in the Southern Cameroons and also in French Cameroon, before it was abolished by Ahidjo. As events in the 1990s were subsequently to demonstrate, segments of the population were not indifferent to the second 'wind of change' that was blowing across Africa. The continent-wide movement for political liberalisation inspired many Cameroonians, particularly Anglophones who demanded a return to political plurality, some demanding a return to the federal structure that was abolished in 1972, while others demanded outright secession. Biya's defiant rejection of this popular clamour for political reform, particularly of demands for a 'sovereign' national conference to discuss these issues further, stoked the flames of revolt. The political genie that was let out of the bottle in the 1980s came back to haunt Biya in the 1990s, forcing him to concede to a measure of political liberalisation.

3.5 Political Turbulence and 'Governance' Reforms

The focus of mass protests moved from general dissatisfaction with the effects of corrupt and authoritarian rule to a much more specific demand for the democratisation of the political system through the introduction of multipartyism (Wiseman 1996, 65).

As the above quote shows, the stranglehold of one-party dictatorships in Africa had by the late 1980s "lost its narcotic power on the populace" (Mentan, 1998, p. 43). By the 1990s political monopoly had outlived its usefulness, making the imperative for change on the part of the masses irreversible. Even the Bank acknowledged that 'political renewal' (The World Bank, 1989) was inevitable. Meanwhile debate about the provenance of the pressures that forced autocratic African 'big men' to accept political reform in the 1980s and 1990s has been quite extensive. Some argued that political reform was driven by external actors, principally western governments acting through the IMF and the World Bank (Young, 1993). Both institutions were alleged to be "pushed by their shareholders towards a more explicitly political stance under the rubric of governance" (Gordon, 1997, p. 154). On the other hand, there were many including Bayart (2009), Chazan (1992) and Clapham (1993) who acknowledged the role of donors and other external influences, but contended that political reform in Africa was largely driven by internal forces. Accordingly, local stakeholders influenced the democratisation process in Africa to varying degrees; they included churches, trade unions, professional associations, human rights groups, the media, old politicians, university students and youth associations (Wiseman, 1996). The activities of these myriad groups all coalesced into massive street protests, boycotts and other civil disobedience campaigns designed to force entrenched dictators out of their fortifications and down the path of democratic reforms

The successes of pro-democracy movements in Eastern Europe, symbolised by the toppling of the statues of Soviet-era leaders, the collapse of the Berlin Wall, and the trial and execution of Nicolai Ceausescu in Rumania, proved to many Africans that popular uprisings could overturn authoritarian rule (Wiseman, 1996). As in Eastern Europe, African leaders felt the 'democratic wind of change' in many ways. Some ordered the army and police to crush protesters, as did Moussa Traoré in Mali (van de Walle, 1997). In Chad, on the other hand, Hissène Habré was chased from power by an armed rebellion and Samuel Doe of Liberia was subjected to execution and dismemberment by rebel forces in 1990 (Mentan, 1998). And of course South Africa's ruling National party released Mandela in response to the same developments elsewhere.

In Cameroon, the mass euphoria that greeted the peaceful handover of power from Ahidjo to Biya in 1982 was punctuated by a failed putsch in 1984. The economic situation began deteriorating in 1985, as did enthusiasm for Biya's 'New Deal.' The political situation became volatile when the drastic cuts that accompanied structural adjustment began to bite. Paradoxically, the patronage system put in place by Ahidjo, was reconfigured by Biya to enable him to "monopolise political space, and resource allocation in the country" (Mbuagbo & Akoko, 2004, p. 242).

However, political patronage under Biya was largely and selectively doled out to fellow ethnics (Mentan, 1998).

Frustrated by economic hardship and disappointed in the political leadership, Cameroonians began calling for political liberalisation, inspired in part by "[t]he wave of democratisation in Eastern Europe which was broadcast daily on Cameroon television" (Schilder, 2011, p. 331). In the 1990s, calls for an end to one-party rule and also for constitutional reforms gained momentum because of intransigence by the authorities, prompting events to explode into street protests and violence. At the time, calls for multipartism and constitutional reform were quite popular across the continent. As a result, many autocratic regimes, like Banda's and Kaunda's (see above), were forced to undertake the democratic test by organising pluralistic elections. Unlike in Zambia, change in Senegal took the form in 1991 of a coalition government between President Abdu Diouf and the main opposition *Partie Démocratique Sénégalais* (PDS) (Schilder 2011).

The situation in Cameroon was quite similar to that in Senegal, not because the main opposition Social Democratic Front party was persuaded to form a coalition with the ruling Cameroon Peoples Democratic Movement party, after losing the controversial 1992 presidential elections, but because President Paul Biya (just like Diouf in Senegal), despite his "failed populist mission of popular mobilisation" (Schilder, 2011, p. 331), successfully maintained himself in power through the turbulent years. The next section examines how the continent-wide democratisation movement manifested itself in Cameroon in the 1990s, how it affected the political landscape and how the government turned the tide of events in its favour.

3.6 Political Reform in Cameroon: 'Wind of Change' but No Change

Everyone seeks power by every means, legal or otherwise and those who already control state power try to keep it by every means (Ake, 1996, p. 7)

Most African leaders who were swept out of power by the democratic 'wind of change' in the 1990s were at the helm of state affairs following the anti-colonial 'wind of change' in the 1960s or some time thereafter. According to Ottaway (1997, 10) "few [of these] leaders embraced the cause of democratisation unambiguously." Unlike many on the continent, the President of Cameroon was in many respects a relatively new head of state. In *Communal Liberalism* (1987), Biya expressed his desire for a 'strong' democracy whereby the elite led the masses. He also shunned 'chaos' and 'anarchy' and advocated a "Cameroonian democracy [that] must be strong in order to survive" (Biya, 1987, p. 41). In what Delancy (1989) described as his 'paternalistic attitude' towards the population, Biya declared that Cameroonians have to be shepherded from anonymous elements in a shapeless and passive mass into mature and responsible individuals under the aegis of an enlightened and committed elite.

According to Ottaway (1997: p. 5), 'the problem with democratization particularly in a purely political transition is the problem of power.' Unlike during the monopolistic era where everything boiled down to one-man rule, power in the context of multipartism ideally involves redistribution among those with vested interests such as 'political parties, interest groups and formal government entities'. This is the reason why national leaders have to accept 'institutionalised uncertainty' and the presence of a 'loyal opposition' that plays its traditional role as the conscience of the executive (Ottaway, 1997).

At the grassroots level, local governments were portrayed by donors as more democratic and quite effective at promoting local development. Hence, they "enthusiastically promoted national policies of decentralisation and administrative devolution" (van de Walle, 2003, p. 6), which was represented as a means of democratising social and political life, and ensuring effective provision of public services. Advocates of these lofty ideals, particularly those emanating from countries with well-grounded democratic practices and sound democratic cultures spanning many generations might be forgiven for thinking that 'what's good for the goose is good for the gander.' However, in real-life politics the ideal can often be at odds with the facts.

Times of crisis can be opportune moments for the implementation of radical reforms. The democratic wind of change that swept across Africa in the 1990s was certainly one such moment and there was no shortage of momentum or enthusiasm for change on the part of the masses; but it was not the case for most African leaders. The long period of autocratic rule had also significantly depleted the institutional capacities of most African countries, leaving very little infrastructure in place to accommodate the needs of the people. This is the reason why some countries which showed early promise in the 'wind of change' subsequently succumbed to military coups, and others relapsed to 'novel' forms of authoritarianism.

That said, democratisation for many African leaders was the stuff of nightmares (Mbembe, 2001). According to Mwenda and Tangri (2005, 450): "Donor-sponsored reforms [not only] threatened to curtail the opportunities of African leaders to mobilise and distribute patronage to maintain their regimes in power", but in some cases were a contributing factor in sweeping incumbent African regimes out of power. However, for the likes of Paul Biya and with the clarity of hindsight, the 'donor sponsored reforms' were both a nightmare and an opportunity for the elites, as he told us in *Communal Liberalism (1987)*, to lead the masses in an 'orderly transition' to an outcome determined by the elite.

According to Gordon (1997, 154): "Autocrats who sustained themselves through the initial crisis of authoritarianism have learned how to manipulate the politics of democratic transition." A man who came to power in 1982 and successfully shook off a threat in the form of a failed *coup d'état* in 1984 and subsequently purged the army and higher administration of Northerners, most of them promptly replaced by his kinsmen (Eyoh, 1998), Paul Biya certainly felt that having thwarted a coup that was widely perceived by people from the South as an attempt by the North to regain power, a *putsch* which he survived by a whisker, nothing could or should shake him off the 'throne' he inherited from the 'father of the nation.'

Seen from another angle, the new predominantly Southern ruling elite also presumably felt that, unlike other African leaders who had been in power for decades, their kinsman (Paul Biya) was a mere novice and had not savoured power long enough to risk losing it. Or better still, going by the rate at which other long-serving autocrats were defeated in multiparty elections which they 'voluntarily' organised, these elites likely felt that Biya did not deserve to lose power.

This was likely the mind-set of the ruling clique at the time, particularly because a lot of people from Biya's region of origin in the Central-South Province[30] felt they now had their rightful turn to 'eat the state' after having lost out to the North , thanks in part to the

---

[30] The Centre-South Province was split into Centre and South Provinces (now Regions) by Presidential Decree in 1983.

manoeuvrings of the French colonial authorities. Conspiracy theories that Ahidjo's French doctors advised him to resign the presidency after having groomed Biya to take over was just a restitution of the rightful order of things by France. It should be noted that French governments are generally believed by many in Cameroon and across Francophone Africa to be "active manipulators who, when they realised they could not maintain a firm grip on their colonial empire, deliberately sabotaged the future progress of their former territories, just to make them ready to be exploited for French economic interest" (Keese, 2007, p. 594).

I now proceed to unpack political developments in the 1990s. Specifically, I will analyse the events that culminated in the constitutional reforms of 1996 which were seen by many as the genesis of a transformation and adaptation of the structures of the authoritarian regime into a democratic environment or, perhaps more accurately, I will show how the governing elite manipulated the politics of democratic transition in Cameroon.

3.7 People vs. Power I

3.7.1 Political Liberalisation or Entrenched Status-quo

African states have been caught in a double squeeze of declining economic performance and pressure from various segments of society to deliver on the promise of Uhuru (Nyang'oro and Shaw 1992, p. 5).

According to Biya (1987, p. 18), "the genuine reality of the country is to be found in the rural areas and villages." Because the vast majority of the population of Cameroon in the 1970s and 80s inhabited the rural areas, the challenges facing such areas at the time was a rural exodus manifested as young people flocked the big cities, mainly Douala and Yaoundé, in search of employment opportunities. Inasmuch as Biya's objective was to stem the tide of this rural exodus, his intention to tackle the 'realities of rural areas' was quite visionary.

The goal was therefore to democratise government at the local level by decentralising authority, and in the process provide village communities with ample opportunities and *'real responsibilities'* (Biya, 1987) (my emphasis). However, this leaves out the entrenched mind-set of the regime in place, notably the strong tendency for centralisation inherited from French colonialism, accentuated by Ahidjo and legated to Biya. The latter's aversion to chaos required a strong party and a committed elite dedicated to lead the masses on the road of democratisation; this meant that talk of "decentralization, democratization, and devolution of power to local communities [therefore] required almost revolutionary undertakings" (Delancy, 1989, p. 78).

Because urban dwellers are often viewed less romantically by the state than rural folks in terms of the potential for political trouble-making, it certainly makes sense that Biya envisaged containing people in the rural areas rather than have to face a rabble rampaging the urban landscape. However, conscious of their rights amid a rapidly deteriorating economic situation that was largely blamed on Biya's poor handling of the economy and buoyed by events elsewhere, Cameroonians never waited for Biya's gradualist vision for multipartism to manifest itself, nor did they stay put for the Bretton Woods institutions to prescribe the conditions for political change, as was the case with economic reform.

I have listed the different categories of local stakeholders that were involved in the struggle for multipartism in Africa in the 1990s. In Cameroon the democratic flame was ignited by a group of ten lawyers headed by Yondo Black. In January 1990, Black organised a meeting in Douala to examine the plight of democracy in Cameroon and to explore modalities for the creation of an association to bring pressure for a return to multipartism. He was promptly accused of being a 'crooked lawyer' and of taking advantage of his position as a "traditional tribal chieftain to organize the takeover of the government" (Monga, 1996, p. 37). Black and his colleagues were arrested and charged "with holding clandestine meetings and circulating seditious tracts" (Mentan, 1998, p. 44). In response to the 'Douala ten', the CPDM organised nationwide anti-demonstration marches during which Black and his colleagues were denounced as "trouble-makers, adventurers, and selfish demagogues" (Takougang & Krieger, 1998, p. 104).

Not long after what became popularly known as the 'Yondo Black' affair, "John Fru Ndi, launched the first opposition party the Social Democratic Front in Bamenda" (Konings & Nyamnjoh, 2003, p. 8). In fact, on 16 March 1990 Fru Ndi declared his intention to form a political party, but his application was dismissed by local authorities in Bamenda

(Awung & Atanga, 2011). In defiance of administrative injunctions, heavy troop deployment, a campaign of intimidation and threats of violence, Fru Ndi went ahead to launch the SDF on May 26 1990.

According to Bayart (2009, p. 152), "Anglophone Cameroonians particularly those in the North West Province, felt alienated by 'Reunification' since it destroyed their hopes for autonomy." The launch of the SDF[31] in Bamenda was therefore no coincidence, since most Anglophones increasingly felt marginalised by the system. Interestingly, the people of the North West overwhelmingly voted to join French Cameroon in the UN-organised plebiscite in 1961 and therefore felt betrayed by the assimilationist actions of the Francophone-dominated governments under Ahidjo and then Biya. It was therefore not surprising that a vast majority of the population in this area were at the forefront of opposition politics in the 1990s.

The launch of the SDF turned violent. According to Mentan (1998, 44): "The bloody clash, which left six dead, was a strong indicator that the Biya regime was not going to give in to pluralism without a fight." The government eventually succumbed to popular pressure and on 6 November 1990 parliament passed a bill dubbed 'liberty laws', paving the way for political parties and other freedoms, notably for the media and associations. The bills were promulgated into law in December 1990; but, just like the proverbial *Oliver Twist* (Charles Dickens, 1838), the hunger of Cameroonians for change did not subside following the promulgation of the so-called liberty laws. The mood at the time was for things to be taken much further. In fact, popular demands at this stage were for the convening of a 'sovereign' national conference to discuss fundamental constitutional reform.

3.8 People vs. Power II

3.8.1 Growing Demands for a 'Sovereign' National Conference

The use of the national conference in the transitional phase [was] almost exclusively a Francophone phenomenon; so much so that it may be tempting to

---

[31] One of its founding principles was and still is to return Cameroon to a federal structure, albeit not the two state federation that was put in place following reunification. For more details see Social Democratic Front (SDF), Proposed Constitution for Cameroon. Bamenda December 16, 1994.

see it as representing a partial resurrection of the French political tradition of the States General (Wiseman, 1996, p. 84).

Some of the most popular slogans used by the new social leaders have to do with organizing public trials of those who were in charge of the country since independence (Monga, 1996, p. 103).

In the 1990s, African leaders reacted to popular demands for change in myriad ways. These included: "outright rejection of multipartyism (Kenya); continued dialogue with uncertain outcomes (Tanzania); half-hearted attempts at dialogue with strong indications against reforms (Zaire, Zambia and Zimbabwe); and acceptance of multipartyism in principle (Côte d'Ivoire, Mozambique)" (Nyang'oro, 1992, p. 23). Most of these regimes eventually succumbed to popular demands for change, albeit grudgingly, at different paces, using different yardsticks, and in most cases with rather superficial outcomes.

According to the UNDP (1993, 65): "The movement towards democracy in [Africa] was partly a result of internal weaknesses in authoritarian regimes, [whose] claims to rule had been based on the promise of firm government that could establish order and promote economic growth." Failure of authoritarian regimes to live up to the expectations of the masses therefore generated a lot of public resentment. The situation was no different in Cameroon where the impact of the economic crisis caused profound hardship and general disillusionment amongst a vast majority of the population. This was because of perceived failures by the government to redress the social impact of a crisis that was largely blamed on ineptitude, corruption and nepotism.

Demands for political liberalisation in the 1990s were the articulation of deeply entrenched feelings of frustration with one-party rule which was widely perceived as responsible for failings on the economic as well as political fronts. On the other hand, intransigence by the authorities over opposition demands provoked popular street protests and sometimes carefully choreographed counter protests by government supporters. As noted in the quotes above, opposition movements in predominantly Francophone Cameroon, as in other former French colonies, resorted to civil disobedience to force the government to organise national conferences to discuss constitutional reform. The idea of a national conferences was made popular by Benin's successful experience (Southall, 2003). These forums served as open trials for authoritarian regimes and were also viewed as appropriate arenas for organising the transition from authoritarianism to democracy.

In 1989 the military ruler of Benin, Mathieu Kerekou, was forced to abandon Marxism as the official state ideology, to legalise opposition parties and to convene a national conference. Given autocratic regimes' penchant for prevarication, the establishment probably thought that a national conference was merely another talking shop that would lead nowhere. The opposition on its part justifiably viewed the whole idea with much suspicion. The conference took place in Cotonou from February 19 to 28, 1990. Participants included representatives from the government, opposition parties, trade unions and religious leaders (Wiseman, 1996).

The conference elected the Archbishop of Cotonou, Isadore da Souza, to chair the proceedings. A few days into the meeting delegates made an unprecedented move by voting to declare the conference 'sovereign' and replaced the government as the 'supreme political institution of the state.' This was much to the chagrin of President Kerekou who described it as a "civilian *coup d'état*" (Wiseman, 1996, p. 86), but eventually succumbed to the popular will. The conference went on to appoint an interim Prime Minister and cabinet which presided over the transition and organised elections in March 1991 which Kerekou contested and lost.

Outside Benin, national conferences were also held in Burkina Faso, Chad, Comoros, Congo Republic, Gabon, Mali, Niger, Togo and Zaire, now the Democratic Republic of Congo. Of these ten countries, three share borders with Cameroon and had varying experiences with national conferences. In the Congo Republic, for example, the conference was almost a copycat of that held in Benin. It declared itself sovereign and organised elections in July 1992 that culminated in the defeat of incumbent Marxist-Leninist leader Denis Sassou-Nguesso (Wiseman, 1996, p. 88).

In Cameroon, the opposition also demanded a 'sovereign' national conference.[32] Fearing that conceding to a national conference in Cameroon will be tantamount to a "civilian *coup d'état*" like Benin's and

---

[32] Just like in Benin, the opposition in Cameroon adopted the name 'sovereign' indicating its intention to take over the government and rule by the popular will, something which President Paul Biya vehemently opposed.

in the Congo Republic next door, President Biya made a defiant speech in the National Assembly on June 27, 1991 during which he declared: *"Je l'ai dit et je le maintiens: la Conférence Nationale est sans objet pour le Cameroun.... Seules les urnes parleront.* I have said it and I maintain it: The National Conference has no purpose for Cameroon.... Only the ballot boxes will speak" (Takougang & Krieger, 1998, p. 125).

According to Ake (1996, p. 12), "in the face of the global resurgence of democracy, they are bending democracy into a strategy of power, using elections to disempower the people. And they are succeeding." Having thrown down the gauntlet, Biya swiftly brought forward to 1992 presidential elections scheduled for 1993. However, unlike elsewhere on the continent, the anticipated or 'rapid elections' did not remove Biya from power; rather, he won by a narrow margin of '38% against 35% for his main challenger, John Fru Ndi' (Geschiere, 2009). The latter rejected the results, proclaimed himself president and called for public demonstrations against the 'stolen victory.' The government responded by imposing a state of emergency in Bamenda and placed Fru Ndi under house arrest.

Against all the odds, the political elite successfully manoeuvred through the transition years and was still in place at the time of writing in 2015. According to Gabriel (1999, p. 188), "Cameroon's transition was consequently flawed [because] some [economic] liberalisation occurred, but democratisation failed."

3.9 Discussion and Conclusion

Reacting to Biya's defiant rejection of the national conference, the opposition intensified its civil disobedience campaign which eventually forced the government to the negotiating table. In November 1991, the government proposed a 'tripartite conference' involving opposition leaders, civil society, independent personalities and the administration (Mentan, 1998). Unlike what obtained in Benin, the government largely controlled the show. Nevertheless, "non-governmental representatives succeeded in forcing constitutional reforms on the agenda" (Eyoh, 1998, p. 260). In circumstances reminiscent of the Fumban constitutional talks, deliberations at the tripartite conference revealed profound differences between Anglophones and Francophones over the type and form of state. Whereas Francophones advocated a measure of decentralisation within the unitary state, Anglophones demanded a return to federalism (Takougang & Krieger, 1998).

According to Eyoh, (1998, p. 348) "the regime's determination to control the agenda and outcome of the debate on constitutional reform" caused deadlock in the discussions, which ended without agreement. As a result, a technical committee on constitutional matters was set-up; this committee met regularly from November 1991 to February 1992. It was composed of eleven members (seven Francophones and four Anglophones). It was chaired by Professor Joseph Owona, who at the time was the Secretary General at the Presidency, and an ardent Biya henchman (Konings & Nyamnjoh, 2003).

In the course of the constitutional discussions, the government lived up to its reputation as a 'sorcerer state' (Mbembe 2001 and Nyamnjoh 1999) which often leaves "its audience in the dark for as long as possible before sweeping away the magician's cloak to reveal its decisions" (Page, 2002, p. 9). Barely two weeks before the anticipated October 1992 presidential election (which it should be recalled was moved from its scheduled date in 1993) and despite deadlock in the constitutional discussions, Owona declared that a new constitution was ready. However, three of the four Anglophone members of the committee refused to sign the document because "it preserved the fundamental elements of the unitary state with its domineering executive" (Eyoh, 1998, p. 352).

Anglophone resentment over perceived injustices in Cameroon was nothing new (Konings & Nyamnjoh, 2003 and Takougang & Krieger, 1998). According to (Bayart, 2009, p. 165), "the Anglophone elite tried to reintroduce political plurality in 1972, once it was certain it had been swindled by the UNC." Despite having been 'deceived' by Ahidjo, many Anglophones never gave up the quest for a return to federation or outright secession; this demand continued right into the Biya era and became very vocal in the 1990s. Likewise, it is often argued that the government introduced decentralisation reforms in the 1990s not only as a strategy to diffuse generalised discontent among Cameroonians, but also to thwart Anglophone separatist sentiments (Njoh, 2011 and Konings & Nyamnjoh, 2003) The government therefore used the rhetoric of grassroots autonomy as a carrot to placate diverse forces and stamp out moves to split the country by portraying itself as the guarantor of the unity and territorial integrity of the country, while pressing ahead with a highly centralised bureaucratic set-up (Fombad, 2012).

Against this backdrop in March 1993, the government suddenly announced a *'Grand Débat'* to discuss revising the 1972 constitution. Around May 1993, the controversial chairman of the constitutional committee produced a draft constitution which purportedly emanated from the tripartite conference. Not surprisingly, the above-mentioned dissident committee members condemned the draft constitution and "charged that the committee had not met for a year, and that the text was Owona's own, unmediated by any consultation" (Takougang & Krieger, 1998, p. 183); the document was later dubbed the 'Owona Constitution.' Despite dissenting voices, the document was adopted by the National Assembly and promulgated as Law No. 96-06 of 18 January 1996 to amend the Constitution of 2 June 1972.

The 1996 constitution states in Article 1 (2) that: "The Republic of Cameroon shall be a decentralized unitary State." Concerning local municipalities, Article 55 (1) states: Regional and local authorities of the Republic shall comprise Regions and Councils. However, a change of appellation from Province to Region only occurred in 2008, three years before the end of the president's final constitutional term limit, as per Article 6 (2). Being an adept political manipulator, Biya, amid protest by the opposition (violently put down by the army), promptly took the opportunity to revise this constitutional clause, effectively removing obstacles placed in the path of the continuation of his then 26 years rule which his apologists described as 'contrary to the democratic spirit.' This enabled him to be eligible for re-election indefinitely.

Other articles of relevance to this study include: Article (3): "The State shall exercise supervisory powers over regional and local authorities, under conditions laid down by law." Article (5): "The organization, functioning and financial regulations of regional and local authorities shall be defined by law." Article (6): "The rules and regulations governing councils shall be defined by law." All three provisions, which reluctantly came into force in 2004, will be examined in greater detail in chapter VIII. Finally, the rather ambiguous language employed in these statutory provisions was a calculated move by the government to give itself ample discretion and adequate room for manoeuvre in the application of the laws (Fombad, 2012). According to (Schilder, 2011, p. 319):

The so-called democratisation movement has not fundamentally changed the situation. Parliament is as powerless as before. Political power is still centralised and concentrated in the hands of a small ruling group. Politics is still an elitist struggle for personal rewards with minimal or no benefits for the common people. And the raison d'être of the powerful police and army forces is not primarily to guarantee law and order [despite being called that], but rather to control the masses and push them to political conformity and indifference.

Chapter IV

Self-Reliance in Anglophone Cameroon: The Bali Community Water Project

History figures in two forms in this [chapter]. On the one hand it is an analytical category of how historical legacies of colonial rule, power struggles, legislative changes after independence, and the like impinge on local dynamics. On the other hand, history as an object of study, as a central part of the idioms and logics of local contestation where people conjure up historical interpretations to back certain claims to power and property (Lund 2008, 3).

4.1 Introduction

Bali subdivision (hereafter referred to as Bali), is situated approximately 16 km from Bamenda, the chief town of the North West Region of Cameroon. It is also one of the seven administrative subdivisions that make up Mezam Division. Unlike most towns in Cameroon, Bali owns a potable drinking water supply system which was constructed by the community in 1957. This water project has gone through a number of transformations over the years. Before reunification in 1961 it was managed as a non-profit scheme by the community under the supervision of the Public Works Department (PWD) of the government of the Southern Cameroons.

Following reunification, the project fell under the jurisdiction of the Ministry of Mines, Water Resources and Power. In 1984, the ministry surreptitiously handed over the water project to a state-owned parastatal, the National Water Corporation or *Société Nationale des Eaux du Cameroun* (SNEC). According to Page (2003, 492): "What the shift from Mines and Power to SNEC undoubtedly did signify was a determined marketization of water supplies." The marketization of Bali community water was very much at odds with its founding principle as a self-help project. Tired of being exploited by SNEC, the population violently expelled it in January 1994. This chapter shows how the people of Bali, through the Native Authority, developed and successfully managed a local project for close to three decades with little or no external support.

4.2 Background

You are by this letter notified that your role of distributing Bali water ends at midnight (12:00 HOUR), on Saturday 15th January 1994 and that the Bali population will resume the distribution of their water with effect from Sunday 16th January 1994.[33]

It was by this ultimatum on January 11, 1994 that the population of Bali, under the auspices of the Bali Community Water Committee (BCWC) and the Bali Traditional Council, issued marching orders to the local chief of SNEC to restore the water installations to the community. At the time SNEC had been in charge of distributing water in Bali for a decade. The company was accused, among other things, of "infrequent shutting up of public taps and/or supplying muddy and untreated water."[34]

The violent expulsion of SNEC from Bali came at a time when Cameroon was undergoing profound socio-political change. As noted in chapter III, the 1990s were marked by opposition calls for civil disobedience campaigns, dubbed 'Operation Ghost Towns' or *villes mortes* (Konings 2006; Konings and Nyamnjoh 2003; Takougang and Krieger 1998). At the time, the government was widely unpopular amongst Cameroonians because of its perceived failure to tackle the economic crisis, and its negative effects on people's livelihoods. Consequently, its legitimacy was seriously undermined in many parts of the country. The government's credibility was further dented by corrupt and overtly nepotistic proclivities in the management of public affairs which were starkly at odds with pledges made by President Biya to fight corruption and promote open and accountable governance when he took power in 1982 (Mentan, 1998). It should be recalled that corruption, mismanagement and nepotism were the order of the day in many state-owned parastatals, especially SNEC which served as a classic example of a neo-patrimonial regime dolling out patronage (Page, 2002)

The economic crisis also laid bare the ineptitude and/or unwillingness of the government to meet the needs of many

---

[33] Ultimatum issued to the local the chief of centre SNEC, by the Bali Community Water Committee (BCWC), and the Bali Traditional Council on 11 January 1994.

[34] Ultimatum issued to the local the chief of centre SNEC, by the Bali Community Water Committee (BCWC), and the Bali Traditional Council on 11 January 1994.

Cameroonians. As a result, people in Bali, taking their cue from precedents set three years earlier by compatriots in Kumbo, (roughly 80km away), violently dislodged SNEC and reclaimed 'their water.' To better comprehend how Bali acquired an autonomous potable water supply system and also to lay the groundwork for other contentious issues that will be elaborated on in subsequent chapters, I dig deep down memory lane here: first, to unearth how Bali Nyonga found itself in the present location; second, to recount why its presence unravelled a chain of events culminating in a concerted onslaught by its surrounding neighbours in 1952; finally, to demonstrate how the outcome of the conflict engendered the Bali community water project which I argue was a showpiece of community development through self-help in Anglophone Cameroon.

4.2.1 The Bali Chamba: Migration and Settlement

The Bali Nyonga are a Chamba[35] group that migrated southwards from the Benue and Adamawa plateaus in Northern Cameroon into the Grassfields (DeLancey, Mbuh and DeLancey 2010; Rubin 1970 and Johnson 1970). The broader Chamba group originated around the borders between Cameroon and Nigeria at the foot of the Alantika Mountains (Fokwang, 2009). The Chamba are said to have begun their exodus around 1770 and settled in the present site around 1830. The south-westerly migration of the Chamba was described as 'an army on the move' in which all able-bodied men and some women were involved in fighting (Nyamdi, 1988). In their downward march, the Chamba incorporated smaller groups such as the Dagha, Muti and Tikali (Fardon 1983; Chilver and Kaberry 1970; and Jeffreys 1957).

After failing to conquer the powerful Bamoum Kingdom with the aid of the Bati,[36] they continued their southward march, further swelling ranks with other subgroups that sought freedom from Bamoum domination (Geary 1988 and Warnier 1980). Upon arriving in the Grassfields, they attacked and wreaked havoc on already established communities, permanently altering the settlement patterns in the area

---

[35] The greater Chamba group consisted of Bali Muti, Bali Gham, Bali Kumbat, Bali Nyonga, Bali Gansin, Bali Gaso and Bali Kontan that was subsequently absorbed by Bali Nyonga (Fokwang, 2009 & 2011 and Nyamdi 1988).

[36] The Bati were settled around the Noun valley and were constantly harried by the Bamum (Nyamdi 1988).

(Argenti, 2007). This brought Bali to its present location. I will now proceed to examine colonial rule in Bali, discussing how colonial officials attempted to deal pragmatically with the repercussions generated by the presence of Bali in the area and their ramifications beyond the colonial era.

4.3 Bali under German Colonialism

Colonial administrators devoted considerable time and attention to demarcating administrative boundaries to define their own jurisdictions; territorial boundaries to resolve competing claims to land and office and social boundaries to define arenas of authority and obligation for chiefs and commoners alike (Berry 2001, 7).

The impact of the migration on Bali Nyonga in the late 19th century was such that by the time it settled on its present location its society consisted of people of varied backgrounds, brought together through confederation, conquest or assimilation (Fokwang, 2009). By the time the first German explorer, Dr Eugene Zintgraff, arrived in the Grassfields, Bali Nyonga was already firmly established in the area. Zintgraff arrived in Bali on 16 January 1889, opened a German post and also signed a 'blood pact'[37] of brotherhood with the traditional ruler, Galega I. Unlike others in the Grassfields, such as the people of Kom and Bafut who resisted the Germans (Nkwi, 1997), Galega welcomed the Germans and used an alliance with them to pursue an expansionist agenda. This enabled Bali to extend its sphere of influence over vast expanses of land, to the detriment of its neighbours who never accepted this as a *fait accompli* and always yearned for freedom from the yoke of Bali domination and to recover land (Mbah 2009 and Geary 1988).

German actions consolidated Bali as the centre of mutual 'imperial' activities in the Grassfields (Fokwang, 2009). German missionaries

---

[37] This blood pact was a prelude to a formal treaty signed in August 1891. Under this treaty Galega was to surrender to Zintgraff all his powers of 'life and death and of peace and war within the Bali empire' and he will implement all decisions in those matters taken by Zintgraff, in return Galega's position as the paramount chief of the surrounding tribes of the Northern Kamerun hinterland was to be assured' (Nyamdi,1988, 99-100).

adopted Mungaka[38] as the medium of evangelisation. Mungaka was also introduced into formal schooling and gradually became the common language of the entire Grassfields. Finally, the alliance with the Germans also enabled Galega to transform Bali Nyonga from a tribe of mounted Chamba raiders into an effective mini-state surrounded by a string of tributaries and a wider sphere of commercial and diplomatic influence (Fisiy 1995; Chilver and Kaberry 1970; Fowler and Zeitlyn 1957).

Galega died in 1901 and was succeeded by Fonyonga II. In 1905, Fonyonga was formally proclaimed paramount chief of 37 villages and was officially installed by German emissary, General Hauptmann in the presence of 47 Grassfields chiefs (Fokwang, 2009). According to a German surveyor, Adametz Hauptmann,[39] cited in Geary (1988, p. 19), the mother of Fonyonga, was a *Ba-Nten*[40] woman, most likely from the Bati group[41] and, on Fonyonga's invitation coupled with pressures on the land, the Bati headed by chief Fomben Nguigong moved from Bansoa to Bali in 1906 (Geary, 1988). Following on the heels of the Bati were the Bawock, another Bamilike community led by chief Nana who originated from near Bangante and fled to Bali in 1906-7 because of persecution by Bangante.[42] Apart from persecution by Bangante chiefs, Bawock's choice to settle in Bali was motivated by matrimonial links between the two chiefs.[43] However, around 1911 the relationship between Bati and Bawock turned sour, forcing Bati to leave Bali in anger[44] and taking the Bawock chief Nana hostage. The rest of Bawock subsequently followed, but returned to Bali around 1912 (Chilver 1964).

---

[38] This is the language spoken by Bali Nyonga, which sharply contrasts with Mubakoh, the original Chamba language spoken by the other Balis. One of the causes was the dilution of Mubakoh by the languages of the different tribes that Bali Nyonga absorbed during its migrations (Nyamdi, 1988).

[39] Explored plans for the extension of the railways beyond Nkongsamba via Chang (Dschang), to Bagam and probably Bamum.

[40] A general name for the non-Chamba tribes that were incorporated or joined Bali Nyonga in the course of its south-westerly migration following the death of its leader Gawolbe II.

[41] According to Kaberry and Chilver (1961), she was from another non-Chamba tribe, precisely from Kefad.

[42] For details see: *The History of a People; The Secret Behind the Bali Nyonga and Bawock Nfeu Gai Nfai Affair* (nd; p12, 15, 17, 19)

[43] The chief of Bati was married to the sister of the chief of Bawock.

[44] During fieldwork in Bali, I came across a peculiar anecdote about the Bati people in relation to their precipitate exit from Bali. The Bati are said to have informed Bali people that they were going to perform a very important traditional ceremony which nobody except a few initiates could witness. People in Bali were politely asked

The relationship between Bali and Bawock over the years has turned sour and sometimes violent. At the centre of this rocky relationship were the latter's claims to land vacated by Bati following its precipitate exit from Bali. Bawock argues that by virtue of its historical ties with Bati they are entitled to the land and are therefore not indebted to Bali. On the other hand, Bali also claims very strong historical ties with Bati; in fact Mungaka is a variant of the Bati language which Bali Nyonga adopted sometime in the 19th century (Fokwang, 2009). Although Bati left Bali in 1911, segments of the *Ba-Nten,* have over many generations coalesced into a harmonious unit and are well-established and fully integrated into Bali society (Page, et al., 2010). On another note, many people from Bawock I spoke to during fieldwork, including chief Quoimon Nana Wanda Théodore III, constantly cited their 'refusal to be assimilated' like the *Ba-Nten,* as a cause of rocky relations with Bali.

Meanwhile, "colonial governments developed alliances with chiefs to secure labour and taxes" (Amanor 2008, 132). Such understandings were a common practice during the colonial era and things were made easier in situations where there was collaboration between the colonial authorities and a local chief. Just like other Grassfields chiefs, notably those that were nominated 'auxiliaries' by the Germans, Fonyonga II exercised the functions of tax collection and forced labour recruitment (Rowlands, 1979).

As tax collector, Fonyonga received tax tickets for all 37 villages[45] in his dominion and got a 10% stipend in return (Nyamdi, 1988). Fonyonga's function as auxiliary was a mixed blessing. On the one hand, it worsened relations with vassal communities and on the other it degenerated into conflict with the colonial administration whose actions were at times clumsy, if not confused. For example, in 1906 the Germans forcefully uprooted and resettled[46] eleven Widekum

---

to stay indoors and the sound of gunshots would signal the end of the ceremony. Upon hearing the echoes of gunshots and coming out of their houses, they realised Bati settlements were in flames and only then did they find out to their amazement that they had been hoodwinked, so as not to witness the hasty, unannounced and unexplained exit of their guests. So in Bali, whenever someone makes a sudden or unexpected departure, reference is always made to the eloping Bati.

[45] The 37 vassals also served as a labour pool for German plantations on the coast of Kamerun.

[46] This was not an unusual practice by the German colonialists in the area; for example in 1912 the Germans uprooted the Kedjom Keku people from their hilltop settlements into the valleys purportedly for easier administration (Diduk, 1992).

chiefdoms into Bali for the smooth collection of taxes, adding to the number of disgruntled tributaries under Fonyonga's belt (Nyamdi, 1988). From 1908, agitation by the Widekum villages boiled over to the point where the Germans decided to relieve Bali of control over a number of them (Fokwang 2009, Fisiy 1995; Kaberry and Chilver 1961). This among other issues was the state of Bali-German relations on the eve of the First World War. The frosty rapport between the two erstwhile allies continued on a downward spiral until the Germans were defeated by British and French forces and their military garrison in Bamenda Station captured in 1915.

4.4 The First World War and the Partition of Kamerun

The British and French partition of the former German protectorate into two spheres was carried out within the framework of the Simon-Milner Agreement (Achankeng, 2014). Both territories were governed as League of Nations Mandates and Bali came under British administration. The arrival of a new colonial administration reignited the Widekum's quest to leave Bali. In October 1915 the chiefs of three villages (Bambunji, Bamenjong and Bamyensi) abandoned their settlements within Bali and moved into the nearby hills, where they were joined by others (Nyamdi, 1988). In appreciation of the support they got from Bali to oust the Germans, the British felt obliged to stem a further exodus (Fokwang, 2009). This was easier said than done. Nevertheless, to demonstrate commitment to Bali, the British sent out an expeditionary force which promptly brought back the 'runaway' chiefdoms into Bali. They were however determined to remain free and soon fled again. As a result, the District Officer (DO) personally led another patrol bent on forcing them back. Despite the patrol's storming of their hilltop villages, they refused to return and instead fled further afield. A third expedition achieved little (Nyamdi, 1988).

The tenacity of the Widekum's desire to leave Bali gave the British pause for thought. At the time it was fashionable for colonial authorities in Cameroon and elsewhere in Africa to commission anthropological studies and surveys to identify and describe 'customary polity and law' (Lund, 2008). The British ordered an enquiry into the exact nature of the relationship between Bali and neighbouring tribes. The investigation was carried out by the DO, W.E. Hunt, who concluded that the main cause of constant rebellion was the ill-conceived German policy of forcefully resettling the Widekum people into Bali (Nyamdi 1988). It must also be added that the Widekums, as noted at the beginning of this chapter, were the original inhabitants of this area and were displaced by Bali in the 19th century at a time when might was right.

Britain was faced with a dilemma: they should respect commitments to uphold the territorial integrity of Bali, yet they did not want to appear to perpetuate the Germans' arbitrary practices. So they leaned on Fonyonga to renounce his tributaries (Nyamdi, 1988). There was however a caveat for the Widekums which was to have far-reaching implications. This came in the form of a warning that they could have no claims *"to the land in Bali on which they lived and farmed during their compulsory detention and which they have now vacated"* (Nyamdi, 1988, p. 136) (my emphasis). This admonition from the colonial official was not something the Widekums were prepared to adhere to; and decades later they mounted a concerted attack on Bali in a bid to recover territory. The level of animosity between Bali and its neighbours was such that none were prepared to associate with it when the British decided to introduce Native Authorities.

4.4.1 Native Authorities in British Cameroons

Britain governed the Southern Cameroons by indirect rule which, according to Mandani, (1996, p. 17) represented a form of "mediated decentralised despotism." Out of political expediency, indirect rule did not radically alter the traditional status-quo of indigenous societies in the Grassfields (Johnson, 1970). Instead Native Authorities (NA), which were constituted by the traditional institutions colonial officials encountered in places such as Bali, Bafut, Nso, Kom and Mankon were legitimated (Vubo & Ngwa, 2001). It is important to note that most of these NAs were headed by powerful hereditary traditional chiefs who controlled hundreds of people and vast territories.

In 1949, Bamenda was carved into 23 Native Authority areas. Twenty two out of twenty three agreed to pull together into a federation of four groups.[47] Bali remained outside this federation because no other NA wanted to be part of a group to which it belonged. The reason for the animosity against Bali was that most villages in the federation were

---

[47]This grouping was known as the Bamenda South Western Federation.

still bitter about events in the last century when Bali conquered their lands, exacted tribute from them and was declared 'suzerain power' over them by Germany (Kaberry 1962). They were fearful of continued domination, as summed up in the words of a local leader; "if you federate with Bali, you might just as well cut your own throat" (Kaberry 2004, 3).

The creation of NAs marked the entry of chiefs and other local people into the colonial administrative structure. Likewise, NAs also served as 'incubators' for the promotion and dissemination of progressive ideas and veritable arenas for community participation in local development in the Grassfields (Page 2007 and Rubin 1970). On the other hand, the federated NAs also imbued a feeling of unity amongst the Widekum. Because Bali was in their middle, the sense of unity was more palpable on their flanks. Nevertheless, it was good enough for them to combine forces and resources to attempt to recoup what they lost to Bali in 1908 and possibly what they had lost many generations back. In the 1950s, they sought redress for past 'injustices', first through petitions to the colonial administration, then through applications to the courts, and eventually through violence (Bejeng, 1985).

4.5 Widekum Action against Bali

The first attempt at administrative redress was launched by Baforchu immediately after the British took over in 1916. They laid claim to the land they had been occupying in Bali, following their forceful incorporation by the Germans in 1906. Because of the First World War and the time it took the British to settle down and administer the territory, the outcome of the dispute was only pronounced in 1923. The verdict was not to the satisfaction of Baforchu which only got its 'independence' from Bali upheld, but not its claims to land.[48]

Fifteen years after this ruling, the Ngyen-Mbu tribe brought another action against Bali. This time they did not present their problem as an outright claim for land, but as a boundary dispute with Bali. The DO ordered an inquiry to determine the facts of the Ngyen-Mbu claim and,

---

[48] A.D.B Manson (1953), Government Notice No 794: Report of an Inquiry held under the Commissions of Inquiry Ordinance (Chapter 37): Nigeria Gazette Extraordinary p 565-57

as in the Baforchu case, the colonial administration persisted in its ruling that "the Mungen Mbo [Ngyen-Mbu] people had lost all rights over the land in dispute with the Bali people who had acquired the land from them by conquest sometime before 1890 and therefore it was not possible to fix a boundary between them."[49] Not satisfied with DO Goodliffe's response, they moved a step higher and appealed to the Chief Commissioner who upheld the decision of the DO, but opened a window of opportunity by suggesting that they seek legal redress for a declaration of title over disputed land via the courts. They duly obliged and in 1950 launched a series of legal actions against the *Fon* of Bali, commencing at the Bali Native Court, which ruled itself incompetent and shifted the matter to the Supreme Court of Nigeria's Calabar Judiciary Division. Other Widekum villages also joined the lawsuit against the *Fon* of Bali (Nyamdi, 1988).

The court action was a complete debacle for the plaintiffs. In the joint suits they claimed title over large expanses of land, sought an injunction prohibiting Bali from entering the said land and requested damages amounting to £1000 sterling. The case was heard in February 1952 and immediately collapsed on a technicality. The court ruled that they had not filed their motion over a title to land under the 'Land and Native Rights Ordinance' and as a result their claims to an injunction and damages could not be entertained. The court dismissed the case and asked the Widekums to pay Bali £150 pounds sterling in costs. The court further informed the plaintiffs that the land title they sought could only be obtained from the Governor (Nyamdi, 1988). The Widekums therefore found themselves caught in a game of 'ping pong' between the courts and the governor. It was as if both institutions had made a vicious conspiracy against them. Having exhausted all legal avenues to obtain redress, they sought to recapture territory through violent means.

4.5.1 The Bali-Widekum 'Disturbances'

The term disturbances, as applied by the colonial authorities, represents a 'typically British understatement' to the actual events that occurred in Bali on 3 March 1952. Events of that day set off violent clashes during which surrounding Widekum tribes went on the rampage

---

[49] A.D.B Manson (1953), Government Notice No 794: Report of an Inquiry held under the Commissions of Inquiry Ordinance (Chapter 37): Nigeria Gazette Extraordinary p 565.

against Bali. Armed with Dane guns, machetes, spears and other implements, they launched a ferocious assault on Bali, catching the latter and the colonial officials off guard. Skirmishes raged on for several days before Bali eventually gained the upper hand. The immediate outcome of the war was significant property damage and loss of life and livelihoods on all sides. Fatalities amounted to a total of fifteen people, four of them Bali. Regarding property, Bali lost over 1500 dwelling houses and 370 store houses, while the Widekum lost 130 dwelling houses and 20 store houses (Nyamdi, 1988, p. 148).

The colonial government drafted troop reinforcements from nearby stations and also from Nigeria to stabilise the situation. It immediately set mechanisms in place for a 'post-mortem' of the conflict by appointing Justice A.G.B. Manson to investigate the crisis. He began work on 18 March 1952 and within three months produced a report which laid blame for the violence on the doorstep of the Widekums, specifically the leadership. Accordingly, "the Widekum communities have been ill-advised, misguided and misled by unscrupulous agitators who have for personal motives persuaded the great majority of simple Widekum people by encouraging false hopes of re-acquiring all or part of their land from the Bali."[50] The commissioner further stated, "the Widekum claims of occupational rights over the area in dispute cannot be entertained as there are no grounds either legal or equitable or compassionate which justify any such rights being granted to them" (Nyamdi, 1988, p. 150). Colonial officials therefore accepted the Commissioner's findings and imposed a collective fine of £10,000 sterling. A significant amount (£9000 sterling), was paid to Bali as compensation for damages incurred during the violence. The compensation money was put to collective use in the form of a potable water supply project.

4.6 Self-Help in Anglophone Cameroon: The Bali Community Water Project

Community Development was enormously successful in Anglophone Cameroon. In no sector was this more true than water supply (Page 2003, 486).

---

[50] A.D.B Manson (1953), Government Notice No 794: Report of an Inquiry held under the Commissions of Inquiry Ordinance (Chapter 37): Nigeria Gazette Extraordinary p 565-57.

During British rule in the Southern Cameroons, native authorities were the main source of local decision-making. According to Johnson (1970), Britain's limited moral commitment to radically altering the traditional status-quo of indigenous societies meant colonial policy was tailored to ensure that local needs did not constitute much of a strain on the financial resources of the crown. As a result, local people funded community development through local taxation and other income-generating schemes.

Around 1950, the British authorities began implementing a "new welfare-oriented colonial development policy" (Page, 2002, p. 16). Community development through 'self-help' initiatives was the *modus operandi* of this policy. The scheme initially focused on mass education and adult literacy, but later evolved to include projects in the domains of agriculture, healthcare, infrastructure, buildings, and road construction (Page 2003). Community development was a trade-off mechanism whereby local people provided labour and materials and colonial officials sometimes provided cash and technical support. In the view of colonial officials, community development through 'self-help' was to "induce in the people a desire for progress and the will to achieve it by their own efforts" and by cultivating a 'work ethic' which in the process "preserved an historic African tradition of co-operation" (ibid, 486).

Missionaries also played active frontline roles in developing infrastructural projects in the Southern Cameroons. According to Nkwi (1997, 72), "they raised funds from their home parishes and with labour supplied by Christians were able to build these institutions and improve the quality of life of the people." In Bali, missionaries were prominent in evangelisation and also in the realisation of social projects, including schools and hospitals. The Basel Mission, for example, was well-established in Bali, having arrived there during the German colonial period. During fieldwork, I was informed that Basel Missionaries in Bali had excellent working relations with *Fon* Galega II and were involved in the decision to use the damages from the Bali-Widekum conflict to construct a community water project.

4.6.1 Historical Timeline of the Bali Community Water Project

During fieldwork in Bali in 2013, I sought to fill gaps in the history of the water project. Specifically, I attempted to piece together the process that led to the decision to use the £9000 sterling damages awarded to the Bali Native Authority headed by *Fon* Galega II in this way. I consulted documents (some handed to me by frontline members of the movement to expel SNEC from Bali), conducted interviews and held informal conversations with various personalities. These included managers of the water project, current and former members of Bali Council, traditional notables and some people living around the original site of the water pumping station in Mbatmandet neighbourhood.

Because there were no known legal or other precedents on which to fall back regarding the amount of damages to pay to people who were killed, injured or suffered property damage, Galega II inevitably found himself in a dilemma. This was made worse because the concerted Widekum attacks affected large areas of Bali (see the figures above) and consequently affected almost every household. In the end, a decision was reached to use the money to provide potable drinking water for the community.

I could not find any recorded evidence of how this decision was made. However, speaking to people in Bali, I got the sense that it was a well-thought out process reached by the *Fon* in collaboration with the traditional council and with inputs from some missionaries stationed in Bali. The Basel Mission station was established in Bali in 1903 during the German colonial period and served as a base for missionaries to fan out and spread Christianity throughout the Grassfields (Fokwang, 2009). I was also informed that the main sources of water for the population were a number of naturally occurring springs dotted around different areas of Bali, wells or boreholes and a handful of streams. However, the unreliable nature of these water sources meant people in some places had difficulty accessing water, mostly in the dry season.

There was one major stream that cuts across the entire length of Bali and, unlike the others, it flowed all-year round. The stream or *Tsi* in *Mungaka* was named differently depending on the neighbourhood through which it flows; thus, at a place called *Mbat Matua*, it is known as *Tsi Matua*, at Mbatmandet it is known as *Tsi Munyam,* and at the main water pumping station it is called *Tsi Gola*. This stream constituted the main water source for many people. It was accessed at many points and was used for diverse purposes, including drinking water for humans and animals, laundry, bathing and other household purposes. Its multi-purpose use potentially exposed the population to water-borne diseases. According to some accounts, one of the factors that concentrated the minds of the traditional authorities to provide pipe-born water was the potential and actual occurrence of water-borne diseases, especially cholera. I did not find any evidence of a cholera epidemic in Bali around 1957, when the water project was constructed.

4.6.2 Construction of the Community Water Project

Once the decision to use the money for the water project was reached, a German engineer was charged with the actual construction work. The bulk of the cash was therefore used to purchase material and some to pay the engineer and his crew. Given that Germany was kicked out of the Grassfields around 1915, the choice of a German engineer to construct the water project is intriguing. I met an old man in Mbatmandet neighbourhood who said he was a teenager when the water project was constructed and that he worked as a labourer in the initial pumping station at *Tsi Munyam,* where the engineer resided during construction. He recalled that one of the foremen at the construction site was from Nsongwa, (a neighbouring village). The said foreman recounted how they had worked on similar projects around the Grassfields which therefore implies the company was selected for its competence.

True to the spirit of self-help, the population of Bali eagerly participated in the construction process. This was done by way of manual labour for transporting construction material and digging trenches to lay down asbestos pipes which transported water from the pumping site to the main storage tank in *Jamjam* neighbourhood. The tank was strategically placed on a high plateau and, once full, water could easily be resupplied to other areas by gravitational pull. In addition to labour costs, the storage tank and asbestos pipes, among other equipment purchased for construction, everyone I spoke with who grew up in Bali around that time vividly remembered a famous sound emitted by two hydraulic rams,[51] which were purchased from Westminster, UK

---

[51] A hydraulic ram, or hydram, is a cyclic water pump powered by hydropower. The device uses the water hammer effect to develop pressure that allows a portion of the input water that powers the pump to be lifted to a point higher than where the

and were used to pump water at *Ntsi Munyam*. Purchasing the hydraulic ram was appropriate considering that at the time Bali did not have electrical power.

Construction was completed in 1958 and the project handed over to the Bali Native Authority. Being the principal local government institution in the area and given the circumstances that brought about the development of the water project, the NA managed the water as a not-for-profit scheme for the entire community. It constructed a number of standpipes that were dotted around Bali from which people collected water for free. Individual connections was possible; but the vast majority of the population used the public standpipes.

Many informants commended the 'charitable' nature of the project, although some argued that it was not entirely free because people paid poll tax to the NA which used part of it to run the system. Other informants wondered how feasible it would have been for the NA to treat the water with chemicals, maintain the equipment and network of pipes without a regular source of income, especially from the much dreaded poll tax. The above discussion pretty much sums up the situation that prevailed in Bali prior to the arrival of SNEC.

4.7 'Modernisation' and Expansion of Bali's Water Supply: Enter SNEC.

Following reunification of Cameroon, the Federal government sought to supply potable drinking water to urban and rural areas. This involved the creation of the Ministry of Mines, Water Resources and Power, the Rural Engineering or Public Works Department, and the Community Development Department (CDD) (Nchari, et al., 1997). The CDD mostly operated "in the English-speaking part of the country, where most of the successful self-help and community-managed projects [were located]" (Nchari, et al., 1997, p. 2).

As the Bali Community Water Project shows, self-help and community participation in local development were long ingrained in

water originally started. The hydraulic ram is sometimes used in remote areas, where there is both a source of low-head hydropower and a need for pumping water to a destination higher in elevation than the source. In this situation, the ram is often useful, since it requires no outside source of power other than the kinetic energy of flowing water. Source http://en.wikipedia.org/wiki/Hydraulic_ram

the mind-set of the people in the Southern Cameroons. This was the spirit most Anglophones brought into the Federation, following reunification in 1961. The stark difference between the Anglophone and Francophone ways of doing things was often cited as a source of tension on both sides of the linguistic divide (Konings & Nyamnjoh, 2003). Unlike Francophone Cameroonians who were tightly controlled by a stifling central authority, Anglophones were accustomed to a measure of grassroots autonomy. Because Native Authorities in the Southern Cameroons were precursors of the municipal councils in present-day Cameroon, the Bali Community Water project, which was successfully managed by the Bali Native Authority for decades before the central government surreptitiously handed it over to SNEC, clearly indicated the capacity of municipal officials and communities to manage local resources effectively.

Created on 13 May 1967, SNEC was a state parastatal with a monopoly to manage water resources in predominantly urban areas. Other organisations such as the Swiss Association for Technical Assistance (SATA-HELVETAS), the Cooperation for American Relief Everywhere (CARE), the Cameroon Industrial and Civic Contractors (CIACC), and SCANWATER were active in rural areas (Nchari, et al., 1997). SNEC's shareholding structure consisted of the government, the national electricity corporation or *Société National d'Electricité* (SONEL), and the French Development Fund or *Agence Française de Développement,* (AFD) (Page, 2003, p. 489).

There are varying accounts about the circumstances surrounding SNEC's take-over of the Bali community water. According to some informants, because Cameroon in the 1980s was under an autocratic regime, the state sought absolute control of everything. As a result, it could not stand the sight of a 'proud Bali man' successfully managing its own water, hence it decreed that all such assets be handed over to the government-controlled utility supplier. This begs the question why the water project wasn't taken over earlier during the dictatorship of Ahmadou Ahidjo whose legendary obsession for control meant he would not shy away from using brutal means to attain his objectives. That question remained unanswered.

Another controversial issue concerning the takeover was whether SNEC paid compensation to the people of Bali. Some informants said that SNEC actually paid damages before taking over the water project, but the money was syphoned off by the Divisional Officer and the Municipal Administrator of the Bali Rural Council. This version of events was hotly disputed by others who claimed that, if any negotiation about handing over the water installations was ever contemplated, it had to be with the *Fon* who at the time was Galega II the reigning monarch, founder of the project and the only person with the 'natural mandate' to engage in such a process on behalf of the people. As one informant recalled:

> *SNEC came in and compensated Bali people, by paying money to the Fon, because according to tradition the Fon is the head of the community. If he took the money and ate it, we couldn't question him. Hence, if we had found out that SNEC paid compensation to the Fon or to the Council, which was the local government, then we would not have taken back the water. But what was the basis of SNEC managing the water and making profit out of the property of Bali people? None!!! This is why we decided to take back our water.*[52]

No claims of compensation was raised during talks between Bali, state officials, SNEC and representatives of the Ministry of Mines, Water Resources and Power, following the violent takeover of the water installations by the community in 1994.

Another grievance people in Bali expressed about the circumstances surrounding the takeover, was that they had requested the authorities to help them explore possibilities of extending the water supply network, not to appropriate it. Some people were still fuming over the fact that SNEC completely changed everything, including the canalisation system, even though with hindsight it was a good decision because the asbestos that had been used in making the pipes transporting water was found to contain cancerous properties. Walking through Mbatmandet neighbourhood, I noticed remnants of the pipes that were abandoned when SNEC took over and replaced them with Polyvinyl chloride (PVC) pipes. It also replaced community standpipes with metered public taps. Further, SNEC also moved the pumping station from Mbatmandet upstream to Gola. At Gola, it constructed an ultra-modern water catchment, treatment and pumping station that is still in use. SNEC controversially removed the much-vaunted hydraulic rams which were

[52] Interview with a frontline member of the uprising against SNEC in Bali on 19/12/2013.

used at the *Tsi Munyam* and replaced them with electrical engines. At the time, the sole supplier of electricity in Cameroon was another state-run parastatal, SONEL, which incidentally was a shareholder in SNEC.

Unlike the hydraulic rams which were mechanical and incurred minimal costs, the use of electricity to power the engines at the water treatment plant could only mean high water bills, which as expected were passed on to the council. The municipal authorities became alarmed at the exorbitant amount they were regularly charged by SNEC. It got to a point where the council could no longer afford to pay the water bills. This resulted in SNEC shutting down public taps in Bali, leaving many people with no option other than to fetch water from unreliable sources. This generated great resentment against SNEC in Bali.

4.8 Build-up to the Revolt against SNEC in Bali

While piecing together the story of the expulsion of SNEC from Bali, I visited the North West Regional Delegation of the Cameroon Water Utilities Corporation (CAMWATER) in Bamenda. Created in 2005,[53] CAMWATER is a parastatal which took over from SNEC after it came out of 'temporary administration' in 2002. Because SNEC offices in Bali were ransacked and razed to the ground during the violent uprising, I wanted to find out from CAMWATER officials in Bamenda whether they had files relating to SNEC operations in Bali. They did not and I was directed to Mr Kongnyuy (pseudonym), who had been posted to Bali as a clerk in 1989. As an Anglophone from Kumbo in Bui Division, he said he felt at home in Bali and interacted well with the people. Unlike the chief of centre, who lived and worked at the water treatment site in Gola, he was at the SNEC administrative offices in Bali central town, where bills and other customer service issues were handled.

Not long after arriving in Bali, he started getting complaints about high water bills. Most of them were unhappy about SNEC's management of 'their water' and resented the exorbitant bills they were charged. People were also fuming that water supply was intermittent, often muddy, and unfit for human consumption. According to

---

[53] Presidential decree N° 2005/495/ of December 31 2005.

Kongnyuy, "every encounter I had with a Bali man, even outside my workplace, the issue of water came up, and they always reminded me that this is their water and not SNEC's. People often threatened to kick out SNEC because of the exorbitant bills."[54] To buttress this point, when the Governor visited Bali following the ouster of SNEC, he was told that despite persistent appeals by "the population against poor services, including provision of muddy water, frequent water cuts, reduction of public stand-taps, and frequent shutting of the public taps to force people to connect water into their homes, the administration never sent anybody to resolve the problems."[55]

Meanwhile, the management style of the local chief of centre did not help improve SNEC's negative image in Bali. The rash and somewhat cavalier attitude of Mr Nguenang (pseudonym) precipitated the revolt. According to Kongnyuy, the incoming chief of centre, like his predecessor, was a Bamiléké from the West Region of Cameroon. Just like his colleague and fellow Bamiléké in Kumbo, where the population rioted against SNEC and took over 'their water' in 1991 (Page, 2003), the chief of centre in Bali also recruited fellow Bamilékés to perform menial jobs such as mending broken pipes, digging trenches and reading water metres. This greatly incensed many locals who resented the fact that SNEC not only usurped their property and was making profit out of it while delivering poor services, but also excluded them from any potential spin-offs. I subsequently found out that the only local person working at the water treatment site was an ex-policeman who served as a night watchman.

In the 1990s, Bamenda was the centre of opposition against the regime of President Paul Biya. Because the leader of the opposition was an Anglophone, he was loved and loathed in equal measure by some Francophones. This was because *Ni* John Fru Ndi defied the government and launched the SDF party in Bamenda, an action that stunned many and presumably angered the likes of Mr Nguenang. Generally, prejudice against Anglophones and people from the North West in particular was translated into phrases such as *les Bamenda, les Anglos*. For admirers this was synonymous with bravery and defiance, and for haters it symbolised insubordination to established authority.

---

[54] Personal communication with Mr Kongnyuy in Bamenda, on 18/12/2013.
[55] Welcome address to the Governor of the North West Province (now Region) by the Chairman of the Bali Water Committee on 7th June 1994.

Upon taking charge of the treatment centre in Bali therefore, Nguenang dismissed a key staff member at the Gola treatment site. According to Kongnyuy, the new chief of centre erroneously thought *Ni* Fogam was a relative of the SDF leader *Ni* John Fru Ndi.

In many parts of North West Cameroon, the male prefix *Ni* (female *Ma*) is generally employed as a mark of respect for seniors. The story goes that *Ni* Fogam from Batibo was the sole qualified person in charge of water treatment at the Gola station. Without much ceremony and in complete disregard of his pivotal function, *Ni* Fogam was fired on the presumption that the prefix *Ni* automatically meant he was a relative of the SDF party chairman, *Ni* John Fru Ndi.[56] It is quite possible that there was more to the dismissal than this; but, unbeknown to Nguenang, the repercussions of this action were very dramatic.

Apparently, the chief of centre was in no hurry to find a replacement for *Ni* Fogam. This created acute water shortages in Bali and the water that occasionally flowed through the taps was untreated and dirty. According to Kongnyuy, the chief of centre, who lived on site, could have acted promptly to save the situation by standing in temporarily for the dismissed colleague, while seeking a replacement so as to ensure uninterrupted and drinkable water supply in Bali. However, he "completely abandoned his responsibilities and spent his time drinking beer in *Ntanfoang*."[57] To make matters worse, the water crisis occurred in December at the peak of the dry season when alternative water sources were scarce. December is also a very sensitive period in Bali because it is the season for the annual Lela festival which pulls in hordes of Bali people from around Cameroon and abroad. The shortage of water during this sensitive period caused outrage.

To confound things further, the previous chief of centre had prior to his departure issued what one informant described as a "fantastic bill" to the *Fon* of Bali and also sent a notification threatening to cut-off water supply if the *Fon* did not pay the bill. Because traditional rulers in the Grassfields, and Bali in particular, are "near-deities and containers of ancestral spirits" (Awasom, 2003, p. 103), this threat to stop supplying

---

[56] In the midst of the political upheavals that shook Cameroon in the 1990s, there was a popular anecdote about why the SDF chairman Ni John Fru Ndi lost the 1992 presidential elections to Paul Biya. It was believed that the authorities felt, '*Ni John, Ni Fru, Ni Ndi,*' or Neither John, Nor Fru, Nor Ndi, was qualified to govern Cameroon. Ni being the French equivalent for neither or nor.

[57] Personal communication from Mr Kongnyuy in Bamenda, on 18/12/2013.

water to the palace, the highest institution of the land and incarnated by the *Fon*, was deeply offensive. In fact, many saw it as a "slap in the face of Bali people",[58] something they could not tolerate. For all these reasons, the ultimatum mentioned at the beginning of this chapter was issued. This not only threatened to forcefully expel SNEC from Bali, but also requested it to pay damages based on the following claims:

1. Damage to 250 standpipes and concrete protective slabs amounting to the sum of: 170.000.000 francs.

2. Damage to our network of pipelines amounting to the sum of: 150.000.000 francs.

3. Depriving the Bali people of their water supply (a basic necessity of life), and frequent inconveniences for the duration of 10 years amounting to: 200.000.000 francs.

4. Rent for our water tank for 10 years, amounting to: 100.000.000 francs (up until now you refused to pay either royalties or compensation).

5. Exploitation of our quarry at Njenka quarters amounting to: 50.000.000 francs.

6. Cost of 3 rams collected by SNEC after taking over, amounting to: 30.000.000 francs.

7. Destruction of Bali water office when you took over, amounting to 7.000.000 francs.

8. Compensation for damages to property in Bali during the construction of High Tension line for SNEC system of water pumping, amounting to 31.000.000 francs

TOTAL SUM DUE: 748.000.000 (SEVEN HUNDRED AND FORTY EIGHT MILLION FRANCS CFA).[59]

The expiration of the deadline on midnight 15 January 1994 passed without reaction. On Monday 17 January 1994, the population sprang into action, ransacking and burnt down the SNEC branch office in Bali town. It appeared that the chief of centre and his staff were 'tipped off' and discretely fled over the weekend, not without "breaking doors, and

---

[58] Interview with a frontline member of the uprising against SNEC in Bali on 19/12/2013.

[59] Ultimatum issued to the local chief of centre SNEC by the Bali Community Water Committee (BCWC), and the Bali Traditional Council on 11 January 1994.

windows, pulling off toilets, wash basins and electrical fittings."[60] According to Mr Kongnyuy, the slogan adopted by the movement to oust SNEC was dubbed 'the global fight' and the leaders of this movement issued clear instructions that no staff member of SNEC was to be physically harmed. This was so as not to give the government an excuse to intervene forcefully and reverse the people's gains.

The actions of the people of Bali came in the wake of the devaluation of the CFA which took place on 12 January 1994. The CFA was devalued by 50% to the French Franc so as to boost Cameroon exports by making them cheaper on the world market (ODI, 1995). Devaluation of the CFA occurred at the peak of austerity measures that were implemented within the framework of the IMF-World Bank Structural Adjustment Programme. Some of the measures required privatisation of state-owned parastatal companies. This process was rather slow and lacklustre because parastatals, notably SNEC, were a major vehicle for patronage. Restructuring SNEC would have significantly disrupted a vital source of patronage to ethnic kin, whose loyalty was a crucial pillar of the regime of President Paul Biya during the precarious 1990s. As Page (2002) noted, privatisation of SNEC was quite intractable and only occurred decades after the structural adjustments.

The action by the population of Bali therefore occurred at a time when the legitimacy of the government in most parts of Cameroon was at its lowest ebb and quite possibly its moral authority too. This was due mainly to its perceived failure to tackle the economic crisis and its blatant refusal to meet popular demands for a national conference (Takougang & Krieger, 1998, p. 125). The government's lack of credibility presumably sapped its will to use force on this occasion, unlike what had happened in Kumbo. That notwithstanding, the population of Bali did not leave anything to chance. Short of avoiding a bloodbath, I wonder how the security measures taken by them would have stopped the state from overrunning Bali with troops and forcibly reinstate SNEC.

4.8.1 Triumph over SNEC: The Aftermath

On January 19, 1994, two days after the expulsion of SNEC, several meetings were held at different locations in Bali to draw up plans to manage the water project. Key issues discussed included security of

---

[60] Welcome address to the Governor of the North West Province (now Region) by the Chairman of the Bali Water Committee on 7th June 1994.

facilities, finances and alternative water sources. According to the minutes of one such meeting, the prime objective was the *'Resumption of Water Distribution by the Bali Population,'* (my emphasis). Several themes were discussed under the rubric General Affairs; these included:

Work on Alternative Water Sources: The main objective here was to clean and revive all water catchments in Bali including; Bangu, Bacali, Munuga, and Chaibo amongst others.

General Maintenance of Facilities: This plan outlined a rotating schedule of cleaning activities by different neighbourhoods around the water source in Gola.

Anti-Gang/Vigilante: This plan had two main objectives, first to station six guards at the Gola site (two during daytime and four at night), three guards at the storage tank in Jamjam (two at night and one during daytime). Second, to mobilise all vigilante groups in Bali and put them on maximum alert. Moreover, the neighbourhood watchers and guards at Gola were to "be equipped with all necessary instruments suitable for the execution of their duties. They should be provided with alarm instruments to alert the villagers in the event of any confrontation."[61] This was probably because at the time there were wild rumours that the government was planning to send in troops to retake the water installations and hand them back to SNEC, as it did when the population of Kumbo made their first attempt in April 1991, only to be thwarted by massive troop deployment from a military base in Koutaba in the West Region (Page, 2003). The people of Kumbo nevertheless successfully retook 'their water' in October 1991.

Strategy for General Mobilisation: In the 1990s, Bamenda was highly militarised. This was because it was the bastion of the main opposition SDF party and also the epicentre of the civil disobedience campaign, dubbed 'Operation Ghost Towns', which aimed to force the government to organise a 'Sovereign' National Conference and carry out electoral reform. This campaign urged citizens to stop paying utility bills (water, electricity, and telephone), civil servants to desert their offices, and markets/businesses to open only on weekends to enable the population to restock on essential supplies. This campaign was largely effective in Bamenda and other opposition strongholds, notably

---

[61] Minutes of the Bali Nyonga Elites meeting held on 19-01-1994 at the Bali Community Hall.

Bafoussam and Douala. There were also weekly rallies and regular protest marches organised by the SDF, most often violently dispersed by the 'forces of law and order.'

Bamenda being located around 16km away, it meant troops could be deployed to Bali within a twinkle of an eye. Fearing a repeat of the Kumbo scenario, the people of Bali decided to take preventive measures to alert the population in such an event. The strategy went thus: "Alarm instruments should be installed in all quarters of the village, which have to respond to [any distress signal] from Gola, Jamjam or the *Fon's* palace in the event of any confrontation."[62] Upon the alarm signal going off, the population was urged to come out "in readiness for necessary action."[63] It appears that the people of Bali, in a somewhat desperate attempt to counter possible government action, were prepared to revive their historical legacy as warriors. Other measures were taken to address possible or even imminent financial constraints.

While the general affairs meeting was taking place, another conclave was brainstorming about the immediate and long-term modalities to raise funds for the smooth functioning of the water project. The members of the finance committee were drawn from people with a wide range of backgrounds, including 'economists', 'accountants,' and businessmen. In the short term, they sought voluntary donations from individuals and from all Bali meeting houses or *Nda Kums* throughout the country. The committee also recommended the production and sale of support badges with the slogan 'I SUPPORT THE BALI WATER PROJECT.' In the long term, they proposed sending out letters appealing for funds to Bali elites at home and abroad, foreign embassies and consulates, donor organisations and the elites of the other communities in Bali, i.e. Bawock and Bossa. They also envisaged a scheme whereby individuals and groups would pay annual subscriptions.

The price per unit of water consumption was significantly reduced from CFA 286 francs per cubic meter (cm^3), as charged by SNEC, to CFA 100 francs per cm^3. It was decided to continue with the metered public taps installed by SNEC with the bills to be footed by the Council. They also scrapped the CFA 545 francs that was charged monthly by

---

[62] Minutes of the Bali Nyonga Elites meeting held on 19-01-1994 at the Bali Community Hall.

[63] Minutes of the Bali Nyonga Elites meeting held on 19-01-1994 at the Bali Community Hall.

SNEC for meter rent to households with private connections and instead recommended a once-off fee for meters payable during the first installation. On the vexing issue which evoked enormous passion and outrage, the 'fantastic bill' to the *Fon* of Bali, it was decided that; "the paramount *Fon* of Bali will enjoy 25 cm^3 free every month."[64] Finally the committee recommended opening accounts with "banks over which the government has little or no control."[65] This indicates that faith in the state was at this juncture in very limited supply among the population of Bali.

4.8.2 Government Reaction to Community Action

Unlike in Kumbo where a "Government minister, Francis Nkwain, was sent from Yaoundé to try to persuade the people of Kumbo to allow SNEC to return, and operate the water supply" (Page, 2003, p. 493), no such high state official was sent to Bali. Instead the local authorities, notably the North West Provincial Governor, summoned the population for a meeting in his office on 1st February 1994, to discuss what he termed the 'SNEC-Bali Water Problem.'[66] Delegations at the meeting included members of the security forces, representatives of SNEC, SONEL and the Ministry of Mines, Water Resources and Power. Unsurprisingly, the main item on the agenda was a request by the authorities for SNEC to be allowed to return and continue managing the water project.

Before this encounter, the people of Bali held a meeting and designated Mr Ndangoh (pseudonym), a frontline leader of the movement to oust SNEC, to speak on their behalf. They also opted to send a delegation instead of attending the governors summons en-masse. As recounted by Ndangoh, the governor used the opportunity to demonstrate state authority and power. "They brought in colonels, lieutenant colonels, and even generals, some of them from Bafoussam…, they were there in their uniforms, looking fierce. Then

---

[64] Minutes of the Finance Committee (Committee No 2), during the Bali Water Supply General Meeting 19th January 1994.

[65] Minutes of the Finance Committee (Committee No 2), during the Bali Water Supply General Meeting 19th January 1994.

[66] A brief Report by the Steering Committee Secretary of the Bali Community Water Supply, (undated).

the governor entered the hall, introduced the matter and totally condemned the action of Bali people."[67]

References to military generals in this instance could be a gross exaggeration on the part of Ndangoh. However, during the 1990s, the government mobilised the military and carved up the country into operational command units (Mentan, 1998). The North West and West Provinces (now Regions) were headed by a gendarmerie general based in Bafoussam, roughly 60km by road. Given that the actions of the people of Bali was seen in official circles as a 'treacherous challenge to state authority', it is not unreasonable to think that the presence of General Oumarou Djam Yaya, and other senior military officers was solicited to intimidate the people of Bali, and cow them to back down.

After delivering a rather fiery sermon, the governor 'calmed down', but not without demanding that the Bali Water issue be resolved forthwith. He then rhetorically asked the delegation from Bali: "So what is the solution…?"[68] It seemed as if the governor's remarks 'threw a cat amongst the pigeons', because in disregard of the arrangement that one person would speak on behalf of the delegation from Bali, the local Member of Parliament (MP)[69] from the governing CPDM took to the floor and, according to Ndangoh, controversially stated that "he wants to join the government and the governor to condemn what happened…, for people should not think they can re-enact what happened in Nso.[70] He went on to dissociate himself from what happened and stated that the people of Bali were prepared to return the water project to SNEC."[71]

A visibly elated governor quickly jotted down the MP's remarks with some satisfaction and then asked the audience if anybody had something

---

[67] Interview with a frontline member of the uprising against SNEC in Bali on 19/12/2013.

[68] Interview with a frontline member of the uprising against SNEC in Bali on 19/12/2013.

[69] The SDF party boycotted the 1992 legislative elections citing the refusal by the government to reform the electoral code. As a result, the CPDM party won all 20 seats in the North West Province (now Region) including Bali. The North West therefore had CPDM MP's in an area where majority of the population supported the opposition SDF. This rift was certainly at play in this meeting.

[70] Nso or Banso is commonly used to refer to people from Bui Division in the North West Region; the chief town of this division is Kumbo.

[71] Interview with a frontline member of the uprising against SNEC in Bali on 19/12/2013.

else to add. At that juncture, Ndangoh raised his hand and was asked to speak:

> *I said the governor is saying we should sit here and decide that we are handing over this water…? He said yes. I said no, it's not possible because we are here as a delegation representing the people of Bali and in order for us to do that we have to consult those who sent us here. They said voila, you are leaders, you take the decision here then go and tell your people that you have decided on their behalf. I was still standing and said your Excellency, no we will do it the other way. We will go back, call the population of Bali and tell them what you have proposed. If they say yes then we will hand it over. I also said we are not going to hold the meeting in private. It will be held in public on a specific date at the Fon's courtyard. You can send your representatives and your security people to watch how we put the matter to the public. So he accepted my suggestion and we agreed on a date.[72]*

Soon after this meeting, the authorities embarked on a misinformation campaign, issuing radio communiques saying that the people of Bali had agreed to hand back the water and the forthcoming meeting was simply to get the population to endorse a decision agreed upon by their leaders. It also appeared that the local MP had secretly reassured the governor to this effect.

It was against this backdrop that on 25th February 1994, the *Fon* of Bali summoned the population to his main courtyard, also known as *Ntan Lela* or *'Lela* Piazza. The agenda of the meeting was to examine the issue that was raised at the meeting with the Governor on 1st February, i.e. whether the population wanted SNEC to return and continue managing the water project. In the weeks preceding this meeting, information about the 'understanding' with the governor spread like wildfire in Bali and the population eagerly waited for the 25th of February to publicly express their true feelings on the matter. Early that morning, the population thronged the *'Lela* Piazza, determined to take a final stance on the matter. According to Ndangoh:

> *When the crowd had assembled, I stood up and narrated exactly what happened at the meeting with the governor. Then I said as a spokesman of the*

---

[72] Interview with a frontline member of the uprising against SNEC in Bali on 19/12/2013.

delegation that met him we are here to publicly present you what happened. So I said, the governor told us that it was better for us to hand back this water, do you agree...?. Before I finished my statement they started shouting, no, no, no, no, no, no, no...!!! I pleaded with them to stay calm and stated that we have to decide whether we are handing back the water or we are keeping it. Do we want to hand back the water, they shouted no way, no, no, no, no!!! I asked three times, and they said no. Then I emphasised, is there anybody who is in favour of handing back this water to SNEC. Nobody spoke. I also asked this three times and everyone stayed quiet. At that point, I said we had told the governor to send his representatives to this meeting, I hope they are around. They should write their reports of this meeting and submit to the governor, we will also submit ours.[73]

It is clear from the above that the resolve of the people of Bali to oust SNEC and take over 'their water' was a "laudable action against corporate exploitation of man by man."[74] The authorities were not impressed. Curiously, they seemed somewhat powerless to do much about it. Why? Remember they had sent troops to reinstate SNEC in Kumbo in April 1991, albeit temporarily, so why didn't they do the same in Bali?

4.9 Discussion and Conclusion

When the people of Nso took back their water supply from SNEC, the Governor of the N.W. Province rushed from Bamenda to Nso, and held a meeting with the people there. The Minister of Mines and Power drove from Yaoundé to Nso and held meetings with the population and the Fon of Nso. By contrast, after the people of this subdivision took back their water supply from SNEC, they and their Fon have been summoned to Bamenda thrice now. What an insult to a peaceful people!!![75]

---

[73] Interview with a frontline member of the uprising against SNEC in Bali on 19/12/2013.

[74] Resolutions of the Third Plenary General Assembly of the Bali Sub-divisional Population on the Self-Reliant Management of their Water Supply held on 25 February 1994.

[75] Welcome address to the Governor of the North West Province by the Chairman of the Bali Water Committee on 7th June 1994.

Judging from the above, from the outset of the Bali water crisis the authorities underestimated the tenacious will of the people to retain control of the water supply and also their capacity to manage it sustainably in the long term. The authorities presumably felt that sooner or later the people of Bali would come begging for SNEC to return, so they waited with bated breath, ready to celebrate the capitulation of the Bali people.

On 25th March 1994, exactly a month after the population overwhelmingly turned down the request by the governor to allow SNEC to return, the SDO of Mezam Division visited Bali. The chairman of the community water management committee prepared a welcome address to be read for the event. The issues highlighted in the speech included a brief history of the water project, as well as motivation behind the decision to retake it from SNEC.[76] However, the SDO refused to listen to the speech that was prepared for him and categorically rejected any suggestions about visiting the storage tank in Jamjam or the treatment and pumping station in Gola.[77] As if refusing to visit the water installations was not enough, the authorities also embarked on a smear campaign. According to Ndangoh:

Suddenly, we heard rumours that the government had taken samples of the water we were supplying to the public, got them tested and the results showed that the water was horrible. According to reports from the laboratory, if this was the water people in Bali were drinking, then there is an imminent risk of an epidemic. They wanted to use the results as a pretext to arrest me. I conferred with a number of lawyers and we concluded that, if the water that was purportedly from Bali was indeed from here, did the government get anybody to witness when it was collected? Did they actually test the water? And if so, can they make the results public? This was our position and when they heard this, the whole matter just died.[78]

Despite this apparent setback, the authorities were still hoping the population of Bali would not only fail, but return to them cap in hand.

---

[76] Welcome Address Presented to the SDO Mezam by the Chairman of the Bali Community Water Committee on 25 March 1994.

[77] Welcome address to the Governor of the North West province by the Chairman of the Bali Water Committee on 7th June 1994.

[78] Interview with a frontline member of the uprising against SNEC in Bali on 19/12/2013.

Their trump-card was the high cost of electricity needed to power the engines for pumping water. In fact SNEC admitted in the course of the meeting with the governor that it was running the centre at a deficit.[79] However, this was out of its own doing. It should be recalled that when SNEC came to Bali it removed the low cost hydraulic rams that were installed by the community and replaced them with electric engines which inevitably hiked the cost of producing water and also the price paid by consumers.

What the authorities failed to realise (as detailed in the above-mentioned contingency plans), was that ousting SNEC was not a spontaneous action by a disgruntled population eager to take advantage of the volatile political situation in the country to challenge the state. In fact, the two crucial elements that unite all Bali Nyonga people, irrespective of political leanings, are land and the community water project. For during the uprising against SNEC in 1994, "pro and anti-government factions united to drive the water corporation out of town" (Page, 2002, p. 12). Consequently, the views expressed by the local MP during the meeting with the governor were described by one informant as similar to the act of the biblical Judas, even though nobody knew whether he was bribed to sell out.

During the meeting with the governor, SNEC strenuously argued that what happened in Bali was a spontaneous act by a handful of disgruntled individuals who could not afford to settle outstanding bills. But we have seen that it was a well-planned movement. The revolt was born out of frustrations following SNEC's stubborn silence and administrative officials 'refusal to heed the complaints of the people of Bali. Further, managing the water project, especially in the immediate aftermath of the takeover, was a rather daunting task, not least because of a lack of skilled staff, finances and the constant fear of the government sending in troops to retake it forcefully.

What SNEC and the authorities failed to realise was that the community previously managed the water project for twenty seven years and were determined to return it to its founding principle as a not-for-profit scheme. Hence, when the governor visited Bali later that year, he heard the following: "If the government truly stands for ensuring that

---

[79] Resolutions of the Third Plenary General Assembly of the Bali Sub-divisional Population on the Self-Reliant Management of their Water Supply held on 25 February 1994.

its citizens have potable water, then we expect the administration to stand by the population of Bali in their self-reliant effort. After all, the Bali Water supply was constructed in 1957 as a self-reliant project."[80]

The government finally backed down, leaving the community to manage the water project until 2013 when it was handed to Bali Council amid controversy over whether it was another prelude to a takeover by government and by extension CAMWATER, because the Bali municipality was now under the control of the ruling CPDM party.

---

[80] Welcome address to the Governor of the North West Province (now Region) by the Chairman of the Bali Water Committee on 7th June 1994.

Chapter V

Land Tenure and Inter-Community Politics: The Perils of Municipal Planning in Bali

As a primary and fundamental but also highly symbolic resource for most African peoples, land holds a unique position within the so-called traditionalist societies and economies (Ward and Alden 2010, 4).

5.1 Introduction

In 2004, the government of Cameroon introduced policies to empower local municipalities to take decisions in the domains of economic, health, social, educational, and cultural development. These policies received strong donor backing, ostensibly because local government was perceived to be more democratic and quite effective in promoting development (van de Walle, 2003). Section 17 of the rules applicable to Councils devolves powers to 'prepare land tenure plans, town planning documents, urban rehabilitation and land consolidation plans.'[81]

In line with this regulation, in April 2005 the authorities of Bali Council in North West Cameroon with the technical support of Helvetas[82] commissioned a research project designed to produce a monographic database. This survey documented information on the economic, socio-cultural and developmental potential of Bali and also chronicled 'the culture of all ethnic groups, and their interaction with each other.'[83] Information for the survey was to a large extent collected by municipal councillors who received training in field data collection techniques. These councillors were elected representatives from the three main communities in Bali: Bali Nyonga, Bawock, and Bossa.

Themes explored in the study included culture, demography, administration, infrastructure, economy, environment and land tenure. These will be highlighted to varying degree in this chapter. Emphasis will be placed on the administrative and land tenure structure of Bali

---

[81] Law N° 2004/18 of 22 July 2004.
[82] Swiss Inter-cooperation agency
[83] Bali Council Monographic Study August 2005.

subdivision, which resulted into a dispute between Bali Nyonga and Bawock. The friction stemmed from the fact that the findings of the survey split Bali into seventeen neighbourhoods and all but two belonged to Bali Nyonga.

Prima facie, this is a reasonable repartition, considering that Bali Nyonga had 6,796 out of 7,582 houses, Bawock 477 and Bossa 309; and a population of 75,282 out of 85,058, Bawock 5,341 and Bossa 4,435.[84] At the time of the study, Bali Council was managed by the opposition Social Democratic Front party, which had been at the helm following the first multiparty municipal elections in Cameroon in 1996. As discussed later, the outcome of this survey reduced the chances of the SDF retaining Bali Council in the 2007 municipal elections.

5.2 Background

There is of course no single land question; the burning issue varies from country to country and between various groups within different societies, but the mere fact that land questions are so contentious is a clear indication of the political and social transformative dynamics in the negotiation of property (Lund 2008, 10).

Bali is bounded to the North by Chomba, Nsongwa, Mbatu and Mankon in Bamenda II subdivision; to the East by Pinyin, Baforchu and Baba II in Santa subdivision; to the South by Njaitu, Osum, Ngemuwah, Guzang and Ashong in Batibo subdivision and to the West by Ngyen-Mbu and Bome in Mbengwi central subdivision.[85] As discussed in chapter IV, the relationship between Bali and surrounding Widekum tribes was tumultuous because Bali was embroiled for over a century in intractable land conflicts with many of its neighbours. There were numerous attempts by administrative officials from colonial to present times to address this problem. Whereas these efforts have brought lasting solutions in some cases, in others they have created confusion and exacerbated tensions, often degenerating into bloodshed. This chapter will examine these conflicts in general, with specific emphasis on recent incidents involving Bali Nyonga and Bawock.

---

[84] Bali Council Monographic Study, August 2005.
[85] Bali Council Monographic Study August 2005.

Unlike Scott's (1998, p. 3) description of abridged maps which "did not successfully represent the actual activity of the society they depicted," the picture painted by the monographic survey not only illustrated growing urban expansion in Bali, which like most small towns in Cameroon is semi-urban at the centre and rural at the periphery, but also the demographic, socio-economic and cultural potential of the area. However, the new administrative setup which was yet to be approved by the state reignited a quest for land and territorial demarcation by Bawock and in the process opened a 'can of worms' which degenerated into a series of violent incidences in 2006 and 2007. As a subsequent rendition of events will demonstrate, conflicting historical narratives and centuries-old tribal discord combined to create an explosive situation between Bali and Bawock.

The people of Bawock arrived in Bali around 1907 while fleeing persecution from a kin group in *Nde* Division of the present-day West Region of Cameroon.[86] The chief of Bawock, however, disputes this, saying they were party to another Bamilike group (the Bati) which migrated to Bali around 1904. He further argues that, just like Bali, they came to the present site as a 'conquering army' and therefore deserve respect and a clearly defined and demarcated territory. It was on these grounds that in 2005 a plot was orchestrated to actualise Bawock's territorial claims in Bali. This was planned with the connivance of traditional chiefs from Santa subdivision known to be among Bali Nyonga's age-old foes, and with the collusion of administrative officials from the headquarters of Mezam Division.

The goal was to conduct a *"successful and peaceful installation of boundary pillars between the village of Bawock in Bali subdivision and the villages of Mbu and Pinyin in Santa subdivision"*[87] (my emphasis). This theme raises a number of issues: For example, where is the boundary between Bali and Bawock on the one hand, and Bali, Mbu, and Pinyin located? What are the statutory provisions governing land tenure in Cameroon? Why was the

---

[86] For details see: *The History of a People; The Secret Behind the Bali Nyonga and Bawock Nfeu Gai Nfai Affair* (nd; p12, 15, 17, 19)

[87] Letter addressed to the SDO for Mezam Division, on November 14, 2006; with the subject: The installation of Boundary Pillars between Mbu, Bawock, and Pinyin Fondoms.

Fon of Bali, who is the paramount traditional ruler[88] of the administrative subdivision where Bawock is situated not involved in preparations for the 'peaceful installation'? What was the role of administrative officials in the demarcation saga? Finally how did Bawock get to the point where it aggressively sought a delimitated domain?

This chapter seeks to establish how administrative decisions and actions, prescribed as a panacea for territorial disputes, inadvertently causes others to spring up sometimes from unexpected angles. I will also explore how local actors have responded to state policy of decentralisation implemented in Cameroon since 2004. Specifically, I will demonstrate how the unveiling of a municipal town planning blueprint intended as a master plan for future development activities in Bali rapidly degenerated into a violent land dispute. First, I will unpack the relationship between land tenure and land-use practices in the Bamenda Grassfields.

5.3 Land Tenure and Traditional Land-use Practices

> *Being a valuable and immovable resource of limited quantity, land is not only fundamental to the livelihood of most Africans, but also represents a precious reservoir of natural resources (Ward and Alden 2010, 2).*

Land is a very important asset for peoples and communities around the world. According to (Hart, 1982, p. 10) "if there was a scarce factor of production in traditional agriculture, it was not land." The relative abundance of land in precolonial Africa ensured a sustainable balance between livelihoods and resources. The value of land for many Africans was not only because of its ability to sustain life, but also because of its importance as a source of religious power and inspiration (Mope Simo 2002). This combination of spiritual and material values was such that land in precolonial Africa could neither be bought nor sold (Diduk, 1992), because it was generally believed that "land belongs to the dead, the living and generations yet to be born" (Njoh, 2006, p. 27).

Because land in most traditional African settings was held by groups or communities and not individuals, the former were often recognised

---

[88] According to **Arrêté N° 36/A/MINAT/DOT OF 19/01/1982,** Bawock is a 2nd degree chiefdom attached to the 1st degree chiefdom of Bali in the Mezam Division of the North West Province (now Region).

as the 'land owning or controlling' units, and responsibility for protecting land against outsiders was often bestowed on chiefs, family heads, and community elders (Ndjio, 2006 and Rodney, 1982). Moreover, traditional land holding systems in the Grassfields consisted of farmland for subsistence agriculture, land for housing and land for hunting and gathering (Engard 1988). These activities, according to Egbe (2002, p. 62) "imposed little stress upon the environment."

Abundant land in antiquity meant that acquisition of or claims to territory in the Grassfields, as elsewhere in Africa, was generally conducted via a number of methods, including conquest, first settlement, confiscation following punitive judgements, habitual visitation and spiritual sanction amongst others (Njoh, 2006). At the time, rivers and mountains were deemed appropriate physical barriers that demarcated one territory from another (Fisiy, 1992). Plentiful land also encouraged shifting cultivation, whereby a piece of land was cultivated for some time and when soil fertility depleted it was abandoned to fallow (Hart, 1982). As a result, one could reasonably argue that by the time the Germans arrived in the Grassfields, there was "no single tract of land [that] could be said to be without an owner" (Fisiy, 1995, pp. 58-9). Hence, if the line *'chiefs know their boundaries'* (Berry, 2001) is anything to go by, Fonyonga II of Bali was certainly playing the territorial card when he presented a list of several villages under his belt to the new British administration in 1915 (Nyamdi, 1988).

Colonial officials needed land for the smooth functioning of imperialist ventures, much of it located in hostile terrain; so it was unsurprising that they introduced "new rules of tenure in order to claim access to land" (Fisiy, 1995, p. 59). However, because Bali Nyonga fought its way to dominance in parts of the grassfields and welcomed Europeans with open arms, there was no need for the latter to acquire territory by force because abundant land was readily available. Moreover, colonialism was a game of self-interest and alliance with Africans was quite tenuous and often marked by duplicity. For example, the terms of the German-Duala treaty of 1884 stated that no land would be alienated from native inhabitants. However, the ink had hardly dried on the piece of paper when Germany began expropriating lands for the establishment of plantations (Chiabi 2011; Eyongetah and Brian 1989; Diduk 1992; Fisiy 1992; Austen and Derrick 1999).

Britain and France took over Cameroon under a League of Nations Mandate. Both powers managed land differently and each made provision for registration of customary land. This practice was known in French Cameroon as *livrets fonciers* and as 'certificates of occupancy' in British Cameroon (Javelle, 2013). Britain divided Southern Cameroons into smaller administrative units known as Native Authorities (NA) and each was responsible for settling local disputes, collecting taxes and directing local services such as road works and health centres (Vubo & Ngwa, 2001).

As in the Matatiele district in South Africa, where "most land in the district [was] held under communal tenure administered by chiefs and headmen who presided over tribal authorities" (Sharp & Spiegel, 1985, p. 136), land control in the Grassfields was vested in NAs headed by chiefs and their council of elders. They presided over native courts that adjudicated land disputes and claims through customary land tenure systems. Access to land in the Grassfields was generally viewed as an inalienable individual right within broader kin groups (Diduk, 1992). Consequently, the advent of new land tenure rules following independence meant that very few individual Cameroonians formerly registered lands (Javelle, 2013).

5.4 Changing Land-use Patterns in the Grassfields

Over time, a number of factors distorted traditional land use patterns in the Grassfields; these included colonialism, population increase, cash crop cultivation, animal husbandry, land sales and individual titling, which together "conferred a very different economic status and symbolic value upon land" (Diduk, 1992, p. 195). As a result, traditional practices became untenable. For example, the introduction of cattle into West Africa by the Fulani led to what was described as "an ethnic division of labour between pastoralists and the bulk of agriculturalists" (Hart, 1982, p. 53). Across the grassfields one of the most prominent forms of land disputes in the second half of the 20th century was between farmers and graziers. The arrival of the Fulani in the Grassfields around 1916 was a mixed blessing. First, their presence provided local chiefs with an opportunity to settle new clients on hilltops because of their suitability for pasture in return for tributes. Secondly, nomadic grazers introduced new products such as beef and dairy into the local economy and dietary habits which in themselves constituted rich sources of protein for many households. The presence of cattle rearing Fulani also provided the colonial administration with a valuable source of income in the form of *Jangali* or cattle tax (Dafinger and Pelican 2006, Fisiy 1992 and Mbah 2013). By the 1930s however, enthusiasm for the Fulani presence in the Grassfields began to wane.

According to Egbe, (2002, p. 62), "traditional methods of utilising resources were generally well-adapted to local conditions." Because the majority of the population in the Bamenda Grassfields were subsistence farmers producing food crops mainly for household consumption with surpluses sold-off to local markets, the descent of the Fulani from the hilltops did not bode well for local cohesion (Rambousek, 1982). The Fulani migration was due mainly to overgrazing and denudation of the landscape; as a result, pasture land became scarce, pushing herders into the fertile lowlands where food crops was cultivated. The immediate outcome was farmer-grazier conflicts which, according to Njeuma & Awasom, (1990), was the subject of almost every administrative report from the Bamenda area to the administrative headquarters of the Southern Cameroons in Buea from the 1940s onwards. This led Fisiy (1992, p. 72) to conclude that "land which was still abundant in the 1920s became an intense battleground for struggles over ownership access and control," something which today constitutes a major thorn in the side of administrative officials in many parts of North West Cameroon.

During fieldwork in Bali, I spent time consulting files at the local sub-divisional office. There I stumbled on correspondences documenting complaints by farmers against cattle rearers going back decades. I also observed the Divisional Officer shuttling between meetings and field inspections, while attending to complaints by local farmers about crop destruction by Fulani cattle. Farmer-grazier problems constituted a sizable proportion of petitions in the DO's in-tray; but like most his predecessors he had other pressing land issues to contemplate. It should be recalled that Bali is located in an area where land and boundary disputes go back generations and efforts to settle them were a major preoccupation for colonial and contemporary officials.

Prior to attempting a solution to the land situation in Bali, the state of Cameroon sought to codify customary practices as formal law. In

1974, the government of Cameroon issued a law[89] establishing the rules governing land tenure. In principle, this land ordinance abolished all customary arrangements and nationalised all lands (Konings 2003 and Amungwa 2011). Paradoxically, both customary and nationalised systems are still operational in Cameroon and the confusion this generates is often cited as a potential source of land conflicts (Mope Simo 2011 & 2002). In Bali, the state attempted to solve the land problem by issuing decree N° 77-525 of 23 December 1977 carving out large expanses of land from Bali Nyonga and awarding them to neighbouring areas. It then requested the people of Bali, under the leadership of the traditional ruler, to apply for a land certificate for the remaining parcels.[90]

To understand the context of these decrees, I draw the reader's attention to a few historical facts about the area in question. First, Bali conquered and occupied its present location sometime in the 19th century (Fokwang 2011; Nyamdi 1988; Fardon 1983; Rubin 1970 and Chilver 1964). Second, it used its alliance with Germany to further expand and entrench its hold on a vast hinterland (Kaberry 1962; Kaberry and Chilver 1961). Third, most of the displaced tribes agitated against Bali hegemony, yearned for freedom from Bali domination and sought to recovery lost territory (Fokwang, 2009). Fourth, when Britain and France split the territory after World War I, the former took over present-day English-speaking Cameroon. Britain tried but failed to entrench Bali domination over neighbouring Widekum tribes whose land claims became increasingly vocal (Fokwang, 2011). Finally the Widekums took a number of ultimately futile legal actions against Bali in an attempt to reclaim land (Nyamdi, 1988). Left with little other option, they mounted a concerted attack against Bali in 1952 causing loss of life and property. In the aftermath of the crisis, British colonial authorities appointed a commissioner to investigate[91] the 1952 Bali-Widekum violence. The commissioner's report blamed the Widekums for aggression and singled out specific individuals for rebuke.

---

[89] Ordinance 74-1 of 6 July 1974
[90] Decree N° 77-525 of 23/12/1977.
[91]A.D.B Manson (1953), Government Notice No 794; Report of an Inquiry held under the Commissions of Inquiry Ordinance (Chapter 37): Nigeria Gazette Extraordinary p565-57.

5.4.1 Bali-Widekum Crisis: Aftermath

Amongst the Widekum leaders cited in the commissioner's report was one S.T. Muna who, prior to election into the Eastern House of Assembly in Nigeria, was a teacher in Bali. According to the commissioner, the Honourable Muna "produced no new historical data to support the Widekum claim."[92] He was "vague, uncategorical [and admitted to having] no personal grievances."[93] Considering that the Widekums were in a position of weakness after the war, what good would have come out of saying otherwise? Moreover, the Honourable Muna did not have a bone to pick at this time, presumably because the Widekums were licking their wounds from their disastrous failure to capture land from Bali. Likewise, if Muna had any grievances, he probably was not in a position to divulge them just yet.

Over a decade later, the Honourable S.T. Muna went on to become a prominent political figure in Cameroon as Prime Minister of the federal state of West Cameroon from 1968 to 1972 and President of the National Assembly of the United Republic of Cameroon from 1973 to 1988, then second only to the head of state in protocol (DeLancey, et al., 2010). Muna's spectacular rise was linked to his staunch support for Ahidjo's centralisation drive which led to the dissolution of the federation following a referendum in 1972 (Konings 2011; Eyongetah and Brian 1989; Delancy 1989; Takougang and Krieger 1998,). Occupying such a strategic position of power in a one-party dictatorship would offer considerable leverage and unlimited opportunity to pull strings behind the scenes.

Meanwhile, the opinion of Bali Kumbat[94] on the decision by the Federal Court of Justice in Buea to rule in favour of Bafanji over a land

---

[92] A.D.B Manson (1953), Government Notice No 794: Report of an Inquiry held under the Commissions of Inquiry Ordinance (Chapter 37): Nigeria Gazette Extraordinary p 568.

[93] A.D.B Manson (1953), Government Notice No 794: Report of an Inquiry held under the Commissions of Inquiry Ordinance (Chapter 37): Nigeria Gazette Extraordinary p570.

[94] Bali Kumbat is one of 7 villages that make up the Chamba group. Bali Kumbat and Bafanji are located in the Ngoh-Ketunja Division in the Northwest Region of Cameroon. According to (J. Mope Simo 2002, 45): Counter petitions had been made about the ownership of an agriculturally fertile area called Mbangang which is at their common border. In 1969, the government of the former West Cameroon set up a land consultation committee, which demarcated the area in favour of Bafanji, and pillars marking the boundary were erected. However, under the reign of the most influential *Fons*, Bali-Kumbat challenged the terms of the decision, and sued the Bafanji at the

dispute is quite revealing. "We have been deprived of our land because Hon. Muna who is Prime Minister influenced the courts because of a grudge that we supported the Bali Nyongas against the Widekums" (Nyamnjoh & Rowlands, 1988). As a result, many in Bali did not have to look far for the provenance of a presidential decree signed in 1977 that effectively carved out with almost surgical precision virtually all the territories the Widekums went to war with Bali in 1952 to conquer. This decision led many to believe that land issues in Bali were effectively laid to rest. Before the 1977 decree, the state issued an ordinance appropriating all but a limited quantity of land in the country. I now examine the 1974 Land Ordinance, followed by the 1977 decree and the implications of both on Bali's enduring land issues. These legal texts will contextualise the decision of Bali Council to commission a monographic database.

5.4.2 The 1974 Land Ordinance, and Customary Land-use Practice

> *However simple and uniform the new tenure system was to an administrator, it flung villagers willy-nilly into a world of title deeds, land offices, fees, assessments, and applications. They faced powerful new specialists in the form of land clerks, surveyors, judges, and lawyers whose rules of procedure and decisions were unfamiliar (Scott 1998, p. 48).*

Within its broader framework of nation-building and national integration, the state in Cameroon is often criticised for using legislation as a hegemonic tool to spread its tentacles into far flung areas of the country, enabling it to capture "divergent interests and local communities" (Egbe, 2002, p. 65). The 1974 Land Ordinance falls within this domain. These reforms were controversial because they undermined "customary communities [who perceived them] as unwarranted interference with their rights by the government" (ibid, p. 68). Meanwhile, the North West Region has for several decades witnessed "an increasing number of often violent conflicts over access to land, a resurgence of boundary issues, and insecurity of tenure over commercial and subsistence farmland" (Mope Simo, 2002, p. 37). These

---

Federal Court of Justice in Buea. Again the judiciary ruled in favour of Bafanji. In 1994, the two villages were at war, and all the pillars were knocked down.

issues were attributed to the impact on farming communities of ambiguities inherent in the 1974 Land Ordinance.

Like most developing countries, subsistence farming was (and still is) the cornerstone of Cameroon's agricultural sector (Mope Simo 2002 and Auty 1988). In the Grassfields, farming was still dominated by small-scale crop cultivation practised mostly by women who largely depended on customary land tenure systems for access to and control over land. However, by alienating land tenure from customary into state hands, the 1974 Ordinance threw customary practices into disarray. From antiquity, the majority of people in the Grassfields were governed by centralised chieftaincies and land tenure rights were often held by the chief in trust for the people (Diduk, 1992).

According to Mope Simo, (2002, pp. 38-9), the *Fon* "is the most senior title holder in the highly stratified social, political, economic and religious structure, and wields much political, symbolic and spiritual power... The *Fon* is [also] custodian of all land and natural resources under his jurisdiction, and guards the sacred sites." It is tempting to speculate that, with the passage of time, the advent of the modern state and the practical implementation of the above-mentioned land ordinances, the position of the *Fon* as 'custodian of all lands' was no longer tenable. However, this is certainly not the case in the Grassfields, not least in Bali:

> *The common goal of every Bali man is defending the territorial boundaries of our community. Now that our Fon is senator, it gives him a bigger platform to effectively carry out this task. And if he allows the Ngyen-Mbu people or other neighbouring villages to take Bali land while he is in that house where major decisions can be taken about land tenure then he has failed the people who entrusted him with custodianship over our land.*[95]

The *Fon* of Bali has been tirelessly working to uphold his customary obligations to his subjects vis-à-vis the 1974 Land Ordinance and also decree N° 77/525. As a member of the Central Committee of the governing CPDM party, Ganyonga III has a dilemma that forces him to walk a tight rope and occasionally pits him in open conflict with the

---

[95] Interview conducted with a Bali elite on 03/01/2014.

state. What then is the content of the 1974 Land Ordinance and why has its application been the source of so much acrimony?

According to Njoh (2006, p. 70), "land tenure comprises the system of legal rights and obligations that govern the acquisition, possession, alienation and transfer of land in any given community." The 1974 land reforms were therefore aimed at harmonising customary practices with Western precepts of rational land management (Mope Simo, 2002). The law outlined three categories of land -- State Lands, Private Lands and National Lands (Amungwa, 2011). State Lands were reserved for public uses such as roads, bridges, etc. Private Lands, comprised privately held land and state private land such as de-gazetted lands, lands purchased by the state etc. Finally, National Lands fell in a rather ambiguous category that is neither public nor private. These include "vacant lands, settlements, farms, plantations, and grazing lands manifesting human presence and development" (Egbe, 2002, p. 68).

In principle, the enactment of this policy effectively superseded all customary land rights in Cameroon, with exceptions only in circumstances where land was covered by 'certificates of title' which many ordinary people cannot afford because of the prohibitive costs (Jua, 2011). Paradoxically, the law also states that; "individuals and communities may apply for a title on land that they effectively occupied and used before 1974" (Javelle, 2013, p. 3). To confound things further, the law states that people may continue to effectively and peacefully occupy land without title, meaning "communities and individuals are not required by law to title land." (Javelle, 2013, p. 3).

Meanwhile, Hart (1982, p. 3) contends that "the key to the development of predominantly agrarian states lies in the countryside and not in the cities." In line with this, I argue that the ambiguous nature of the 1974 Land Ordinance, coupled with the equally ill-conceived decree N° 77/525, stoke up land and border conflicts, as seen in disputes in North West Cameroon (Mbah 2009, and Mope Simo 2002), such as that between Oku and Mbessa (CERD, 2008), Bali-Kumbat and Bafanji (Mope Simo 2011 and Erbe, et al. 2009), and Bali Nyonga and Bawock in 2006 and 2007. This does not bode well for developmental prospects in the affected areas. Decree N° 77/525 was crafted as the final solution to the land issues in and around Bali.

5.4.3 Decree N° 77/525: Panacea to Land Issues in Mezam and Momo Divisions

"However precisely they were drawn on paper, boundaries could be remarkably elusive in practice" (Berry 2001, p. 13).

On 23rd December 1977, President Ahmadou Ahidjo issued decree N° 77/525, modifying the Territorial Boundaries of certain traditional communities in Mezam and Momo Divisions, in North West Cameroon. Articles 2, 3, 4 & 5 of the decree carved out large parcels of land from Bali and awarded them to: Baforchu in the East, Chomba, Mbatu and Nsongwa in the North, Ngyen-Muwa in the South, and Ngyen-Mbu in the West. Article 8 (1) of the decree states: "Natural persons in zones affected by the modifications of the territorial boundaries made in this decree may remain where they are on condition that they submit themselves to the authority of the new traditional ruler having jurisdiction over the area in which they reside."[96] (Berry, 2008). Simply put, people from Bali in Mezam division residing in a disputed area known as Kontan were arbitrarily ceded over to the traditional authorities of Ngyen-Mbu in Momo Division. Further, the law permitted them to live and continue farming in the area on condition that they renounced the *Fon* of Bali and swore allegiance to the traditional authorities of Ngyen-Mbu. Bali people in Kontan accepted the spirit but not the letter of Article 8 (1). They continued paying allegiance to the *Fon* of Bali and repeatedly sought his intervention in the dispute and retained claims to the land.

Upon arriving in Bali for fieldwork in 2013, I paid a courtesy visit to the *Fon* and his retinue subsequently joined us to report to him about a visit they had just completed at the disputed site. Throughout my research in Bali there was a flurry of activities over the disputed area and its controversial agricultural project; these involved senior state officials, including the Regional Governor. Meanwhile, in the decades following this decree, numerous clashes occurred around Kontan involving people from Bali and Ngyen-Mbu. A fairly recent incident was a violent disruption of farming activities on the site of an agricultural development project set up by the government on disputed land for a

---

[96] Decree N° 77-525 of 23/12/1977.

group of farmers from Ngyen-Mbu. Another incident in September 2014 resulted in the lynching of a man from Bali, allegedly by people from Ngyen-Mbu. According to Article (9) of decree 77/525:

> *The people of Bali duly represented by the Fon are authorised to have a collective land certificate issued to them for their entire area against the background of the boundaries established in 1954, as modified by articles 2-5 including parts of the area constituting public or private property of the state.*[97]

The prohibitive costs involved in obtaining a collective land certificate notwithstanding, the process itself could be explosive if not deadly. The African continent is littered with cases of land conflicts that often turn violent. For example, Medad (2010, p. 30) discussed how "since the late 1980s different segments of the *Chebyuk*[98] population have petitioned the state in an effort to claim or reclaim land on the basis of community or landlessness." In Northern Ghana, there was a double clash between the *Nanumba* and the *Konkomba* communities in April and June 1981. These clashes, according to Skalník (2003, 72-3), "had not been predicted by state officials, and the state did not manage to prevent them until the first carnage was over." In Cameroon, Bali has since the 1970s witnessed incidences similar to what occurred in the above examples. The attempt by the chiefs of Bawock, Pinyin and Mbu to conduct 'a peaceful installation of boundary pillars' in December 2006 was a poignant illustration of the volatility of such an exercise.

5.5 Timeline of Encounters between Bali and Bawock, 1970-2007

> *Few issues evoke deeper passions and/or account for more bloodshed in Africa and everywhere else than disagreements about territory (Njoh 2006, p. 69).*

As I have noted, there is profound disagreement between the Bali Nyonga and Bawock communities over the latter's historical antecedence, particularly the circumstances that brought Bawock to its present location and subsequent claims to land. This situation has over the years wrought enormous discord on both sides. The decades-long

---

[97] Decree N° 77-525 of 23/12/1977.
[98] Chebyuk is located in the Mount Elgon District in kenya.

differences between both communities could be traced to 1974. In that year, the *Fon* of Bali wrote to the chief of Bawock ordering him to suspend his annual festival until the "Bali Supreme annual festival [known as] Lela is over."[99] This dispute led to an agreement of January 15, 1975 termed: *Communiqué of peaceful co-existence between the peoples of Bali and Bawock communities.*[100] This acknowledged the voluntary choice of the ancestors of both communities to live together and also called for mutual recognition and respect by traditional leaders on both sides.

Despite this agreement, tension simmered unabated and "public opinion in Bawock was that it was better for them to go back to their former land in *Nde* Division."[101] However, the advent of Paul Biya as head of state raised the hopes of many Cameroonians, including the people of Bawock, who subscribed to Biya's 'New Deal' mantra (Delancy, 1989), and were comforted because "when the president said everywhere in Cameroon, a Cameroonian is free because he has the right to enjoy freedom of speech, political, social and cultural development, it was then that the Bawock man had confidence in himself around the area."[102]

In the 1980s and 1990s, Cameroon experienced economic crisis and the government was pressured by donors to liberalise the economy. Internally, it was facing calls from opposition movements for political liberalisation. In order to confront these challenges, the Biya regime employed a divide and rule strategy. It also drifted away from Ahidjo's policy which held that "it was bad taste to mention someone's ethnic affiliation, let alone to qualify someone openly as an *allogène*" (Geschiere, 2009, p. 39). The government encouraged the creation of ethnic and regional elite associations to promote and achieve broader ethno-regional interests. These included *Essingang* (Beti elite), *La'akam* (Bamilike elite), the Southwest Elite Association (SWELA), and the Northwest Elite Association (NOWELA) (Nkwi 2006; Konings and Nyamnjoh 2003). Biya's tactic of employing high-sounding political

---

[99] For details see: *The History of a People; The Secret Behind the Bali Nyonga and Bawock Nfeu Gai Nfai Affair* (nd; p36).

[100] For details see: *The History of a People; The Secret Behind the Bali Nyonga and Bawock Nfeu Gai Nfai Affair* (nd; p39).

[101] For details see: *The History of a People; The Secret Behind the Bali Nyonga and Bawock Nfeu Gai Nfai Affair* (nd; p36).

[102] For details see: *The History of a People; The Secret Behind the Bali Nyonga and Bawock Nfeu Gai Nfai Affair* (nd; p53).

rhetoric and divisive tribal tendencies was not a unique Cameroonian phenomenon. It was a ruse also adopted by some contemporaries across the continent. In Kenya, President Arap Moi's stratagem to garner support from minority groups following the introduction of multipartyism in the 1990s involved the development of *Majimbo* ideology which, according to Medad (2010, p. 25), "promoted an exclusive view of ethnicity defined by territory."

According to Konings and Nyamnjoh (2003, p. 40), "autochthony became the all-overriding issue in Cameroonian politics, and with it claims to special rights for those who "really" belonged in the area where they lived." The outcome of the politics of autochthony was that communities increasingly believed that "it is only by having one's own administrative unit (subdivision, division or province), that one stands a good chance of benefiting from the national cake which different groups wish to appropriate to the detriment of others"(Konings and Nyamnjoh 2003, p. 132). This period also witnessed a surge in appeals for the creation of administrative units in exchange for pledges of support for the governing CPDM party.

It was therefore with renewed zeal that on 30th May 1986, the Bawock traditional Council wrote a petition to the DO for Bali.[103] Though not seeking an administrative unit per se, the motivation was undoubtedly territorial. The complaints in this petition included "encroachments into the village by our neighbours, attempts to wipe [out] our identity and the entire village," and the arbitrary (re)naming of development projects in Bawock with Bali names."[104] This led to another meeting at the end of which both parties restated their commitments to the resolutions arrived at in 1975. The presiding chairman and DO for Bali concluded by stating that people resident in an area known as 'Nted B', which was claimed by both sides, should pay taxes to Bawock and participate in communal work without which "the question of a boundary demarcation would not have arisen."[105]

---

[103] Petition addressed to the Sub-Divisional Officer Bali, by Bawock Traditional Council, dated 30th May, 1986. Titled; *Application for the demarcation of our village boundaries with Survey Pillars*

[104] Petition addressed to the Sub-Divisional Officer Bali, by Bawock Traditional Council, dated 30th May, 1986. Titled; *Application for the demarcation of our village boundaries with Survey Pillars*

[105] For details see: *The History of a People; The Secret Behind the Bali Nyonga and Bawock Nfeu Gai Nfai Affair* (nd; p49).

The 'New Deal' propaganda not only buoyed the people of Bawock, but spurred them on and intensified the campaign for an 'independent jurisdiction', something which Bali Nyonga vehemently opposed. Meanwhile, the location of *Nted* B and *Mbatmandet,* where people from both communities are intertwined, makes it physically impossible to demarcate both communities. Likewise, the potentially lethal consequences of attempting such a venture very close to the centre of Bali prompted the MBU-PIN-WOCK alliance (acronym for Mbu, Pinyin and Bawock villages) to seek a convenient location on the fringes far away from prying eyes. However, in doing so, it failed to countenance the vigilance of Bali Nyonga when it comes to land matters.

5.6 Partition and Annexation of Mantum Village

According to Amanor and Ubink (2008, p. 13), "devolution of land administration to customary-based institutions will result in a more equitable management of land [and] allow rural people to be involved in the negotiation of rights to land." Whereas this is true under certain circumstances, land regulations in Cameroon are fraught with ambiguities, often leading to subjective interpretations that in some cases feed violent conflicts.

In January 2005, an association known as the MBU-PIN-WOCK alliance was founded as a development organisation of chiefs from the above-named villages.[106] The creation of MBU-PIN-WOCK was preceded in 2004 by a pronouncement of the chiefs of Mbu, Pinyin and Bawock villages that was aimed at redrawing the map of Mezam Division. These chiefs unilaterally declared that their communities have "common boundaries in two different Sub-Divisions in Mezam, [and also that] Bali Nyonga village and/or *Fondom* is situated on the West of Bawock *Fondom* in Bali Sub-Division."[107] As Konings and Nyamnjoh (2003) observed, the petition letter ended with warm greetings to the SDO and a reaffirmation of "unalloyed attachment to His Excellency

---

[106]By-laws of MBU-PIN-WOCK drawn up in Bamenda on 11th January 2005.

[107] Letter addressed to the Senior Divisional Officer of Mezam Division on 31 May 2004.

Paul BIYA…"[108] However, its real objective was to actualise the partition and annexation of Mantum village in Bali.

In the years leading up to the formation of the MBU-PIN-WOCK alliance, the SDF party managed Bali Council and, in line with the 'sociological composition' of the subdivision, the municipal executive included councillors from Bawock. It was therefore no secret that all councillors were privy to the monographic study commissioned in April and rendered public in August 2005. Alarmed at the prospective outcome, councillors from Bawock informed their community leaders who in turn registered a protest with the local administration. In a bid to ease tensions, the DO for Bali and his *état major*[109] in November 2005, chaired a meeting of delegates from Bali and Bawock headed by their respective chiefs. The meeting, termed the 'Gwan Summit,'[110] came up with five resolutions, three of them vital for this discussion:

1. The creation of new villages or neighbourhoods by Bali Council, and Bali Nyonga *Fondom* cannot be officially admitted until approved by the competent authority of the state.

2. Bali Nyonga is a 1st class *Fondom* with jurisdiction on the entire Sub-Division, and Bawock a second class *Fondom* attached to the above 1st class *Fondom* with jurisdiction over territory in old Bawock *Fondom*.

3. To uphold and strongly recommend the full implementation of the terms of the communiqué of Peaceful Co-existence between the people of Bali and Bawock communities of the 15th day of January 1975.[111]

These three points succinctly sum up the core issues plaguing the relationship between Bali and Bawock. At the end of the meeting "both parties expressed satisfaction with the resolutions and promised to work for their effective implementation."[112] However, while Bali Nyonga was basking in this apparent success, the MBU-PIN-WOCK alliance had

---

[108] Letter addressed to the Senior Divisional Officer of Mezam Division on 31 May 2004.

[109] The état major or close collaborators of the DO on this occasion included the various security chiefs (police gendarmerie, intelligence services or special branch), stationed in Bali.

[110] This meeting was held at Gwan where the main police station in Bali is located and the reason given for this was to offer an 'undisturbed atmosphere for the talks'

[111] Gwan Summit Resolutions 7th November 2005.

[112] Gwan Summit Resolutions 7th November 2005.

other plans. On 2nd October 2006, it addressed a petition to the SDO.[113] This was followed on 14th November by a follow-up reminding the SDO of its earlier request and asking him to provide "appropriate technicians and experts in land matters to assist in the successful and peaceful installation of boundary pillars."[114] Because the SDO apparently was on leave, the matter was forwarded to the Regional Governor who responded favourably through his second assistant or A2, and lauded the initiative while cautioning that it should be carried out lawfully.[115]

On 3rd December 2006,[116] the SDO's A2 wrote to the *Fon* of Bali inviting him for a brief meeting at his office to prepare for field activities scheduled for 6th December.[117] Despite being kept in the dark during the planning phase, Ganyonga III responded positively to the invitation and 'succeeded in persuading' the A1 and A2 to put off the event 'till after the end of year festivities.'[118] Satisfied that the matter had been resolved, he returned to Bali only to be informed three days later by the DO that the demarcation was proceeding as originally planned, and that a team was already in place at Mantum village with cadastral equipment and signage posts.[119] Ganyonga arrived in Mantum and met a tense scene and an enraged population whose village was the subject of the intended partition by MBU-PIN-WOCK.[120]

According to a report by the Company Commander of the National Gendarmerie in Bali, the irate population of Mantum burnt down a pickup truck laden with signage posts, some reading: 'Welcome to Santa

---

[113] Petition by members of MBU-PIN-WOCK alliance Titled: *The Installation of Boundary Pillars between Mbu, Bawock and Pinyin Fondoms.*

[114] Petition addressed by members of MBU-PIN-WOCK alliance, to the SDO of Mezam on 14th November 2006.

[115] Administrative correspondence No 2456/A/E/GMW.65/SG/DAJ/BFA, done at Bamenda on 24/11/2006.

[116] The fact that this was a Sunday which is a non-working day in Cameroon led many in Bali to conclude that it was a plot concocted in collusion with administrative officials of Mezam Division. Further, many in Bali ridiculed the author and civil administrator to have been so amateurish to the point where he stamped his name signature up-side-down, and instead of saying proceeding to the field he said filed.

[117] Administrative correspondence No 00/L/E29/PS/A2, done at Bamenda on 3rd December 2006.

[118] Statement by the *Fon* Ganyonga III on the incident of 06/12/2006.

[119] Statement by the *Fon* Ganyonga III on the incident of 06/12/2006.

[120] Correspondence addressed to the Governor of the North West Region by the Bali Traditional Council, dated 8th December 2006; and Correspondence addressed to the Prime Minister and Head of Government by the Bali traditional council dated 15th January 2007.

subdivision,' and also wrecked the vehicle of the *Fon* of Bawock. Meanwhile, *après avoir résolu d'évacuer le Fon de Bawock avec le véhicule de la Mairie de Bali, les populations dévoilent leur intention de l'éliminer. Grace à l'intervention énergique des FMO[121] appuyées par le Maire et le Fon de Bali, il est sauvé de justesse[122]/* the angry population began threatening to lynch the chief of Bawock who had his life saved thanks to the forceful intervention of 'forces of law and order' backed by the Mayor and *Fon* of Bali. The chief of Bawock was whisked to safety inside a vehicle belonging to Bali Council.

In the ensuing chaos, the A2 and his team including the chiefs from Mbu and Pinyin fled uphill into Mbu village and disappeared. Later that day, people from Bali and Mantum went on a punitive rampage in Bawock destroying houses, crops and animals.[123] Concluding his report, the military officer admonished officials to tread carefully because, going by the sensitive nature of the dispute between Bali and Bawock, things could quickly degenerate into serious conflict.

5.7 Inter-Communal Politics in Bali: Analysis and Discussion

> *Once a year, at the beginning of the agricultural cycle, when the women have started farming, the palace seals off the country from external malevolent forces in the form of tornadoes, hailstorms, locusts and other pests. This apotropaic ritual is still performed in most Grassfields chiefdoms by putting medicines across the paths and at road junction (Warnier 1993, p. 308).*

In line with this quote, on 3rd March 2007, the Bali Nyonga's sacred traditional cult or *Voma*[124] went out for the ritual of "praying to the gods of the land to bless the community with increased production and reproduction of the species" (Fisiy, 1992, p. 57). On the way from Mantum, it was intercepted in Bawock and its instruments seized by a notable and his sons for allegedly veering off course and heading towards Bawock palace. This version of events is hotly disputed in Bali. When I spoke with the head of *Voma*, he denied that they were

---

[121]Forces des Maintiens de l'Ordre.
[122] Reference: Synthèse N° 167/CIE/BL/4 DU 15/12/2006, done at Bali on 2nd January 2007.
[123] Reference: Synthèse N° 167/CIE/BL/4 DU 15/12/2006, done at Bali on 2nd January 2007.
[124] For more details about Voma see chapter VI

attempting to go to Bawock Palace, but noted that during the reigns of the predecessors of the current chief of Bawock, both communities lived harmoniously and every time *Voma* performed this ritual, the Bawock chief would welcome them at his palace for a stop-over. The Bali traditional council also issued a statement saying that *Voma* was intercepted on the highway which is public space.[125]

Following this incident, Mr Saboh (pseudonym) reportedly sent word that the *Fon* of Bali should personally come and retrieve the seized *Voma* instruments, something most in Bali interpreted as a grievous affront and others saw as a declaration of war. This incident drew an angry response, occasioning a brawl and subsequent violence during which people were hurt and property damaged in Bawock. Prior to this incident, the Bali traditional council reported that the chief of Bawock held a series of meetings with his notables during which the attack on *Voma* and other 'diabolic' plans to destabilise Bali was hatched.[126]The DO of Bali also reported that "the *Fon* of Bawock assembled the Bawock people and told them that if they have any problem, they should report to him [and he] will in turn take the matter to the SDO",[127] effectively side-lining the DO who is the administrative head of Bali.

The DO's report to his hierarchy illuminates the view held by the Bali traditional council that the chief of Bawock was at the centre of a 'diabolical plan to destabilise Bali.' "After the incident of 6th December 2006, there have been persistent calls from the chief of Bawock about alleged destruction of his village by Mantum people and, when verified, it will turn out to be a lie."[128] Persistent phone calls from the chief of Bawock went thus: A week from the incident at Mantum, he phoned the DO to report an arson attack on Government Bilingual Secondary School (GBSS) Bawock. A few days later he phoned the SDO's A2 to complain about an arson attack at his palace. On 25th January 2007, he phoned the SDO's A1 to complain that people in Mantum were preventing Bawock people from going to their farms. On 27th January

---

[125] Understanding the Bali-Bawock problem, pamphlet produced by the Bali traditional council dated; 07/07/2007.

[126] Understanding the Bali-Bawock problem, pamphlet produced by the Bali traditional council dated; 07/07/2007.

[127] Report by the DO of Bali, addressed to the SDO Mezam. Ref N° E29.03/C.82/VO/1/76, dated 5th February 2007.

[128] Report by the DO of Bali, addressed to the SDO Mezam. Ref N° E29.03/C.82/VO/1/76, dated 5th February 2007.

2007, he rang the Mayor of Bali to report that a man from Bawock had wounded another man from Mantum with a machete. On 28th January 2007, he rang the DO to lay the same complaint he made to the Mayor a day earlier. In response, the DO and his *état major* made on-site visits to verify these allegations, all of which turned-out to be 'red herrings.'[129]

In a bid to ease tension, a meeting was convened for 31st January 2007 involving representatives from Bali, Bawock and Mantum. However, Bawock notables reportedly declined to attend the meeting, declaring it irrelevant. The DO also wrote in his report that the local chief of police informed him that the chief of Bawock had instructed his people not to attend any such meeting. Exasperated, the DO declared: "Only God alone knows the intentions of the chief of Bawock."[130] Many informants corroborated the DO's statements and the Bali traditional council's that ahead of the violence several planning meetings were held at Bawock palace during which 'strategies' were elaborated.

It was not an 'act of god' that carried out an early morning raid on 6th March 2007 at the *Fons* Palace in Bali during which an antique shrine containing 'sacred ancestral implements and archives' was razed to the ground.[131] Neither was there an 'alien invasion' of Bawock on that same day that ravaged homes and property, but caused no visible injury or loss in human lives. In the days leading up to the incidents of March 6th 2007, eyewitnesses I spoke to in *Mbatmandet* described scenes evocative of the biblical exodus of the Jews from historic Palestine. Many people recounted how the population of Bawock were observed carting away belongings and boarding public transport cars at the Bali main square to Bamenda, roughly 16 km away. At the time, people in Bali could not understand why the Bawocks were leaving their village en masse, taking along portable items such as mattresses, clothes and other household belongings. However, it was only after the incidents of March 6 that most realised the real motives of the mass exodus. Many people in Bali argued that the strategies discussed during the meetings at Bawock palace included emptying houses of all valuables and subsequently torching them to give the impression of an attack from Bali.

---

[129] Report by the DO of Bali, addressed to the SDO Mezam. Ref No E29.03/C.82/VO/1/76, dated 5th February 2007.

[130] Report by the DO of Bali, addressed to the SDO Mezam. Ref No E29.03/C.82/VO/1/76, dated 5th February 2007.

[131] Understanding the Bali-Bawock problem, pamphlet produced by the Bali traditional council dated; 07/07/2007.

When I spoke to the chief of Bawock, he admitted that it was out of fear that his people "decided to start carrying their belongings and hide them in the bushes, because there were serious rumours that Bali people were coming to burn Bawock."[132] He added that prior to the incidents leaflets were circulated in Bawock urging them to return to Nde division where they originated. He also denied claims by the Bali traditional council that the 'burnings' were carried out by his people to attract public sympathy and government action; rather he pointed an accusing finger at the former SDF Mayor of Bali for orchestrating the whole plot. Accordingly, it was the Mayor "who went round Bawock telling people that peace had returned and that they should bring their belongings from the bushes. But our people did not know that the Mayor had an evil plan, because as soon as they brought their things Bali people came and set everything on fire."

The former Mayor brushed off these accusations, stating that the differences between himself and the chief and elites of Bawock, including some former SDF councillors who served in his team, stemmed from the fact that it was during his tenure that the monographic survey which Bawock strenuously opposes was commissioned:

The Bawocks are totally against the idea of seventeen neighbourhoods in Bali subdivision. These neighbourhoods were not conjured out of thin air, they were simply recognised by way of a monographic study. In fact, they had always existed but were only recognised for the purposes of development. The law on decentralisation gives municipal authorities such powers, and the reason we did it was that when you ask government to give you something as Bali, they erroneously think Bali is an obscure rural outpost. So we embarked upon that study to identify all village communities for the sake of development, so that when government is budgeting for Bali it should be aware that Bali is now a big town.[133]

When I spoke with the chief of Bawock about the 17 neighbourhoods, his appraisal of the move by the former Mayor was scathing:

---

[132] Interview conducted on 02/02/2014.
[133] Interview with former Mayor of Bali on 03/01/2014.

Other than Bossa, Bawock and Bali Nyonga, what other communities do we have in this subdivision? Out of the 17 neighbourhoods how many speak the same language? How many have similar cultures? If there is any other community that needs recognition in this place, it is the Hausa-Fulani who are Moslems. Those people living in Mantum, where is their origins? They are from the West. There was never any such place as Mantum. They all came from Bali Nyonga.[134]

Meanwhile, a CPDM Councillor from Bawock was much more circumspect about the whole affair: "I think it was a good thing to do so that the subdivision can look big, and when we request things from government it will be much more than what we currently receive. But within us we should know that neighbourhoods cannot be villages."[135]

It is clear from these statements that the parties not only have differing positions about the 'burnings', but also differing opinions about the rational for the seventeen neighbourhoods. Interestingly, what everyone agrees upon is the need for increased access to development resources from the government, but how to go about it remains the main sticking point. Meanwhile, the circumstances leading up to and after the 2007 incidents are still very murky. For example, although a few people were arrested in the immediate aftermath of the incidents, nobody was charged in court for perpetrating the attacks and the population of Bawock returned to Bali after a few months as IDPs[136] in Bamenda.

Ambiguity by the state over responsibility for the attacks, but not the jurisdictional location of Bawock confounds things further (Ministry of Justice, 2007).[137] However, many in Bawock have a firm idea about the culprits. According to them, Bali Nyonga is responsible and the motive often cited was that it wanted Bawock out of the area because they are viewed as a thorn on its side. Bali Nyonga insisted that what happened in Bawock was an 'own goal' designed 'to give it a bad name' so as to persuade government to grant Bawock an 'independent jurisdiction' in Bali.

Asked how this was possible, many cited the "uncharacteristic alacrity" (Page, et al., 2010, p. 351) of some administrative officials and

---

[134] Interview with chief of Bawock, 02/02/2014.
[135] Interview with CPDM councillor from Bawock on 22/01/2014.
[136] Internally Displaced Persons.
[137]Source:
http://www.minjustice.gov.cm/pdf_download/droit_homme/English/Rapport_Mi njustice_2007_Ang.pdf

the 'malicious' complicity of traditional rulers from two neighbouring villages involved in the bungled boundary demarcation attempt of December 2006 as ample evidence of a wider conspiracy that harks back to precolonial times. Finally, one informant rhetorically identified Bawock's quest for a boundary as follows: "If Lesotho claims to have a physical boundary with Mozambique, Swaziland or Zimbabwe, then where is South Africa...? Or better still if Gambia claims to have a physical boundary with Guinea, Mali or Mauritania, then where on earth is Senegal?"[138]

5.8 Conclusion

Bawock did not entirely lose out in the furore over the seventeen neighbourhoods in Bali; it achieved some measure of success in the end. The 2007 municipal elections presented Bawock with a golden opportunity to capitalise on its minority status in Bali. It also presented an opportunity for the chief of Bawock to get even with the Mayor, who was gunning for another term at the helm of Bali Council:

> *I was reading this document about decentralisation and the electoral process and a passage that struck me went thus; if in a subdivision all the sociological components is not represented in a council list, then it should be disqualified. I immediately told my people nobody should give their name to the SDF.*[139]

Asked why he did it, he said; "it was because of the person who was once again going in for Mayor of Bali Council.[140]

The story goes that in order to meet the legal requirements for submitting a list of candidates for the municipal elections, the SDF needed candidates from all three communities of Bali subdivision i.e. Bali Nyonga, Bossa and Bawock. But because the chief of Bawock had instructed his people not to give their names to the SDF the outgoing Mayor found it difficult to draw up a list. Realising that the Mayor might circumvent his 'embargo,' chief Nana decided to employ a tactic reminiscent of the ancient Greek subterfuge with the '*Trojan* horse.'

---

[138] Interview conducted with a Bali elite on 19/12/2013.
[139] Interview with the *Fon* of Bawock; 02/02.2014.
[140] Interview with the *Fon* of Bawock; 02/02.2014.

Because tribal affiliation in Bali and Bawock was determined by paternal and not maternal lineage, Bawock used this to its advantage and coached a certain Mr Sama (pseudonym), a resident of Bawock whose father is from Bali but his mother from Bawock, to serve as a spoiler by offering his name for the SDF list. Immediately the list was forwarded to the authorities for scrutiny, the CPDM raised an objection that Sama was not from Bawock because his father was from Bali and as a result the SDF list was illegitimate because it was not representative of the 'sociological composition' of Bali. The Supreme Court agreed and disqualified the SDF list, paving the way for the CPDM to contest the municipal elections in Bali without its fiercest opponent, abruptly ending the decade's long reign of the SDF party at the helm of Bali Council.

Chapter VI

'Wrath from the Gods:' Traditional Institutions and Electoral Politics in Bali

6.1 Introduction

The government of Cameroon introduced changes to the county's constitution in 1996. These changes heralded a major overhaul of the system of governance in the direction of decentralisation and community participation in development activities. This system accorded local municipalities powers to take decisions on a significant number of areas including economic, social, health, educational, cultural and sports development.[141] Following the promulgation of the Law on the orientation of decentralisation[142] and that on the rules applicable to Councils,[143] elected municipal councils that had existed for decades were transformed from bodies with minimal responsibilities, such as performing civil ceremonies, into agents of local development (PNDP 2009 & 2010). These laws also encouraged active community participation in local development; however, community participation through self-help projects was in many respects a way of life in Anglophone Cameroon during the colonial and early independence and reunification eras. The autonomous status of the Southern Cameroons was exemplified by grassroots institutions in the form of Native Authorities which served as natural arenas for self-government and community participation in local development. However, these institutions were progressively and systematically eroded during the monolithic era to the point where local people became increasingly dependent on the central authorities in Yaoundé.

The constitutional reforms of the 1996 were preceded by legalisation of political parties which paved the way for open competition for elective posts. This was in stark contrast to what obtained under the

---

[141] Law N° 2004/018 of 22nd July 2004
[142] Law N° 2004/017 of 22nd July 2004.
[143] Law N° 2004/018 of 22nd July 2004.

autocratic rule of Ahidjo, and also in the early years of his successor Paul Biya. During that era, everyone including traditional chiefs in principle belonged to the single party and any form of dissent was often violently supressed. Likewise, the House of Chiefs served as an arena, as well as an outlet for traditional authorities in the former West Cameroon to engage in national politics; but it was unceremoniously dissolved in 1972 (Chem-Langhee, 1983). Consequently, North West chiefs, most of whom were heads of Native Authorities during colonial rule, could no longer be seen to be politically active lest they be branded subversive (Mentan, 2011, p. 33).

Chiefs therefore channelled their efforts into tackling the day-to-day concerns of their subjects, as well as into development activities in their communities. Prior to the dissolution of the House of Chiefs and the advent of the one party state, some chiefs were very active in politics. A good example was *Fon* Galega II of Bali who was very prominent in national politics in the years leading up to and the immediate aftermath of independence and reunification. He was 'rewarded' with a visit to his palace by President Ahidjo. Although Ahidjo's 'iron rule' is now history and Cameroon is a nominal democracy, keen observation of traditional rulers and politics suggests that chiefs still prefer to ally themselves with the ruling CPDM party for fear of being side-lined or worse denied a share of the 'national pie.'

The advent of Paul Biya, self-styled advocate of the 'New Deal', brought in the reluctant liberalisation of the political landscape and the legalisation of political parties (Delancy, 1989). The new political dispensation provided a platform for national actors, including chiefs, to re-enter party politics, in some cases pitting them against their subjects. As a result, most chiefs no longer limited themselves to local issues as in the past, but aspired to play active roles in national politics. Pluralism heightened the political stakes and reinvigorated electoral campaigns, in some cases transforming them into battlegrounds where a number of actors, including politicians, parties, traditional rulers, and ordinary citizens, fought it out, nonetheless, employing every available means including cash, cults and culinary items to gain votes.

Like elsewhere in Africa, the election timetable in Cameroon is the sole prerogative of the President who is often referred to by state media as *le seul maitre du calendrier électoral* / the sole master of the electoral calendar. Further, political parties usually have no manifestos; rather campaigns are fought on the basis of ethnicity and personality. Opaqueness in the mode of governance implies that decisions affecting the livelihood of millions of Cameroonians are often taken by a select few, the president and his close advisers. This is mostly done behind closed doors, and most often without popular consultation, not even with pro-regime members of the National Assembly or Senate who merely rubber-stamp presidential directives. In Cameroon, as elsewhere in Africa, the "mechanisms for holding elected representatives accountable for the use of resources or for the performance of service delivery are generally weak or non-existent" (Devas & Grant, 2003, p. 307); this is why corruption is rampant. The proliferation of corrupt practices in Cameroon earned it the dishonourable title from Transparency International of 'the world's most corrupt country' in 1998 and 1999.

Meanwhile, the introduction of decentralisation and its explicit focus on municipal councils as hubs for development somehow revitalised local politics in Cameroon. However, despite the general perception of decentralisation as government throwing the governed "off the scent of [centralisation] by dragging red herrings of [decentralisation] across the path" (Greene, 2000, p. 120), Cameroonians in general and people in Bali in particular genuinely believe that given adequate resources and room for manoeuvre, councils could become engines for local development, as was the case during the late colonial and early independence eras, when local government in Anglophone Cameroon enjoyed 'limited autonomy' and were not subject to stringent bureaucratic oversight (Delancy, 1989).

This chapter therefore examines the 2013 municipal elections in Bali, through the prism of political parties, traditional authorities and ordinary citizens. It unearths the strategies employed by these actors to retain and regain control of Bali Council. It further argues that contrary to a commonly held notion that "the variegated process of political institutionalisation is supposed to have reduced the role of the [occult] to the private sphere of the individual citizen… In Africa [occult forces still] impinge quite normally and legitimately on all areas of human activity including politics" (Chabal & Daloz, 1999, p. 65).

6.2 Background

> *Once more Mr outgoing Mayor, I want to thank you and your entire team for all that you achieved for the Bali man for the past six years at the helm of this council. To the incoming team…, I equally want to congratulate you and by extension the councillors and all the militants and sympathisers of the Cameroon People Democratic Movement party for the brilliant success recorded during the last municipal elections. It was indeed a landslide victory, and the victory was not due to the coming out of Voma. It was a vote of the heart.*[144]

In these terms the SDO for Mezam Division addressed the assembled crowd while presiding over the official installation ceremony of the newly elected executive of the Bali Council in 2013. The ceremony took place at the 'grandstand' (where most public manifestations in Bali are staged), situated off the main road intersection in Bali central town, known locally as *Ntanfoang*. Like most public ceremonies of this nature in Cameroon, this occasion was marked by pomp and pageantry. Ubiquitous during this event were different components of CPDM militants (Youth, Women and Men), sporting party gear, bearing the effigy of the head of state and the party logo (a flame).

The occasion had a festive flair interspersed with performances by traditional dance groups bussed in from all the nooks and crannies of the subdivision, competing to outshine each other by way of ostentatious displays. It was also animated by a local MC who, when not announcing the arrival of invited dignitaries, was blasting out loud music. One of the songs aired by the DJ carried explicit messages of praise to the head of state, likening him to the messiah and reminding him (as if any were needed) that *ton mandat n'est pas finir à Etoudi,* / it's not yet time to vacate the Presidential Mansion, *Etoudi* Palace. Another song touched on a pertinent issue that drew almost unanimous approval throughout Bali. The lyrics of this song heaped praise on the head of state for appointing the *Fon*, and paramount head of Bali, senator after elections[145] held earlier in the year.

---

[144] Excerpts of a speech delivered by the SDO for Mezam Division in Bali November 30, 2013.

[145] According to the constitution, senators are elected by members of Regional Assemblies; however, the latter institution does not exist. For the purposes of this election the government decreed that municipal councillors whose mandate had

Ganyonga III entered a list under the CPDM, but it was rejected by the party hierarchy. This was not Ganyonga's first attempt at electoral office. In 1996, he made an unsuccessful bid for Bali Council under the CPDM ticket, but was trounced at the polls by the main opposition SDF party (Fokwang, 2009 and Takougang & Krieger, 1998) His appointment was therefore received with great joy and a profound sigh of relief, because there were fears of impending 'war' in Bali.

This was because the traditional ruler of nearby Bawock village, was elected alternate Senator in a list headed by a former PM. The latter, by dint of his alleged support to the sub-chief in boundary claims (amongst other 'crimes'), is generally viewed in many quarters as an arch-enemy of Bali Nyonga. Many in Bali viewed the rejection of Ganyonga's list and the election of the chief of Bawock as alternate Senator to former PM Simon Achidi Achu, as a malicious conspiracy aimed at humiliating the *Fon* and the people of Bali. The chief of Bawock disputed this charge, saying no individual in Bali was courageous enough to form a list with the former PM for fear of challenging the *Fon* who had earlier expressed his interest in becoming senator and had gone ahead to compose a list despite being advised to the contrary.

Conspiracy theorists in Bali advanced reasons ranging from outright cynicism to the banality of the order of arrival at public events to justify their invectives against the former PM and his alternate senator. Many believed that the ageing former PM (alleged to have suffered a stroke) was, to put it bluntly, 'a dead man walking' and therefore handpicked the chief of Bawock (who is in his late 40s) as an alternate to replace him upon his demise. This would place the chief of Bawock in an incredible position of power in Bali. Supposing this were the case, popular belief in Bali was that the second degree chief would then become titular Senator and by dint of that outrank the first degree *Fon* of Bali. The implication was that on public occasions such as the installation of the Mayor or on May 20th, National day in Cameroon, the *Fon* of Bali would precede that of Bawock to the grandstand and upon the latter's arrival rise up to welcome him. However, contrary to the fears of many in Bali things turned out to be quite the reverse on May 20, 2013, as shown in the following newspaper report:

---

expired and been prolonged several times were to constitute the electoral college for the election of 70 out of 100 senators, the remaining 30 being appointed by the President.

Before the arrival of the Divisional Officer for Bali at the ceremonial grounds, Senator Fon Ganyonga deliberately created anxiety. He kept people waiting for his arrival at the Municipal grandstand situated near the palace. The impresarios of the occasion heightened expectations with several announcements, calling on the population to focus their eyes on the road to the palace. Then a black Prado car emerged from the palace flanked on both sides by eight "royal guards".

The car moved slowly and stopped where the country's flag was hoisted. Then, Senator Ganyonga, gathering the loose ends of his "gandura" and fixing his green-red-yellow sash, waved at the population with a smile. He moved to his seat where his wives and notables were positioned. The population applauded ceaselessly and gave him a standing ovation, but for the Fon of Bawock, Fon Nana Wanda, alternate to Senator Simon Achidi Achu, who never stood up. (CameroonPostline.com, 2013).

The appointment of Senator Ganyonga was seen as a magisterial prestation by the president that saved the people and their leader from potentially unbearable humiliation at the hands of the 'enemies' of Bali Nyonga. Others saw it as a just reward to the *Fon* for the role his father played in the reunification of Cameroon, and also for his vocal support to the ruling CPDM party of which he is a Central Committee member. Interestingly, Achidi Achu had dangled the prospect of appointing North West *Fons* into the yet-unborn senate as a ploy to get them to campaign 'vigorously' for the CPDM in municipal elections held in 1996 (Awasom, 2003). President Biya's gesture was heartily welcomed by a cross-section of the population of Bali, including members of the opposition SDF party.

The festive atmosphere of the installation ceremony of the Mayor and his team somewhat mirrored that held three weeks earlier (November 6), marking the 31st anniversary of the accession of Paul Biya to power, only this time around without the SDO as chief celebrant. Nevertheless, CPDM militants also took the opportunity of this anniversary celebration to declare the 'end' of the opposition SDF in Bali. In fact speaker after speaker triumphantly declared the invincibility of the CPDM in Bali and called on 'those who are still with the SDF' to realise that the game was up. Some went further to lampoon the SDF party, its district chairperson and the former Mayor of Bali Council for being 'a tree that cannot bear fruit,' and praised Bali people for their 'political maturity,' and for making the wise choice in the last elections by sticking to the 'winning team.'[146]

References to a tree that cannot bear fruit was reported to have been made by the Prime Minister Philemon Yang, during his stopover in Bali on the campaign trail. 'Barren tree' in this context can also be seen in the light of the following question posed by Chabal and Daloz (1999, 151): "What word might be attached to the function of the leader of the opposition, who in the real world, has no resources allocated to his position," and by dint of that cannot adequately 'scratch'[147] the people's back in exchange for replication of such gestures by the people in the form of positive votes on polling day.

Although the SDO[148] did not make any specific reference to Paul Biya on this occasion, his omnipresence, manifested by effigies on party paraphernalia, loomed quite large. The SDO began his speech by acknowledging the presence of the Senator, cum *Fon*, cum PhD holder, and other dignitaries including his local subordinate and DO of Bali, and the heads of different units of the 'forces of law and order' (gendarmerie and police), as well as members of the judiciary. The speech delved into many topics, including the career and political profiles of the in-coming Mayor, the duties assigned to the latter and his team by law, the challenging road ahead, and the need for close collaboration with the administration. On this latter point, he urged the Mayor to contribute his own 'quota' in maintaining peace and order in and around a disputed 'farming area' and to make sure that perpetrators of wanton destruction of crops at a controversial agricultural development project on disputed land in Kontan be identified and brought to justice; for "your council cannot be a CPDM council and the people are against a CPDM

---

[146] CPDM militants often refer to the party as the 'winning team', and the reason cited is that the party chairman Paul Biya has never lost any election contest since the return to multiparty politics in Cameroon in the 1990s. Another reason is that the party on average always manages to record better scores in municipal, legislative and presidential elections than the opposition. Election results are always highly contested by the opposition on grounds of fraud and other malpractices.

[147] The pidgin phrases, "politics na Njangi" and "scratch my back, I scratch your own" is often associated with former PM Simon Achidi Achu. He repeatedly used these phrases in the 1990s as a campaign strategy to get people to vote for the CPDM in the North West Province (now Region), in exchange for gifts and other political favours. For more on this see (Chiabi, 2011, p. 43 & 57)

[148] SDO's are by law the supervisory authorities over councils in their areas of command and all decisions taken by the council are subject to prefectural oversight.

government development project."[149] It should be recalled that the dispute in Kontan was a result of Presidential decree N° 77-525 of 23 December 1977 carving out large expanses of land from Bali and awarding them to neighbouring villages.

The administrator's address touched on two topical issues in Bali. First he highlighted the intractable land disputes between Bali Nyonga and neighbouring villages, and second he attempted to exonerate the Bali Nyonga[150] traditional cult known as *Voma* from widespread allegations of 'influencing' the outcome of the municipal elections and drawing the ire of the ancestors. The SDO's references to *Voma* and land issues on this occasion highlighted two fundamental components of Bali Nyonga society, both of them having contemporary overtones but at the same time deeply rooted in history. As noted in chapter V, the origins of numerous land disputes in and around Bali can be traced to the 19th century when Bali Nyonga migrated and settled in the present location; likewise the history of *Voma* is not unrelated to these movements. In fact, its rituals are firmly embedded in issues of land, farming, and witchcraft. *Voma* therefore is a 'deity' that performs a dual role; on the one hand, it is a "vengeful god that destroys wrong doers" and on the other it is "responsible for fruitful harvest" (Fochang, 2011, p. 28). Before delving in greater detail into the role of Voma in Bali society and accusations about its meddling in the 2013 elections, it is worth presenting a cursory overview of what democracy means to some Cameroonians.

6.3 *Démocratie Avancée* in Cameroon and President for Life

In their eyes, democratization is a mere cosmetic; thus, they busy themselves with the elaboration of a "new" ideology to explain their refusal to adopt the principle of alternation of power (Monga, 1996, p. 35).

In the 1990s, President Biya gave an interview to a French local radio station in which he is reported to have said he would love to be remembered as the person who brought democracy and development

---

[149] Excerpt of a speech delivered by the SDO for Mezam Division in Bali November 30, 2013

[150] The use of Bali Nyonga in this context is to distinguish it from the non-Bali villages such as Bawock and Bossa situated in Bali sub-division.

to Cameroon (Mentan, 1998). Since then CPDM militants and sympathisers never miss an opportunity to remind Cameroonians that the national chairman of the party, Paul Biya, is the man who brought democracy to Cameroon and is the only person capable of maintaining peace and unity in the country. It is not uncommon to hear party stalwarts, praise singers and other sycophants refer to Cameroon as an 'island of peace in tumultuous central Africa.' Political turmoil in the Central African Republic, oil militants in the Niger Delta, maritime pirates off the coast of the Gulf of Guinea, interminable rebellions in the Democratic Republic of Congo and some time ago in Chad and Congo Brazzaville provide fodder for their hyperbole.

That said, rising insecurity around the Lake Chad basin prompted by an upsurge in cross-border attacks by the Nigerian terrorist group Boko Haram on Cameroonian soil and the decades long entrenchment of the regime of Paul Biya in power raise a lot of questions about the democratic and peace-making credentials of the CPDM party chairman. On the other hand, conspiracy theories within but not limited to the CPDM attribute incidents involving armed groups to a plot by France[151] to destabilise Cameroon and force Biya out of office. This situation reflects French authorities' resentment of Biya's diversification of his foreign partners and sources of external investment in Cameroon. Accordingly, France views Biya's actions as violating a colonial-era pact and also as a threat to its privileged economic status in a country which Paris still perceives as its 'exclusive preserve.'[152] Attacks by Boko Haram in Northern Cameroon are also attributed to a plot by some Northerners in cahoots with France to foment chaos and ignite a Northern-led rebellion with the aim of toppling Biya and replacing him with someone from that region who will better serve and protect French interests.

---

[151] Ever since attacks by the terrorist group Boko Haram and occasional deadly cross-border incursions by rebels from the CAR onto Cameroon soil became intense, there have been accusations levelled at France for attempting to destabilise the country. For example, on November 28th 2014, an MP from the *Mouvement pour la Renaissance du Cameroun* (MRC) party accused France in parliament for being the source of troubles in the CAR; this prompted representatives of the French Embassy present during the parliamentary session to walk out in protest. On March 28th 2015, the French Ambassador to Cameroon was assailed by an angry mob wielding placards containing anti-France messages at an anti Boko Haram demonstration in the capital Yaoundé. The anti-France messages included: "*La France dehors*" "*On ne veut pas la France*" France Out. We don't want the French.

[152] For details see Keese, 2007 and Renou, 2002.

Controversy aside, and going by the lyrics of the praise songs cited at the beginning of this chapter, CPDM militants not only want Biya to remain head of the party, but to be everlasting president of Cameroon. Given that during fieldwork in Mbankomo the CPDM was described as a religion (such sentiments are also expressed in other parts of the country), Biya certainly is God. On his part, the president is also famous for having described his style of rule as *démocratie avancée* or 'advanced democracy' (Songwe, 2011, p. 14). However, Biya did not voluntarily decree the return to multiparty politics in Cameroon, as noted in chapter III; his apologists staged nationwide demonstrations vehemently denouncing calls for a return to multiparty politics, saying it was "models imported from abroad, and not suitable for Africa" (Awasom 2003, p. 114).

Biya's hands were eventually forced by John Fru Ndi who proceeded to launch the SDF party in Bamenda on 26 May 1990 (Konings and Nyamnjoh 2003, and Takougang and Krieger 1998). On that day, six people were shot dead in Bamenda around a place called 'City Chemist Roundabout', termed 'Liberty Square' by the SDF in honour of those 'martyred' on that fateful Saturday. The SDF eventually gained legal recognition following the so-called 'liberty laws' in December 1990. It boycotted the March 1992 parliamentary elections, citing lack of an independent electoral commission, but took part in and lost the October 1992 presidential elections under very controversial circumstances.

After losing the presidential elections, the opposition made a strong showing in the 1996 municipal elections (Mentan, 1998). The results gave the SDF party control over a significant number of councils in the country, notably in major urban areas including Douala, Bafoussam and Bamenda (Takougang & Krieger, 1998). However, in line with its quest for total control and desire to thwart the popular will, "the government continued its practice of imposing a presidentially appointed *'délègue urbain'* who exercises the real power" (Gabriel, 1999, p. 179). Until now, appointed government delegates continue to lord it over elected Mayors in these urban centres.

Following the municipal elections of 1996, the SDF party won 30 out of 32 municipal councils in the North West Region, including Bali Council (Awasom, 2003). Henceforth, the party reigned supreme in Bali until 2007 when its candidates list was disqualified for violating the electoral code. The SDF, according to its district Chairperson, could not compete in these elections and therefore lost out to its arch-rival the CPDM by 'forfeiture.'[153] As seen in chapter V, there was more to the disqualification of the SDF list than meets the eye. Coincidentally, the two themes identified in the SDO's installation speech (Land and *Voma*), had a lot to do with disfranchising the SDF, and also the 'disturbances' between Bali Nyonga and Bawock in 2006 and 2007. The next sections will examine why *Voma* became enmeshed in a do-or-die electoral battle in Bali, but first an overview of past electoral practices in Cameroon.

6.4 Election Management in Cameroon

During the presidential, parliamentary, and municipal elections of the 1990s, MINAT[154] devised and applied additional conditions and diversionary tactics before approving candidacies. In practice, the complicated electoral laws provide the government with precious opportunities to manipulate the electoral roll in its favour while making matters extremely difficult for the opposition (Geschiere 2009, 52).

The state apparatus and its administrative auxiliaries expend enormous resources to ensure electoral success, including the resort to tactics similar to gerrymandering.[155] On occasion, they go to great lengths to prevent individuals from contesting elections. The following tale recounts the ordeal one informant endured while attempting to get his nomination papers confirmed for what was described as "the first time in Cameroon's history that local elections were contested" (Gabriel, 1999, p. 179) i.e. the 1996 municipal elections:

Following primaries held by the SDF, five of us won party nominations for the forthcoming parliamentary elections. So we went Up-Station to the SDO's office with our complete dossiers. We sat at the SDO's office and the files were

---

[153] Interview with SDF Bali Chairman; 03/01/2014

[154] French acronym for the Ministry of Territorial Administration. It is now known as the Ministry of Territorial Administration and Decentralisation (MINATD).

[155] Gerrymandering here refers to the manipulation of the boundaries of an electoral constituency to suit vested interests. A good example occurred in Bali in 1996, when the parliamentary constituency was moved to nearby Santa subdivision in the expectation that the CPDM will win, because the area was the hometown of the Prime Minister Simon Achidi Achu. However, despite frantic campaigning by an armada of CPDM officials, traditional authorities and State bureaucrats, the SDF still won the seat.

checked one after another, and all five were declared complete and approved. We greeted the SDO and were about to leave when he called me back and the others wanted to join but he said he wanted to speak to me alone. When I got in, he began by stating that our chat has nothing to do with the files because they are complete and in order, but he nevertheless wanted to have a quiet word with me the next day at 09:00. As I left the office, it hit me that the day he mentioned was a non-working day. I dashed back in to check if he was aware that the next day was Sunday! He said oh yes, but I should come nonetheless.

I got to his offices on Sunday at 09:00 prompt, he invited me to sit down and informed me that party-wise everything was fine, but he would advise against my involvement with the Southern Cameroons issue. He requested that I dissociate myself from that movement. I sought to know his reasons for trying to dissuade me from my political convictions, but he just said no, it is not good for the country. He wanted me to renounce my sympathies for the Southern Cameroons cause on the spot, failing which my file would not proceed to Yaoundé. I said no this sounds like a threat…, and I was shocked that the SDO was bullying me out of an election. I was further stunned when I realised that we were not alone, people were listening to our conversation. In fact, I soon realised that our conversation was relayed to other people, most likely the Governor and presumably some higher authorities at the ministry in Yaoundé. This is because after I rejected his offer, he immediately started speaking in French and said to somebody who I think was the Governor that I was proving difficult, and the governor immediately replied and said if I don't want to comply the SDO should let me go. And the man in Yaoundé also made a comment which I can't remember now. I felt a little bit intimidated, then I said ok fine I have heard your proposal, can you give me a few days to think about it? He said oh yes that will be fine. I said it could take 2-3 days, he said that's fine. So I said ok, if in 2 or 3 days I have made up my mind to do what you have proposed I will came back and tell you. If you don't see me it means I have stood my ground. So I left and never went back there, I decided not to go back and talk about the thing. I decided to give up my candidature for the elections.[156]

The above story demonstrates the lengths to which the state will go to thwart attempts by the opposition to contest electoral office. However, it is not only pre-election manoeuvring that impacts election management in Cameroon. The period of the publication of results is

---

[156] Interview conducted with a Bali elite on 19/12/2013.

also quite precarious. Most often, election results cause public uproar, not least among opposition party members and civil society, but also among ordinary people. This because people's hopes for meaningful change are often raised when elections are announced, but they have over the years been dashed repeatedly by electoral engineering *à la Camerounaise* / Cameroon style. As a result, popular discontent over rigged or 'stolen elections' has often turned violent.

Violence, according to (Chabal & Daloz, 1999, p. 77), is not only in "situations where law and order have broken down entirely, but also where conditions are deemed to be relatively stable;" Cameroon arguably falls within the latter category. However, when it comes to situations where the regime perceives a threat to its existence, such as during the popular uprisings in February 2008 dubbed 'food riots' or when election results are contested on the streets, as has been the case in almost every elections since the 1990s, the level of brutality and bloodletting from 'the forces of law and order' i.e. Police, Gendarmerie, Army and specialised units, can be quite severe. As a result, election periods in Cameroon are full of apprehension, with the spectre of fraud, intimidation and violence looming in the air.

Municipal elections are often organised under a system whereby political parties are required to group candidates on a single list. The number of lists in a constituency reflects the number of political parties contesting the council seats. Any list that obtains an absolute majority in a particular constituency grabs all available seats. However, cohabitation might occur in situations where no single party obtains an absolute majority. In such a case, seats are repartitioned proportionately amongst contesting parties, according to the results obtained at the polls (Awasom, 2003).

Decades after the return to multiparty politics, municipal, legislative and presidential elections have featured regularly on the political landscape of Cameroon. On many occasions, elections results have been the subject of bitter contestation, amid accusations of electoral malpractice, vote rigging, vote buying, ballot box stuffing and outright intimidation. Very often accusations are levelled against administrative officials acting on orders from above, or against ruling CPDM party officials.

The CPDM is often accused of having developed a 'sophisticated rigging machinery' that has ensured continued electoral success in national and local elections in Cameroon since the 1990s (Geschiere 2009, Konings and Nyamnjoh 2003, and Takougang and Krieger 1998). It should be pointed out, however, that the opposition is not immune to electoral malpractice. This topic often came up during conversations I held with CPDM militants during fieldwork in Bali. They were often quick to point to allegations of witchcraft and use of the occult by the SDF in Bali as proof of the latter's involvement in electoral malpractice, among other 'iniquities.'

In principle, election campaigns in Cameroon officially run for two weeks. Prior to this, political parties employ a number of methods to select candidates. These include primaries and consensus or a bit of both. In the run-up to the September 30 municipal/legislative elections, the CPDM party hierarchy prescribed consensus lists as the sole method for the selection of candidates. However, party militants in many parts of the country were livid because some consensus lists formed at the base either disappeared along the way or, when they arrived at party headquarters, were thrown out and replaced with hand-picked cronies.

On the other hand, the SDF and other opposition parties conducted primaries, which were designed to give grassroots militants the opportunity to elect candidates to compete in the polls. However, this process was not without controversy; on Monday 15 July 2013, SDF militants from Bui Centre[157] stormed the Bamenda residence of the SDF National Chairman John Fru Ndi to protest against the replacement by the party's national investiture committee of a certain Ruth Ngando by Caroline Mbiybe (Le Messager, 2013).

Because of the winner-takes-all electoral system, cohabitation in local municipalities in Cameroon is the exception, not the rule. Cohabitation has never occurred between the two political parties that have managed Bali Council. The 2013 election contest was therefore a three-horse race between the CPDM, SDF and National Union for Democracy and Progress (NUDP) parties.[158] At the finish however, it was the SDF and the CPDM that were locked in a ferocious electoral battle. The stakes were so high that the *Fon* of Bali personally went out

---

[157] Bui Division situated roughly 100km from Bali, is one of the seven Divisions that make up the North West Region

[158] Elections Cameroon (ELECAM) Bali: A report on the results of the September 30th 2013 Municipal Elections for Bali Council area.

on the campaign trail. His venture into the muddy waters of electoral campaigning was controversial.

The *Fon* embarked on a tour of all neighbourhoods in Bali town to impress upon the population the need to vote for the CPDM, so that it could retain the Council. Then, in what could be seen as a form of 'patronage politics' involving "the distribution of ministerial and other major political and administrative posts" (Erdmann & Engel, 2006, p. 24), the *Fon* urged the population to thank the president for appointing him senator by massively voting for the CPDM party. Ganyonga did not limit himself to merely cajoling potential voters. Turning the other cheek, he "threatened that people who took CPDM money and did not vote will see."[159] Some observers therefore attributed the coming out of *Voma* three days before polling day as an ominous sign of this threat. Such allegations from an opposition member could be shrugged-off as political posturing. However, it bears testimony to the monumental stakes in this election. What then is *Voma*? What is its role in Bali Society? And why did the SDO go out of his way to mention it in his installation speech?

6.5 The Role of *Voma* in Bali Nyonga Traditional Structure

Beliefs in witchcraft assign considerable power to individuals' ability to influence the fortunes of others - and reports of the continued salience of witchcraft in contemporary Africa, as a practice and a system of explanation, abound in both popular media and ethnographic literature. (Geschiere 1992, as cited in Berry, 2001, p. xxv).

Voma and Lela,[160] are two ancient Chamba[161] cults that constitute key components of the traditional 'state' institutions of Bali Nyonga, but nevertheless have contemporary relevance (Page, et al., 2010). Their

---

[159] Interview with SDF official on 03/01/2014

[160] This is an annual festival that takes place in Bali Nyonga every December in which the Gods of the land are thanked for a successful year and requests are made for peace and fertility for the coming year. The festival also serves as a form of social gathering of Bali people at home and in the diaspora is marked by massive gun firing, traditional dancing and opulent displays of traditional regalia.

[161] The Chamba are a group of people that migrated southwards from the Benue and Adamawa plateau areas in present day Northern Cameroon into the grassfields around the late 18th or early 19th centuries (DeLancey, et al., 2010).

hierarchical position in the traditional political setup means that both cults come second only to the *Fon* (Chilver & Kaberry, 1970). Between them, *Voma* has the privilege of being the main custodian of the sacred mystical powers of the land, with the highest point of its activities being the enthronement of the *Fon* (Fochang, 2011). As the following excerpts illustrate, the multi-purpose functions of *Voma* are as relevant today as long ago.

> *Ever since we were children, Voma has always been part and parcel of the traditional institutions of Bali. In the past our mothers were constantly complaining about loss of crops in the farms. It was common knowledge that people from nearby villages were reputed to be witches and wizards; some even transformed themselves into animals or used the wind to enter farms, harvest crops and take them away. There were also moments where bad people or sorcerers would come into the village to wreak havoc. Sometimes badly-intentioned Bali people could be tempted to acquire sinister powers from elsewhere to target fellow tribesmen. Voma's function was that after the Christmas and New Year festivities around February, it would be sent out to cleanse the land and neutralise the potency of any evil objects or spirits present on the land. This period also coincided with the onset of the farming season. Consequently, if any such malicious forces were present on the land with the intention to affect crop productivity or soil fertility, Voma would neutralise their powers, ensure abundant rainfall, and ensure that farming activities are conducted smoothly, culminating in abundant yields and harvests. I should also point out that Voma is something that is only seen by a select few, hence when it comes out people are expected to stay indoors and allow it to perform its cleansing rites after which normal activities can resume. Permit me to stress here that Voma is an organisation whose sole aim is to bring peace to the land, nothing short of that!*[162]

Depending on circumstances, different sections of *Voma* perform different activities at different points in time. Therefore, aside from its role as peacemaker and purveyor of benediction rituals prior to farming seasons, *Voma* assists in resolving disputes between ordinary Bali people, particularly over lost or stolen property. As one informant stated, "if something goes missing here, for instance, say a house is broken into, and the owner goes and brings *Voma*, it frightens people and the thief is

---

[162] Interview conducted in Mungaka with a sub-chief in Bali on 22/12/2013.

unmasked."[163] However, the peace-making role of *Voma* has come under intense scrutiny on a number of occasions in the past decade. First, in 2007 it was embroiled in what was likened by some in Bali to 'the last straw that broke Bawock's back,' and secondly, in 2013 it was caught up in electoral politics. Interestingly, these incidents had implications for the outcome of municipal elections held in both years. The next sections will examine events leading up to the SDO's remarks on November 30, 2013. However, in order to get a better understanding of the situation, it is worth taking a look at the relationship between traditional rulers and party politics.

6.6 Traditional Authorities and Multi-party Politics in Cameroon

Historically, the fons in the North West [Region] of Cameroon were near-deities and containers of ancestral spirits, and the loyalties of their subjects were generally unchallenged, particularly when the rulers were benevolent and projected a positive image (Awasom 2003, 103).

Engagement of traditional rulers in party politics was not without controversy, particularly where the population was on one side of the political spectrum and the chief on another side. Much ink has been expended on the relationship between the colonial state and traditional authorities (Mamdani, 1996), as well as on that between the post-colonial state and traditional authorities (Sithole, 2009). Awasom (2003) has argued that the aftermath of the return to multipartyism in Cameroon in the 1990s landed a devastating blow on the lofty image of traditional authorities' vis-à-vis their subjects. Divergence in the relationship between chiefs and subjects is not a uniquely Cameroon phenomenon, and it dates back to colonial times. In Nigeria in the 1950s, the '*Oba of Iperu*' initially supported the NCNC of Nnamdi Azikiwe, but following elections to the Western House of Assembly in 1951, the population overwhelmingly brought him in line. According to Nolte, (2003, p. 58): "Through the ballot, the townspeople made it clear to their king what his political orientation should be," by voting overwhelmingly for the Action Group (AG), led by Awolowo.

---

[163] Interview conducted with a Bali elite on 19/12/2013.

Since 1996, the population of Fumban in the West Region of Cameroon have consistently voted for the *Union Démocratique du Cameroun* (UDC) party of Adamou Ndam Njoya to run the municipal council, over and above the wishes of his cousin, paramount ruler of the Bamoum, CPDM Political Bureau member, and appointed Senator Ibrahim Mbombo Njoya. In Bali, until 2007, the population made a similar choice to that in Fumban and consistently voted for the opposition SDF over the CPDM, despite *Fon* Ganyonga being a prominent member and vocal supporter. This was quite unlike during the monolithic era (1966-1990) when everyone in principle belonged to the single national party.

Upon assuming power in 1982, and in the context of a one-party state and the logic of eternal monolithism, President Paul Biya argued against the participation of chiefs in national politics. However, the advent of political pluralism, his growing unpopularity, and the strong challenge from the opposition saw him backtrack on this position (Jua, 2011). Multiparty politics afforded ordinary people the luxury to pick and choose between political organisations, sometimes to the chagrin of chiefs. The rift between chiefs and subjects was quite stark in the North-West Region of Cameroon.[164] The launch of the SDF party in Bamenda on 26 May 1990, despite being declared illegal by the government, was well received by a vast majority of the population in this part of the country (Mentan, 1998).

Meanwhile, at the beginning of his rule and in what was clearly a modernist vision, Biya expressed antipathy for customary authorities. In *Communal Liberalism* (Biya, 1987), he forecast the preponderance of local government over traditional authorities, and predicted the disappearance of traditional institutions. However, in the 1990s, desperate to stem the tide of support for the opposition and in line with the view that "central agencies also often support customary authorities because they can serve as vote banks for national elections and are easier to integrate into patronage networks" (Ribot, 2003, p. 164), President Biya appointed some chiefs from the North West into high ranking positions in the party (Awasom 2003; Konings and Nyamnjoh 2003 and Takougang and Krieger 1998). Prominent among them was *Fon* Angwafo III of Mankon who was appointed first Vice-President of the

---

[164] This rift is somewhat reminiscent of the dispute between educated elites and illiterate traditional authorities in British Cameroons in the 1940, details in Chapter II.

CPDM. *Fon* Ganyonga III of Bali was also appointed to the Central Committee of the party. The association of such high calibre traditional rulers with the ruling party did not sit well with the majority of the population; the case of *Fon* Angwafo III of Mankon was quite telling.

According to Awasom (2003, 115), "acceptance of this appointment at a time when many North Westerners and Anglophones already felt betrayed by their leaders brought a lot of trouble for Angwafo." This was because "as Vice-President of the CPDM he had to comply with party politics and subsequent party behaviour." In the 1990s therefore, he was involved in coordinating party activities in that part of the country, including a series of nation-wide manifestations with marchers chanting a song called '*dimabola*' to demonstrate loyalty to the party, and to press for the maintenance of the one party system (Nkwi & Nyamnjoh, 2011). The *Fon* of Mankon was ridiculed for his 'anti-democracy' stance, and also suffered significant property damage which in itself was unprecedented, considering that traditional rulers are highly revered in the North West Region of Cameroon. Interestingly, the passage of time has not dampened aversion for what one informant termed the involvement of 'natural rulers' in party politics, particularly on the side of the CPDM.

The question of chiefs and party politics in the North West once again came under intense scrutiny in September 2013. The dilemma for many in the opposition and even some ordinary people in Bali was where to draw the line between the *Fon* as a traditional ruler and the *Fon* as a politician. Traditional rulers, however, do not see anything wrong in being active in party politics, certainly not Angwafo, who fails "to see why chiefs should be treated as apolitical animals or placed above party politics, when they are citizens just like anyone else." Probed further, he retorts: "How can you deprive a citizen of involvement in politics simply because he holds a traditional title of *fon?*" (Nyamnjoh, 2003, p. 132).

Whereas some do not perceive the role of traditional rulers in politics as anachronistic, others feel that *Fons* are better-off staying away from politics. As the following excerpts from an interview with an opposition member demonstrates, drawing such a demarcation line can be tricky:

Until our Fon retires from politics it will always look confrontational here in Bali. The Fon has almost become a synonym for the CPDM and it is very difficult to offend against him. Some people who are traditionally inclined feel that when you oppose the CPDM you are opposing the Fon. Once the Fon becomes continually active in politics it is very dangerous, for politics can sometimes be like a fight in a pig sty. If you put on the damask of the Fon and you get inside a pig sty to meet somebody who might be wearing a torn rag, both of you must rub mud.[165]

My interlocutor, a senior member of the opposition SDF party in Bali, also likened the political arena to a rather surreal football pitch where *tous les coups sont permis* / all tackles are allowed. According to the rules of this hypothetical soccer match, "sometimes to score a goal, one must use things like sliding tackles, airlock etc. Basically, it is a rough game, so when you give airlock to the *Fon* what will be the outcome? It will be gruesome."[166]

The CPDM party did not wait for the opposition to use any of these 'gruesome' tactics during the September 30th municipal/legislative elections in Bali. Soon after the election was announced, the party went on the offensive by instituting legal action against the local SDF district chairman and former Mayor for alleged misuse of council funds during his tenure of office. Curiously, these charges were laid six years after he left office and on the eve of another election. This, according to most observers (including the person concerned), was a blatant attempt to stop him from contesting the polls by way of fictitious corruption allegations:

They tried to disqualify our list by telling lies that I embezzled Bali council money when I was in office. The second lie was that a certain lady from Bossa who was on our list was a Pinyin woman.[167]

This was not the first attempt by the CPDM in Bali to give the SDF a 'technical knockout.' In 2007, the CPDM successfully arranged for the electoral authorities to expunge the SDF list on grounds of non-conformity with the 'sociological composition' of Bali. In 2013, the CPDM again tried a similar tactic (see the above excerpt). Though it succeeded in arraigning the local SDF district chairperson before the

---

[165] Interview with SDF member in Bali 03/01/2014.
[166] Interview with SDF Bali Chairman; 03/01/2014.
[167] Interview with SDF Bali Chairman; 03/01/2014.

courts,[168] its designs ultimately proved futile because the courts threw out the charges for 'lack of evidence.' "Immediately the Supreme Court annulled it and my list stood, they now descended into the use of money and intimidation, intimidation through the traditional council and money through the local elites."[169] This set the stage for an election battle of epic proportions in Bali. The fight to the death between the CPDM and SDF in Bali involved the use of money, food items (Maggi or stock cubes), and the traditional sacred cult (*Voma*). *Voma*'s peace-making role became very controversial and debate over the rational for its deployment quite acrimonious.

Writing about political transitions in Africa in the 1980s and 1990s, Chabal and Daloz (1999) wondered whether the return to multipartism was not likely to lead to an increase in the importance of the 'irrational,' which they define as a "code word for religious beliefs in its broadest sense" (Chabal & Daloz, 1999, p. 63). As detailed below, the methods employed by both political parties to achieve electoral success went beyond the mundane world of electioneering into the realms of magic and witchcraft accusations and counter-accusations. The 2013 elections therefore presented a unique challenge to both political parties. On the one hand, it was an opportunity for the SDF to attempt to reconquer the council and on the other, it presented the CPDM with a chance to maintain itself at the helm and to consolidate its grip on the council for another five years.

6.7 *Voma* and the 2013 Municipal/Legislative Elections in Bali

Ba-ngwana[170] performed annual sacrifices in September-October at the Voma festival to promote the growth of guinea corn, and again in January; they might also be called upon by the Mfon[171] to sacrifice in times of drought, storms, and epidemics (Kaberry & Chilver, 1961, p. 364).

---

[168] This case went up to the supreme court, and the proceedings were unusually speedy compared to other similar circumstances; particularly post-electoral litigations brought against the ruling party which some observers saw as often deliberately delayed to ensure that by the time a verdict is rendered the case would have lost substance, most likely because of the commencement and or approach of another electoral cycle.

[169] Interview with SDF Bali Chairman; 03/01/2014

[170] Custodians of the sacred cult, which is based at the Dola shrine.

[171] Name of the traditional ruler in Bali language or Mungaka.

[T]he process of voting in a multi-party election must be understood as part of (very informal) relations of political exchange which impinge directly, if sometimes obscurely, on the electoral result (Chabal and Daloz 1999, p. 158).

During the two-week period allotted for campaigning for the 'twin elections,' political parties in Cameroon employed every available tactic to convince potential voters to turn out and cast their ballots for them. As Hansen (2010) observed in Ngaoundéré in 1996: "An important strategy in winning votes was the distribution of material benefits to potential voters during the campaign. These material benefits ranged from political merchandise to meat and money" (Hansen, 2010 , p. 435).

The passage of time, however, has not dampened the appeal of similar forms of largesse by politicians during electoral campaigns in Cameroon and elsewhere in Africa. For example, in the June 2014 gubernatorial elections in Ekiti State, (South Eastern Nigeria), the campaign team of the challenger and eventual winner was reported to have "distributed bags of food and fresh naira notes" to ensure victory for the candidate of the governing Peoples Democratic Party (PDP) (Africa Confidential, 2014). Back in Cameroon, newspapers carried daily reports detailing the largesse by political parties during the 2013 electoral campaigns. One report described how young people in the Bépanda neighbourhood in Douala attended long campaign rallies that often end up late at night followed by the distribution of money to buy the consciences of voters. The article goes on: *"différents quartiers de la circonscription électorale de Douala 5è sont quadrillés par ces émissaires qui, à chaque fois, font des promesses et repartent après avoir distribué de l'argent /* different areas of the 5th electoral district of Douala are patrolled by these party agents whose every stop is punctuated by promises and subsequent distribution of cash (Le Messager, 2013).

In Bali, the CPDM conducted what party cadres termed a 'door-to-door campaign strategy' during which cash, foodstuff, and party regalia amongst other items were distributed to potential voters. The CPDM also held regular meetings at the *Fon's* palace where campaign strategies were elaborated. One of the strategies involved inviting groups and other associations from different areas in Bali to the palace, where they were feted in the expectation that they would vote for the CPDM. However, as the following extract from Hansen (2010, 436) illustrates, generous gifts to party 'members' during campaigns do not always translate into positive outcomes on polling day.

> *By giving people meat and rice, the elite in Ngaoundéré tried to place people under a moral obligation to vote for CPDM. This kind of patron–client relationship required a degree of trust since the patrons had to be generous without knowing if the clients would reciprocate their generosity. In most other situations, the population had to take members of the elite at their word. Over and over again, the elite had deceived the people by saying one thing and doing another, leading to a widespread distrust in politicians and in the political system. During the elections this situation was reversed and citizens had the advantage over the administration and candidates. The population could eat without voting CPDM, since the candidates would never know who had voted for them.*

It seems that the opportunity to 'eat' from the CPDM during electoral campaigns dates back to 1996. This election came in the wake of major political changes that occurred in Cameroon, beginning with the surprise resignation of President Ahmadou Ahidjo, the falling out with his successor Paul Biya, and his attempt to regain power via a putsch (Bayart, 2009; Mbembe, 2001 and Delancy, 1989). A year on from the failed putsch (March 24, 1985), Paul Biya announced the dissolution of the Cameroon National Union (CNU) party and its replacement by the CPDM in Bamenda (Delancy, 1989). At the time, the country was still living in the bubble of the one-party system. However, the launching of the SDF in Bamenda on May 26 1990 not only signified that the bubble had burst, but was also a powerful testament to widespread aversion towards monolithism and its flag bearer the CPDM, whose acronym became popularly known in pidgin English as *Chop People Dem Moni*, meaning; "they eat our money like it's their own" (Takougang & Krieger, 1998, pp. 8-9).

Consequently, association or affiliation with the CPDM in Bamenda increasingly became precarious, if not anathema. This made it quite impossible for the party to get votes from ordinary people. Likewise, anyone cosying up to the party ran the risk of paying with their lives, as was the case of one Al Haji Tita Fomukong who was burnt alive when his residence was attacked and set on fire by an angry mob of opposition supporters. Also, as indicated earlier, the *Fon* of Mankon, Angwafo III, not only suffered public personal invective, but also saw his rest-house in Bamenda town razed to the ground and his traditional palace in the countryside threatened by a similarly irate mob (Awasom, 2003). In Ndu, the *Fon's* failure to condemn a violent incident which left six people dead was interpreted by his subjects as proof of his having 'sold out' to the CPDM. He was publicly addressed by name, something many interpreted as an open sign of dethronement (Fisiy, 1995). The apogee of the violence in the North West, was the declaration of a state of emergency in Bamenda on 27 October 1992 (DeLancey, Mbuh and DeLancey 2010 and Doh 2008).

The 1990s was therefore a period of very intense politics. There was then widespread aversion in Bamenda towards the CPDM party and equally strong animosity towards anybody who openly professed its ideals; this greatly affected support for the party. As a result, support for the party mostly came from civil servants from other parts of the country, especially from the president's region of origin in the South, and from members of the security forces. Outside these two camps, the CPDM could barely garner any vote from ordinary people in Bamenda. In fact, the party was widely viewed as a 'plague' that had to be avoided at all costs (Doh, 2008).

Consequently, CPDM barons from the North West, desperate to maintain cabinet portfolios and other privileges from the state, and to demonstrate a modicum of support for the president from this part of the country, resorted to employing schemes that were not dissimilar to what Hansen (2010) observed in *Ngaoundéré*. It was not uncommon for CPDM elites in the North West, after having successfully manipulated events on the ground and got people to turn up for rallies (mostly at heavily fortified locations), to further entice them with 'unsubstantiated promises, lies, and gifts' to get them to turn out to vote CPDM on polling day (Konings & Nyamnjoh, 2003). It was also very crucial to have such events televised and aired on the lone public broadcasting media, the Cameroon Radio Television (CRTV). Airing images of a CPDM rally from the bastion of the opposition constituted a spectacular coup for the government and party.

The irony of political developments in the 1990s was that people 'ate' from the CPDM and voted their hearts, i.e. they voted for the opposition which in the North West was dominated by the SDF party. Years following the first multiparty elections, Cameroonians were once again called upon to elect parliamentarians and municipal councillors.

Unlike in the 1990s when people 'ate' from the CPDM and voted their consciences, in 2013 the CPDM in Bali, in cahoots with traditional authorities were hell-bent on ensuring that anyone who ate at least a grain of salt should well and truly vote for them.

Meanwhile, in line with the patronage relationships mentioned earlier, and considering that "in an African context, clientele relations are relatively unstable" (Erdmann & Engel, 2006, p. 21), the traditional authorities in Bali resolved to ensure compliance by employing occult methods. The continued salience of occult forces in African societies contrasts starkly with the notion held by colonial authorities and missionaries and some post-colonial African officials and religious authorities that as African societies 'modernise' they will become more secular and adopt Christian and Muslim religious practices based on a 'rational God', in the process abandoning ancestral and traditional beliefs and practices (Chabal and Daloz 1999, p. 63).

One may be forgiven for thinking that occult rituals are the stuff of primitive societies or of a bygone era. However, in reality, during the campaign for the municipal elections in Bali there were strong accusations concerning the use of the occult. One story goes that, having feted meeting groups and associations invited to the palace, the traditional authorities 'compelled' them to swear an oath, 'the *Voma* pact,' pledging to vote for the CPDM failing which the *Voma* curse will befall them. I did not attend any of these 'strategy meetings'; but many informants confirmed they took place, although they would not be drawn on the veracity of the alleged pacts, despite rampant rumours in Bali.

In December 2013, I was traveling in a commuter taxi that plies the Bali-Bamenda highway. In the course of the trip I overheard a couple of women at the back of the car heading to Bamenda from farms in Bali discussing the damaging effects of heavy rainstorms that had for several weeks hampered farming activities. One of the women sounded confused because *Voma* usually comes out in January or February to kick-start farming in anticipation of the rainy season that begins in early March, which incidentally is the planting season. Because *Voma* came out in September, it appeared to them that the rainy season was too soon (mid-late November instead of around March). Consequently, they were uncertain about the fate of some food crops that were nearing harvest and about when to begin preparing the fields for planting new crops.

Meanwhile, in Africa generally, "religious conviction entails a belief in the presence and in the power of those who have departed – hence the prominence of the cult of the ancestors" (Chabal & Daloz, 1999, p. 66). In the views of these farmers therefore, there could only be one reason for the unprecedented[172] rainfall and strong winds that caused damage to property and crops during what was supposed to be the dry season. The cause of what I term 'wrath of the ancestors' was the 'inappropriate' use of *Voma* by the traditional authorities for selfish political ends. Such beliefs feed into a view that "the African peasant combines an empirically earned ecological knowledge (i.e. popular technical knowledge) with his [or her] conceptions about the role that spirits and the ancestors play in matters concerning [soil] fertility (i.e. magical–religious knowledge)", to determine meaning and knowledge (Olivier de Sardan, 2005, p. 160).

The conversation between these women (in which the driver occasionally interjected), not only weighed the potential consequences of the rains but also veered towards another controversial issue over which the women expressed equal alarm. They were aghast at the fact that the traditional authorities invited people to the palace, offered them food and drink and obliged them to vote for the CPDM on the pain of a *Voma* curse befalling them. Interestingly, the driver did not agree with the women on all points, especially over the link between *Voma*, rainstorm and potential harvests.

According to Chabal and Daloz (1999, 69), "on occasions politicians might be held responsible for events outside their control, [such as] drought or ill-health." Whereas those in Bali did not anticipate the unintended consequences of deploying *Voma* on the eve of a crucial election contest, the ramifications of their actions was not only a cause for concern to farmers. There were many others who also thought the ancestors of Bali were not happy because the CPDM elite, including the *Fon*, had openly violated tradition. Those who held such views expressed stronger fears and even raised the spectre of possible famine in Bali. As one informant put it:

---

[172]The rainy season in Cameroon usually runs from late March to early September. The rains in 2013 were seen as unprecedented because never had there been such persistent rainfall in some parts of the North West Region including Bali, that lasted right up to mid to late December.

Just immediately after the elections, all the farms in Bali suffered a terrible wind disaster that has never occurred in this community. I am afraid that we may have famine in Bali. Even in the Voma hosting site at Dola in Payila, the sacred tree fell. That tree fell, those are bad signals!!![173]

Some traditionalists I spoke with including the head of the traditional council, strenuously denied such claims, arguing that *Voma* is not a political party, its deployment on the eve of a major electoral contest bore no political overtones and its cleansing activities that night were meant to protect the whole of Bali subdivision. However, according to Abraham and Platteau (2004, 213), "unfortunate events that befall particular individuals are indeed ascribed to violations of social norms that aroused the anger of supernatural powers overseeing human affairs." Traditional authorities could nevertheless be comforted by the thoughts of Kaberry and Chilver (1961, 364) that "Ba-ngwana performed annual sacrifices in September-October," hence *Voma* coming out in September 2013 was just a routine exercise. However, a *Voma* member intimated to me that the *Voma* festival now takes place in November[174] (the staple diet in Bali is no longer guinea corn but maize).

To confound things further, people in Bawock argued that the CPDM victory in their village had nothing to do with *Voma*, since it is not part of their cultural practice. The same defence is cited from Bossa. Controversy aside, traditional rulers in North West Cameroon base their legitimacy on the supernatural. Therefore, by sending out *Voma* on the eve of an election, the *Fon* was certainly acting in his right as the head of traditional institutions in Bali. Under normal circumstances, local opinion neither questions such actions nor are they in principle susceptible to any sanction or punishment.

---

[173] Interview with SDF member 03/01/2014

[174] I was reliably informed by another highly placed traditionalist that the current *Fon*, who ascended the throne in 1985, made a lot of sweeping changes to the traditional setup of Bali Nyonga (some of which were later rescinded), probably explaining why the *Voma* festival date is now in November.

6.8 'Wrath from the Gods:' Analysis and Discussion

> *Because the council of elders embody the will of supernatural agencies, lower people are inclined to believe that their decisions and rulings have an incontrovertible force. And if they would nonetheless feel that the elite are erring in their judgments or abuse their power they have no choice but to comply.*[175]

While actions by traditional rulers, notably the utilisation of traditional instruments such as *Voma,* may be acceptable under appropriate circumstances, particularly during the launch of the farming season, what obtained in Bali in late-2013 completely turned this view on its head. The combination of unprecedented rainstorms and a threat of possible famine was perceived by many in Bali as collective punishment by the ancestors for 'inappropriate' use of *Voma* for political purposes. The spectre of 'wrath from the gods' generated a lot of anxiety amongst the population, to the point that the traditional council had to act.[176]

In what could be seen as buttressing the "simplistic assumptions made by modernisation theory that the [occult] necessarily withers with modernisation" (Chabal & Daloz, 1999, p. 64), some traditionalists and CPDM members in Bali ridiculed the idea of collective punishment by the ancestors as 'absurd and primitive.' Some attributed the rains to worldwide conditions caused by global warming and climate change. They also drew my attention to severe weather conditions affecting Europe and North America between late 2013 and early 2014, to show that events in Bali were not out of the ordinary. However, critics cited the falling of the tree at *Dola* in *Payila* (the *Voma* hosting site) as proof that the gods of the land were not happy with the traditional authorities and as a result had struck back; first at the base of the foot soldiers who executed the orders and who know where next? However, a *Voma* member I interviewed insisted that the tree fell because of strong winds that occurred before and not after the *Fon* asked them to 'cleanse' the

---

[175] Abraham & Platteau, (2004, p. 217).

[176] Members of the traditional Council, which serves as the main advisory body to the *Fon* and also a native tribunal, went to the weekly Bali main market to publicly denounce rumours linking the persistent rainfall and the risk of famine with *Voma* in an effort to reassure the increasingly agitated population.

land. Accordingly, "if the wind was after then why did we go out? We went out because there were evil people in the village."[177]

When I left Bali in February 2014, debate over *Voma* was yet to subside. People were wondering if the dreaded famine would happen, or if persons accused of bringing evil into Bali, whom the CPDM argued *Voma* went out to counter, would be punished, or further if those who ordered *Voma* to go out and 'intimidate' voters would equally face retribution. To many oppositionists, it was clear that a coincidence of factors including the likelihood of voter 'duplicity', as experienced in past elections, weariness in face of the strong challenge posed by the SDF and a quest for victory at all costs spurred the CPDM party to collude with some elites and the traditional authorities to concoct a novel strategy to ensure the compliance of potential voters, particularly those that ate during the campaigns.

I often heard this when I asked if such claims were justified: The door-to-door campaign strategy employed by the CPDM, in the course of which food items among other things were distributed to a large proportion of households, is evidence of this. The majority of people in Bali strongly uphold traditional values, coupled with a fear of Voma lurking in the shadows; so people were very much ill at ease over the thought of violating its edict. The SDF concluded that people in Bali voted for the CPDM out of compulsion. As one informant put it:

> "The traditional council knew that *Voma* is the most feared and dangerous juju[178] in Bali, and the only way to get people who took maggi to vote CPDM was to threaten them. So when *Voma* came out and mentioned that if you took one maggi, you must vote CPDM or arukwa fabia. Arukwa fabia is in Mubako [the old Bali Language] meaning this is the end of your life… people were terrified!!!"[179]

Such trepidation was reinforced three days before polling day, when *Voma* left its base at *Dola* shrine in the dead of night to conduct 'cleansing activities.' Whereas almost everyone agrees that it is in *Voma*'s

[177] Interview with Voma member 03/02/2014.
[178] Juju in this contexts broadly refers to objects (masks and amulets etc.), worn during public displays by dance groups or by members of traditional cults or secret societies while performing religious and other rites.
[179] Interview with SDF member; 03/01/2014.

right to cleanse the land, why it came out on that fateful night is strongly disputed. The fact that *Voma* came out at night was unprecedented, and its sudden and unexpected deployment was quite perplexing. It should be recalled that besides the *Fon*, *Voma* is the highest traditional institution in Bali Nyonga and only the *Fon* can order its deployment after consultation with his council of elders, also known as the traditional Council. In any case, the population usually gets advanced warning before the deployment of *Voma*. In fact they are advised to stay indoors for the duration of its activities, failing which they are alerted of its approach by the loud shrieking sounds from its gourd trumpets which prompt people to dash for cover. Moreover, local administrative officials, notably the DO of Bali, and local heads of the police and gendarmerie are always notified whenever *Voma* goes out for cleansing activities. Whether or not they were informed on this occasion remains a mystery.

The two political parties in Bali have diametrically opposed views on why *Voma* came out on 27th September 2013. For the CPDM party and the traditional authorities, *Voma* came out to counter the threat posed to peace and tranquillity in Bali by the SDF party. The local district chairman of the SDF party was accused of recruiting pygmies[180] from the East Region of Cameroon and 'importing' witchdoctors from Nigeria to cast magical spells over the population to vote for the SDF, so he could regain the position of Mayor he lost in 2007. As one local CPDM official asked rhetorically:

> *If the Fon learns that some people have gone to the East to bring Pygmies to Bali, as you know those people are noted for witchcraft, wizardry..., If he gets that kind of information that someone has brought them to hypnotise people to vote his party, then the Fon decides to send out Voma to cleanse the land and neutralise the potency of those witchdoctors charms, what wrong did Voma do?*[181]

Belief in the capacity of the ancient traditional cult of *Voma* to neutralise potential threats to the peace and wellbeing of the population

---

[180] The Pygmies in Cameroon are reputed to possess powerful supernatural powers that can be used for healing, and protection from enemy attacks amongst others. For more see Geschiere (1997) *The Modernity of Witchcraft: Politics and the Occult in Postcolonial Africa*

[181] Interview with CPDM member on 24/01/2014.

has long been well-established in Bali Nyonga society. For the opposition however, a combination of 'money, mystic and munchies' was employed by the traditional authorities in concert with local CPDM officials and elite members to get people to vote for them. This according to the SDF at best constituted political intimidation, and at worst amounted to holding the entire population of Bali to ransom. As one prominent oppositionist in Bali stated, "the *Fon* went out to campaign and used traditional things to intimidate people. This Voma is something people fear; just the roaring sound is very frightful! And if you go out to campaign and mention it, you intimidate people and they are not free."[182]

This discussion has laid bare differing perceptions about the rationale for using *Voma* during the municipal-legislative election campaigns in Bali. It supports the argument of Chabal and Daloz (1999, 76) that "as political competition intensifies, witchcraft and religion may become more, rather than less salient" in political activities. That said, the question of Voma's impact on the election result generates only stark contrasts. For the SDF, its electoral defeat was caused by a number of underhand tactics by the CPDM, of which the use of *Voma* to intimidate voters was the apogee, and buying of ballot papers for CFA 5000 francs on polling day from any voter who could provide evidence that he or she voted CPDM by brandishing an SDF ballot paper, came a long way second. The CPDM vehemently denied this charge. The press, however, covered a court case brought by the SDF against the CPDM in nearby Bamenda over accusations that the latter 'bought and cloned' the newly introduced and ostensibly unfalsifiable biometric voters cards of several hundred people there. It then duplicated the cards, recruited over 500 people, paid them huge sums of money, and transported them on polling day to a relatively remote district on the outskirts of town where they could vote multiple times, at different polling stations. It also made sure the ambulant voters did so unchallenged, thereby securing a much publicised landslide victory.

The CPDM also claimed a landslide victory in Bali; but, according to the SDF, the pressure brought to bear on voters left some of its militants with no choice but to vote for their arch rival. Their argument was that, because almost every household in Bali had in one way or

[182] Interview conducted with a Bali elite on 19/12/2013

another 'eaten' from their bitter adversary, with fear of *Voma* lurking in the shadows, they were very ill at ease with the thought of violating its edict. As a result, people had no option than to bow to intimidation and threats from the CPDM and the traditional council, and voted against their consciences. The CPDM rubbished these charges, adding that the SDF was crying over spilt milk, and had itself to blame if its militants had crossed the political carpet. One local party official had this to say:

> *SDF used Takumbeng[183] as a political strategy in Bamenda in the 1990s. Today CPDM uses a similar tradition to counter a threat to the people of Bali and they make political capital out of it? If Voma were to intimidate people to vote, a party like CPDM will not need to campaign. We will use Voma and win easy. In fact even Paul Biya will say I want to win elections and comes and takes Voma.[184]*

6.9 Conclusion

It can only be the stuff of wild fiction to imagine that President Biya could ever require the services of Voma to win elections in Cameroon. However, what most Cameroonians and many observers of the Cameroonian political scene cannot and do not doubt is that Biya is a strong and adept political manipulator. As mentioned earlier, since the 1992 presidential election, when it is widely believed that he lost to John Fru Ndi but was proclaimed victor by the Supreme Court, he has managed to construct a sophisticated winning machinery through a combination of elaborate political, legal, and administrative manoeuvres, which has enabled him and the CPDM party to win every electoral contest in Cameroon.

---

[183] Takumbeng is a female sacred society that wields traditional female power and authority within the Mankon *fondom* of the Cameroon grassfields. The group is heterogeneous and derived from indigenous ethnic structures in adjourning villages and chiefdoms of Nkwen, Chomba, Mbatu, Bamendankwe, Akum, Santa, Bafut, Bambili, and Bambui. The Takumbeng came into the spotlight during Cameroon's troubled transition to multiparty politics in the early 90s, the 1991 "villes mortes" ("ghost town") operations and the state of emergency declared in Bamenda from October 27, 1992. The Takumbeng surrounded the compound of Fru Ndi (Chairman of the SDF opposition party), placed under house arrest in the aftermath of the proclamation of the results of the 1992 presidential election. For more see (Fonchingong & Tanga, 2007).

[184] Interview conducted with CPDM official in Bali on 24/01/2014.

Meanwhile, the mystical activities of *Voma* over many generations have enabled it to stamp its authority as the supreme sacred cult of Bali Nyonga. Its rituals are shrouded in mystery, principally because membership is not open to everyone. Likewise, its real or perceived mystical activities have for countless generations imbued a sense of trepidation in non-initiates, who happen to be the majority population in Bali. No doubt its mythology could be viewed as irrational. That said, the reality for most people in Bali is that the word *Voma* conjures up mixed emotions, some of which are clearly irrational, but the overriding feeling nevertheless constitutes a blanket of fear.

Finally, the SDO's remarks during the installation ceremony echoed tremors generated by events leading up to and after the political earthquake that occurred in Bali on 30th September, 2013. His remarks were clearly designed to dispel the fears of many in Bali that the politicisation of *Voma* by the traditional authorities had not only brought a cherished but fearsome ancestral institution into disrepute, but also that the consequences for the main source of livelihood of the vast majority of the community, subsistence farming, could potentially be catastrophic, even fatal. In the final analysis, whether or not *Voma* had any real impact on the outcome of the elections is still the subject of fierce debate between the SDF and CPDM in Bali.

Chapter VII

In the Name of Investiture:
CPDM Party Discipline in Mbankomo

7.1 Introduction

Mbankomo centre is the main peri-urban agglomeration and chief town of Mbankomo subdivision in the Mefou and Akono Division. It is situated roughly 22km from Yaoundé, the capital of the Centre Region and political capital of Cameroon. Mbankomo is traversed by the economically strategic highway linking Cameroons political capital and its main economic hub Douala. This highway is also the main import-export link for landlocked Chad and the Central African Republic (CAR). According to the *Plan Communal de Développement* (PCD), Mbankomo has a population of around 25,000, predominantly composed of the Ewondo ethnic group and 33 sub-clans. Other communities found in the area are the Eton and Bassa.[185] The main economic activities in this area are agriculture, petty trading, small-scale timber exploitation, and sand digging. Mbankomo municipality hosts many devolved state services including sub-delegations for agriculture, basic education, and social affairs. There are also a significant number of Anglophones[186] living in this area, a few of them civil servants and members of the 'forces of law and order', while others are involved in petty trading and agriculture.

My research in Mbankomo came on the heels of three significant events in the political landscape of Cameroon, two of them directly relevant to this chapter. The first was Senatorial elections held in April 2013, the next was a presidential decree appointing *sous-préfets* and the last were municipal and legislative elections held in September. As is the

---

[185] Plan Communal de Développement de Mbankomo 2011.

[186] Anglophone in Cameroon refers to people from the two English-speaking Regions, North West and South West. The rise in the number of Anglophones in the area led the traditional authorities of Mbankomo to create a headman to serve as a focal point for their activities. It so happened that my arrival in Mbankomo coincided with the creation of this position, and I also witnessed his official installation. I even lived at his residence during my research.

tradition in Cameroon, the president regularly appoints officials to head different administrative units (Region, Division and subdivision). Each administrative area hosts a number of municipalities, most of them headed by elected Mayors. However, despite having elected Mayors, municipal councils in large urban centres such as Yaoundé, Douala, and Bamenda are clustered in city councils and lorded over by Government Delegates appointed by the head of state.

The administrative set-up of the country is also manned by a web of appointed officials, commonly referred to as representatives of the state or supervisory authorities. Sections (66-77) of the law on the orientation of decentralisation outlines various interventions by these 'supervisory authorities', i.e. the Minister of Territorial Administration and Decentralisation (MINATD), Regional Governors, and Senior Divisional Officers, in the functioning of municipal councils. The activities of municipal councils are monitored on a day-to-day basis by SDOs or *Préfets*. These range from approval of council budgets, expenditure, public contracts and development plans. *Préfets* also double as heads of administrative Divisions and coordinators of the activities of devolved government services in their jurisdictions.

At the level of the subdivision, there are Divisional Officers or *sous-préfets* who perform similar duties to the *Préfets*. However, a key difference is that *sous-préfets* head the smallest administrative units in Cameroon and have practically no authority over municipal councils, most of them situated within their jurisdictions. According to some observers, the position of *sous-préfet* is irrelevant and should be scrapped because it is monotonous to have them perform similar functions as the *Préfets*, albeit over a relatively narrow area. In principle, therefore, the only significant differences between both functions is that *sous-préfets* do not oversee the affairs of the most significant political entities in their administrative jurisdictions i.e. municipal councils. Further, the functions of *Préfets* as representatives of the state are said to be anachronistic, given the basic tenet of decentralisation which is to transfer decision-making powers to local municipalities under the authority of elected Mayors. Those who hold this view contend that for decentralisation in Cameroon to be effective, the stranglehold of *Préfets* and by implication the government over municipal councils should also be lifted. It would seem then that anachronism is the norm in the administrative structure of Cameroon, decentralisation notwithstanding.

7.2 Background

On 22 April 2013, President Paul Biya issued decree N° 2013/113 appointing *sous-préfets* to the numerous subdivisions in Cameroon. It was in line with this presidential diktat that on May 10th 2013 the *Préfet* of the Mefou and Akono Division presided over the official installation ceremony of the newly appointed *sous-préfet* for Mbankomo. The scenario at the official installation ceremony of the newly appointed official was quite similar to what obtained during the 'ceremony for the transfer of office to the newly elected municipal administrator in 1987' (Mbembe, 2001, p. 129). The event was animated by a brass band from the Cameroon Customs service, which has an encampment in the Nomayos neighbourhood on the outskirts of Mbankomo. The event was also graced by traditional dance groups from different areas of the subdivision. The arrival of the *Préfet* at the ceremonial grounds kicked off the event. It was immediately followed by singing the national anthem and an inspection of the guard of honour mounted by elements of the 'forces of law and order'. The *Préfet* then proceeded to shake hands with local dignitaries, heads of devolved government services, traditional authorities and local CPDM party cadres. The transfer of the 'baton of command' was preceded by two speeches, one by the Mayor and the other by the *Préfet*.

7.2.1 Welcome Address by the Mayor of Mbankomo Council

The Mayor began his speech by acknowledging the presence of dignitaries, including heads of the local Police and Gendarmerie, representatives of legal political parties, municipal councillors, traditional chiefs, and religious authorities, and also internal and external elites. He proceeded to outline the history of the area, its economic potential and the problems it faces. On the political front, he said the CPDM was the dominant party in the subdivision, but he also noted the presence of other political parties. He added that multiparty politics has not dented the *écrasante majorité* or crushing majority of the CPDM during elections in Mbankomo. This view echoed that of Atangana Ottou, third degree chief of Mbankomo Centre who in the course of a conversation described the CPDM party in Mbankomo as a religion.

The Mayor ended his speech by noting that Mbankomo has a lot of assets, the most significant being the very strong and dynamic elite who contribute positively to the development of the *arrondissement* or subdivision.[187] The overwhelming majority of these elites, who were described by some informants as *les hommes politiques,* loosely translated as political beings, belonged to the CPDM party. Most of them were current or former state functionaries, businessmen and politicians. As discussed later, these elites were quite instrumental in thwarting the Mayor's bid and by some accounts the popular choice to head the CPDM council list for Mbankomo in the 2013 municipal elections.

7.2.2 Installation Speech by the *Préfet* of the Mefou and Akono Division

In his speech, the *Préfet* thanked the Mayor for his warm welcome address. He went on to acknowledge the same invited dignitaries as the Mayor. He also heartily thanked the population for taking time off from their activities to attend the ceremony in such large numbers. This demonstrated their commitment to the President's actions in injecting fresh blood into the state administration. He urged people to support the head of state's grand vision of steering Cameroon into becoming an emerging economy by the year 2035.[188] He further counselled the *sous-préfet* to diligently carry out his duties, including ensuring the security of citizens and their property, supervising various state services in Mbankomo and ensuring law and order.

In line with the above duties, the *Préfet* recommended that the *sous-préfet* pay particular attention to a number of issues in Mbankomo. First, he was urged to coordinate efforts by the security services to stem criminality; second, to revamp agricultural activities; third, to consult with traditional authorities in filling vacant stools; fourth, to oversee the activities of the local branch of the national elections management body or Elections Cameroon (ELECAM). This task according to *Monsieur le Préfet* involved: *Au plan politique, je vous préscrit d'apporter votre collaboration à l'antenne communale d'Elections Cameroon, en assumant l'encadrement sécuritaire des échéances électorales imminents, et en vous impliquant personnellement dans la sensibilisation des populations à retirer leurs cartes électorales biométriques*[189] / at

---

[187] Speech delivered by the Mayor of Mbankomo on 10th May 2013.

[188] Speech delivered in Mbankomo by the SDO of the Mefou and Akono Division on 10th May 2013.

[189] Speech delivered in Mbankomo by the SDO of the Mefou and Akono Division on 10th May 2013.

the political level, I urge you to work together with the local branch of Elections Cameroon, and to oversee security operations in view of forthcoming electoral competitions and also to personally sensitise the population about the need to collect their biometric[190] voter cards.

Emphasis on the distribution of biometric voter cards was because 2013 was an election year in Cameroon and the CPDM-led government traditionally deployed an armada of senior state/party officials to closely monitor the process. Strong mobilisation by the CPDM was aimed at stamping its authority when the electoral landscape was going through profound transformations, following the introduction of a biometric voting system.

During the 2013 municipal/legislative elections then, allegations of sorcery, magic, sacred cults, 'cloned' voter cards and ambulant voters were a key point of discord between the CPDM and SDF in some areas of the North West Region. In Mbankomo and other parts of the country, events took the form of open, internecine and sometimes violent bickering within the CPDM party. This raised eyebrows among Cameroonians and generated debate about the future direction of the party, amid wild speculation about its possibly imminent implosion. The furore within the CPDM party raised a number of issues. First, what was the cause of political discontent within the CPDM party in 2013? Why were CPDM grassroots militants in Mbankomo left fuming over the actions of some party cadres? How did episodes of discontent manifest themselves in Mbankomo and other places around the country? And what impact did these and other events have on the outcome of the elections for the CPDM party in Mbankomo and other municipalities in Cameroon?

7.3 The 2013 Municipal and legislative Elections in Cameroon

In July 2013, the president of Cameroon signed a decree[191] convening the electoral corps. Article (I) stated that an election of Parliamentarians into the National Assembly and Councillors into

---

[190] Compilation of the biometric registration process and production of voter's cards had the full backing of most foreign chancelleries based in Cameroon and also international bodies, notably the Commonwealth and *La Francophonie*; as well as the World Bank and other multilateral donors. The contract for the process was awarded to a Munich-based firm, Giesecke and Devrient.

[191] Decree N° 2013/220 of 2 July 2013

Municipal Councils would take place on 30 September 2013. This announcement raised the hopes and aspirations of many Cameroonians for meaningful political change via the ballot box. The presidential decision also set the ball rolling for a nationwide electoral contest that was full of intrigue, skulduggery and electoral merchandising, among other political machinations.

In the period of the elections, I had exchanges with friends, conducted interviews and listened to media conversations and commentaries on the side-lines involving officials and ordinary people. The general feeling was that with the advent of the biometric voting system, the electoral process in Cameroon might finally be credible. Many were hopeful that this system sounded the death knell for electoral fraud. People were very enthusiastic about the opportunity to effect real change, something that has eluded them for decades.

Expectations of a free and fair electoral contest were not only espoused by members of the opposition, but also within the governing CPDM party. In fact some CPDM militants I spoke to expressed optimism that the biometric voting system would definitively put an end to post-election accusations of vote rigging often levelled against them by the opposition. In the run-up to these elections, the chairman of the CPDM prescribed consensus as the method for selecting candidates. Reaching consensus in Mbankomo and other places around the country was controversial, however, because grassroots militants who expressed a wish to have certain candidates represent them in the municipality were often brazenly thwarted by the party hierarchy.

7.3.1 Presidential Circular on the Selection of Candidates.

The Mayor of Mbankomo corroborated the notion of the CPDM as religion in his speech of welcome during the installation of the *sous-préfet*. From the evidence of past election results in Mbankomo, this had been the case ever since the restoration of multiparty politics in Cameroon in the 1990s. Going into another election, it was not unreasonable to contend that the CPDM was heading for another landslide victory in Mbankomo. What was uncertain at this stage (from an outsider's perspective) was who would head the party list and most likely emerge as Mayor in the end. Three days after decreeing the date of the elections, the national chairman of the CPDM issued a circular letter addressed to militants in which he outlined the mode of selection of candidates to represent the party in the polls.

Paul Biya's note stated: *Comme il est de tradition en pareille circonstance, conformément aux Textes de Base du Parti, en l'occurrence l'article 23 des Statuts, l'investiture des candidates et des candidats du RDPC aux élections législatives et municipales relèvera du Comité Central/* as is the tradition under similar circumstances and going by Article 23 of the constitution and basic texts of the party, the nomination of CPDM candidates for the parliamentary and municipal elections will revert to the Central Committee (RDPC-CPDM, 2013). This directive was reminiscent of what obtained during the monolithic era, when party barons always reminded candidates aspiring for positions that they owed their 'investiture' to the party leadership and not to their own efforts or the support of voters (Geschiere, 2009).

The circular continues by stating that selection by the Central Committee (CC) will be done in conjunction with militants at the base and will aim to encourage the emergence of honest and dynamic men, women and youths who can effectively convey to the grassroots the president's vision of transforming Cameroon into an emerging economy by the year 2035. Moreover, *Ces opérations devront se dérouler dans un esprit d'ouverture, de maturité politique, d'objectivité et de recherche du consensus /* these operations should be conducted in a spirit of openness, political maturity, objectivity and the quest for consensus (RDPC-CPDM, 2013)

Consensus was therefore a key element in the CPDM's strategy for mobilising militants at the base for the 2013 municipal and legislative elections. Within this framework, the party hierarchy dispatched teams to all ten Regions of the country to oversee the 'investiture' process. These teams usually consisted of a president and vice, members, a coordinator, and *chargés des missions*. Within this setup there were two specialised units, one in charge of the legislative and another the municipal elections (RDPC-CPDM, 2013). Other issues also emerged in the run-up to the elections.

7.3.2 Pre-election Manoeuvring

According to electoral regulations in Cameroon, the announcement of polling day effectively puts an end to registration of voters on the electoral list.[192] This also marks the start of overt and covert manoeuvres by political parties to select or elect representatives to compete for various posts. Whereas campaigning officially kicks off two weeks before polling day, many observers felt the governing CPDM was already on the campaign trail as far back as 19th May 2011 (Mutations, 2011).

In his traditional annual speech delivered on the eve of national day celebrated every 20th May, the president announced the issuing of National Identity (ID) cards cost-free to all eligible Cameroonians. Similarly, he ordered the extension of this process a couple of months later in his usual end of year speech for 2012 (Le Messager, 2013). The official reason advanced for this presidential goodwill gesture was to accelerate the registration of voters on the electoral lists, which had been lagging ever since the process was announced in early 2011 in anticipation of presidential elections scheduled for later that year. In Cameroon, the National ID card not only contains details (name, sex, date of birth, region of origin, etc.) of the bearer, but is essential for all official transactions. It is strictly controlled by the 'forces of law and order' stationed at thousands of make-shift checkpoints that litter thoroughfares throughout the country; and woe betide individual(s) who cannot produce one upon request by Police or Gendarmerie officers.

Also, since the 1990s, voter turnout in Cameroon has witnessed a remarkable decline. This was because of voter apathy, largely blamed on electoral fraud and a generalised feeling amongst Cameroonians that the electoral process is fundamentally flawed. Many viewed the current regime as a prolongation of the autocratic system created by Ahidjo which his successor Paul Biya has skillfully adapted into a 'democratic environment' (Mentan, 1998). Over the years, many citizens lost faith in the electoral system because they did not believe that elections could bring about genuine political renewal in Cameroon. Moreover, observers of the Cameroon political scene often argue that, but for the change of leadership in 1982, there has not been any fundamental alteration in the system of governance (Geschiere 2009 and Delancy 1989). In fact, the current president and many key officials have been shuttling round various capacities within the state apparatus for decades. The quest to maintain power in the post-monolithic era witnessed the crafting of a

---

[192] Law No. 2012/001 of 19 April 2012 on the Electoral Code of Cameroon.

'sophisticated rigging machinery' that has ensured continued electoral successes in national and local elections in Cameroon since the 1990s (Konings and Nyamnjoh 2003; Gros 1998, and Takougang and Krieger 1998).

The development of this highly efficient 'rigging apparatus' was not unconnected to the impact of the 'democratic wind of change' in the 1990s. With hindsight, the 1992 presidential election was seen as the turning point when Cameroonians, according to Nyamnjoh (1999, p. 114), "were made to understand that democracy is not necessarily having as president the person the majority wants." This assessment is based on the widely held view that that election was won by the opposition SDF leader, John Fru Ndi, but declared in favour of the CPDM by the Supreme Court (Nkwi and Socpa 2011).

The then president of the Supreme Court was infamously associated with the phrase 'my hands are tied by the law', because of shortcomings in the electoral code which did not grant the court powers to annul a highly contentious presidential election which gave victory to the incumbent Paul Biya. This singular act bounded the fate of millions of Cameroonians to a regime that many people genuinely wanted out of power.

Back to the 2013 elections and free ID cards, the press widely reported how thousands of cards littered Police stations uncollected. One newspaper reported how the *sous-préfet* of Ebolowa II in the president's home Region took it upon himself to tour villages in his administrative unit, personally handing out ID cards that had been abandoned in the South Regional capital, Ebolowa (L'Actu, 2013). As the elections approached, other *sous-préfets* shifted gear from distributing ID cards to distributing voter cards. In Mbankomo, barely weeks after his installation, I accompanied the *sous-préfet* on the last leg of his *tournée des prise de contacte* or meet the people's tour. On this occasion, the *sous-préfet* performed the role of civil administrator and party official; and his call for 'unity' and 'vigilance' was reminiscent to what obtained during political monopoly (Geschiere, 2009). His official delegation included workers from the local branch of ELECAM and during each stopover their functions was to identify registered voters and hand out voter cards.

State officials were not the only ones concerned about potential voter apathy. In a note addressed to party militants, the Secretary

General of the CPDM appointed high-powered delegations of party bigwigs to the 10 Regions of the country to sensitise and mobilise grassroots militants to collect voter's cards (RDPC-CPDM, 2013). This came in the wake of a bruising investiture process in which many at the grassroots level were enraged by the actions of some party barons, CC delegates and also the SG, over what I call the investiture saga. The deployment of such high-powered delegations to the field was not an unusual phenomenon. It is common during election campaigns in Cameroon for the public administration, i.e. ministerial departments and other public institutions, to be drained of high ranking bureaucrats sent to their home regions to campaign for the CPDM.

The deployment of these delegations on the eve of the 2013 municipal-legislative elections came amid generalised paranoia among party top brass over threats of widespread dissent and a possible party split. Despite official denials, it was hard to conceal the fact that these officials were sent out to heal the wounds caused by the investiture saga, and to convince supporters not to desert the party. Acrimony was so widespread that some loyal militants who lost out in the process not only pointed accusing fingers at party big-shots, but also expressed fears for the future of the party.

In Mbankomo, councillor Zele (pseudonym) from the out-going Mayor's team accused the SG of the party of creating chaos and taking advantage of the investiture process to send his friends around to meddle in local party affairs.[193] Despite the rather ignominious manner in which their candidates list was shredded, he nevertheless declared undying loyalty to party leader, Paul Biya, while expressing fears that enraged grassroots militants might transform their anger into negative votes which might cause the party to lose the elections in Mbankomo.[194] Councillor Zele's fears will be explored in greater details later. In the meantime, I will examine how the investiture process played out in Mbankomo.

7.4 In Search of 'Consensus' at Mbankomo Town Hall

On 11 July 2013, the CPDM-CC delegation responsible for the supervision of the investiture process in the Mefou and Akono Division

---

[193] Personal communication 07/18/2013.
[194] Personal communication 07/18/2013.

descended on Mbankomo, where a meeting was scheduled in the municipal hall. This delegation was based at the divisional headquarters in Ngoumou, whence they visited other towns in the area for similar purposes. Initially slated for 13:00 the meeting finally started around 15:00. As I got into the hall, I could hear a member of the delegation reading directives from the party chairman about the rules for investing candidates. The militants present were cautioned that aspirants whose documents did not conform to the electoral code would be disqualified by ELECAM. They were also reminded that candidates would be selected via consensus lists which would be forwarded to the party CC. Militants present in the hall were asked not to pay the requisite caution fee of CFA 50.000 FRS at this juncture, but to have the cash handy and wait for the appropriate moment.

At this point the floor was opened for questions and comments. The first question from the audience sought clarification from the panel about who was authorised to sign the attestation of residence; this person was confused about the statutory authority competent to legalise this document. One of the panellist responded that under normal circumstances it was the preserve of the legal department, but due to time constraints the signature of the *sous-prefet* was sufficient. The next issue was the competent authority to legalise a birth certificate; the panel responded that it was the responsibility of the Mayor or civil status registrar of the person's place of birth. This was confirmed by the Mayor who signalled his availability to append his signature on these documents with speed.

After the Mayor's intervention, the chairperson continued by stating that the committee's job was to collect the list of ruling party candidates aspiring to contest the municipal elections for Mbankomo council. He also added that the party chairman had recommended investiture of candidates via consensus lists. He then proceeded: "we have now come to the most important part of this meeting, and as you know Mbankomo council consists of 25 councillors, and I therefore invite anybody who is head of a list to come up with it"[195] He further stressed that each list should have 20-30% females, in accordance with the party's gender policy and an unspecified number of youths.

---

[195] Statement by the coordinator of the CPDM party delegation in charge of supervising investiture of candidates for the municipal elections in Mbankomo, on 11th July 2013 (field notes).

At this point another member of the panel announced that they were aware that, prior to the arrival of the CC-delegation, preparatory meetings had taken place between different branches of the party (Youth, Women and Men) in Mbankomo. These preparatory meetings were held in the presence of a local elite member and former Minister who urged them to follow the national chairman's directives. He informed the audience that the said meeting had failed to reach a consensus because the individuals who aspired to head the candidates' lists were unwilling to compromise. However, in the meantime, three of the four list leaders agreed to fuse into one, but the outgoing Mayor declined to associate with them because he felt he had achieved a lot during his tenure[196] and sought a new mandate to consolidate his plans.

Next, the CC-delegation chair opened the floor for comments, questions and clarifications. At this juncture, someone stood up and presented himself as the youth-wing or YCPDM president. He argued that not every local stakeholder was invited to the meetings at the former Minister's residence and as a result it was unfair to hold decisions taken at that meeting to be representative of everyone's opinions. He further expressed the hope that, because the chairperson was not from the area, his neutrality would greatly help them reach consensus. He added that any consensus list should take into consideration the hard work of local CPDM youths who had made lots of sacrifices to represent the party at public events in Mbankomo, despite limited support by the *hommes politiques*. He went on to present a file to the delegation chair which he said contained the expectations of the YCPDM about the consensus list. In response, the CC delegation chair acknowledged that he was not from the area, but others in his delegation were and his role was not to make a consensus on behalf of the local party militants. He hoped, however, that the contending lists would contain YCPDM members.

Almost immediately, a man describing himself as a member of the local elite asked to speak and was given the floor. He said the groundwork for the town hall meeting was laid in the presence of everyone and that the YCPDM president's suggestion about the way forward was simply absurd. Everything had been sorted out and the *jeune*

---

[196] The previous Mayor elected in 2007 fled midway in his term over his involvement in a financial scandal linked to a former general manager of the state-run national petroleum storage depot, known by its French acronym as SCDP. The GM was convicted and jailed for 30 years on 3rd October 2012 for stealing public funds.

homme or young man had to accept things the way they are. According to this *homme politique*, democracy is all about majority decision-making and losers have to humbly abide by the will of the majority. If the *jeune homme* was not satisfied by the outcome, he should wait for the next election. After this remark, the delegation chair stated that:

> *We are here to seek solidarity among militants of the party, and not to assess the work of people. We have to designate people who will continue the achievements of the outgoing team. Moreover, it is the Central Committee that will designate the person it deems fit to be Mayor, so fighting about this role at this stage would not serve any purpose.*[197]

In what could be seen as a swipe to the outgoing Mayor, he said:

> *There is a trend for people to invest personal resources to get nominated and when elected they no longer abide by party rules. If challenged, they are quick to point to the fact that they invested their money to get elected and the party did not help them, so we don't want to hear such statements again.*[198]

The following newspaper report about the investiture saga in Mbankomo stated that: *contre l'esprit de la lettre circulaire, ces personnalités ont ordonné aux commissions communales de refuser tout consensus et de ne retenir que les listes conduites par leurs affidés/*contrary to the spirit of the presidential circular, these personalities ordered the municipal committees to reject any consensus and retain only lists headed by their cronies (Le Messager, 2013). The reaction of the CC delegation chair and the *homme politique* to the statement by the YCPDM president sounded the death knell to the outgoing Mayor's ambitions.

The meeting proceeded with calls by the delegation chair for unity and for people to put their differences aside and come up with a consensus list. He also reminded the audience that Mbankomo Council requires 25 not 50 councillors and the numbers cannot be multiplied to suit personal ambitions. At that point, a suggestion was made that the

---

[197] Statement by the coordinator of the CPDM party delegation in charge of supervising investiture of candidates for the municipal elections in Mbankomo, on 11th July 2013 (field notes).

[198] Statement by the coordinator of the CPDM party delegation in charge of supervising investiture of candidates for the municipal elections in Mbankomo, on 11th July 2013 (field notes).

chairman request the list heads to select two people each to enter into a conclave and come up with a consensus list, to which he retorted that it was not his position to direct how things should be organised, but that militants should organise themselves as they see fit.

In line with the above suggestion, leaders of the contending lists selected two people each to join them in a conclave. The Mayor designated the YCPDM president and one other person, the same for the *homme politique*. As both teams were preparing to go into conclave, some people in the hall shouted out about the need for the tribal equilibrium of the area to be respected. Others suggested that the plight of minorities, specifically non-natives, equally be taken into consideration. These opinions captured the divergent positions of the two factions embroiled in the investiture saga in Mbankomo. At this juncture, the committee chair adjourned the meeting for two hours to reconvene at 18:00.

7.4.1 Intractable Conclave: Conversations on the Side-lines

I returned to the hall at 18:00, but none of the rival parties had come back; it appeared that the conclave was taking much longer than expected. I waited for a couple of hours while I struck-up random but ultimately fruitful conversations with three men who said they belonged to the YCPDM. I asked them the reasons for the squabbles within the CPDM in Mbankomo and why it was proving difficult for the militants to form a consensus list, as prescribed by the party chairman.

One of my interlocutors, Onana (pseudonym), started off by listing the two main procedures for choosing candidates for the party, i.e. election or selection. In his view, a third option was always on the cards i.e. consensus, which was the case on this occasion. Mbankomo, he went on to say, was predominantly made up of the Ewondo ethnic group consisting of four main clans or subgroups. These were the Mvog Nnama, Mvog Fouda Mballa, Mvog Tsoungui Mballa and Mvog Ndobo. During elections, CPDM candidates are selected from each of these groupings according to a quota system, which he didn't elaborate upon. Nevertheless, Section 151 (3) of the electoral code states that: "Each list shall take into consideration the various sociological components of the constituency concerned..."[199] However, this law is quite vague about the

---

[199] Law No. 2012/001 of 19 April 2012, on the Electoral Code of Cameroon.

meaning of the term 'sociological components,' leaving it to various interpretations. This hazy clause is often employed by electoral officials mainly as a justification for rejecting opposition party lists.[200] Interestingly, sociological composition was the source of fierce debates amongst jurists in the Supreme Court[201] when examining petitions filed against the rejection of some party lists by ELECAM (Le Messager, 2013).

My next interlocutor, Abogo (pseudonym), was frustrated that other councils in the area had already selected candidates, but Mbankomo always had problems because of meddling by the *hommes politiques* and the CC. However, I later found out that the investiture saga was not only a problem in Mbankomo, but also raged in two of the three other subdivisions in the area, Bikok, and Ngoumou. Probed on the issue of meddling by elites, he cited the furore that ensued following nationwide primaries held by the CPDM in the lead-up to the 2007 municipal elections.

Following party primaries held that year, many CPDM barons were humiliated and denied electoral franchise by militants of the base. A prominent casualty of this revolt was the president of the National Assembly who in 2007 lost the party primaries in his local constituency in the Mayo Sava Division in the Extreme North of Cameroon, but was reinstated by the CPDM-CC. According to Abogo, the actions of the CC on this and many previous occasions were greatly resented by grassroots militants who viewed it as a blatant violation of their right to select credible people to represent them in key state and local institutions. He expressed fears that a similar action might be in the offing in Mbankomo. From the look of things, he went on, it appears grassroots militants always have a rough deal when squared up against

---

[200] There was wild speculation in Cameroon that the entire candidate's files submitted by the CPDM party for the legislative and municipal elections would be rejected by the authorities of the electoral management body or ELECAM for not respecting the midnight 17 July 2013 deadline for all candidates' lists to be registered at its headquarters. As I observed during fieldwork, it was widely reported in the media that the CPDM deposited its documents past that time, and if electoral regulations were to be strictly adhered to, it should not have been received. However, none of that happened. Curiously, out of the 48 candidates list rejected by ELECAM, none of them belonged to the CPDM.

[201] According to the Constitution of Cameroon, the constitutional council is the competent authority to deal with such matters. However, this body only exists on paper, hence the Supreme Court sits in lieu of it.

the party hierarchy and the *hommes politiques*. Such practices by the elite that undermine the role of the masses are not surprising, considering that President Biya's ideology under 'communal liberalism' had from the outset been in favour of a 'strong democracy whereby the elite led the masses' (Biya, 1987).

Unlike in 2007, Cameroon's political calendar in 2013 featured municipal, legislative and senatorial elections. The creation of the Senate wrought fundamental changes in the hierarchical order at the helm of the state. According to Article 6(4) of the constitution, the President of the Senate is next in line to fill the post of State President, albeit temporarily in case of a vacancy for reasons of illness, death or resignation. Prior to the creation of the Senate in 2013, that role was the preserve of the president of the National Assembly who in terms of state protocol was the second personality of the state. This constitutional provision allows the individual at the helm of the state during this delicate period to preside over the transition, but not put themselves up for election; however, they could prove to be a vital king-maker. With the advent of the Senate as the upper chamber of parliament, the role of temporary successor automatically shifted from the National Assembly to the Senate President. [202]

In a desperate and ultimately futile attempt to maintain himself as the second personality of the State: *Le Député du Mayo Sava s'est porté candidat à la Chambre haute. Une candidature qui a malheureusement été rejetée par la Commission nationale d'investiture du parti du flambeau présidée par le Président national, Paul Biya*/The MP from Mayo Sava sought to be a candidate for the Upper House. Unfortunately, his application was rejected by the CPDM party's national nomination commission presided over by the party chairman President Paul Biya (La Nouvelle, 2013). In the months following this rather humiliating experience, there was wild speculation that *Monsieur le Député du Mayo Sava* was heading towards political oblivion. However, just like the mythical phoenix, he made a remarkable comeback following the 2013 legislative elections, this time around in the position of the 3rd personality of the state and president of the National Assembly, a post he has held for over two decades.

Sitting outside Mbankomo council hall with my two interlocutors and contemplating the intriguing investiture saga, we were joined by

---

[202] Article 6 (4a) of the Cameroon Constitution Revised and updated April, 2008.

another YCPDM militant who took an interest in our conversation and decided to weigh in. According to him, the selection of candidates for the 2007 municipal elections began at the level of the *groupements tribales*, during which each tribal grouping comes up with its quota of candidates to make up the requisite twenty five councillors. However, as the list progressed to party headquarters, it was discovered that names of some people elected from below were removed, and replaced with people who neither contested the primaries nor were active at the grassroots. This, according to Mbida (pseudonym), was seen in a bad light by many ordinary militants and almost 'led to a revolution in Mbankomo.' Many people were angry at what they perceived as a deliberate undermining of their choice of candidates by the party hierarchy in favour of those who most ordinary militants viewed as neither working for the good of the party nor the greater good of the community.

In Mbida's view, these *étrangers* or outsiders only think of the base during election periods and, after securing their mandates, quickly scarper off and no-one hears from them until elections are approaching again. Frustrated by such disingenuous practices, grassroots militants in 2007 decided to *les donnez une leçon au cours des primaires du parti,* or teach them a lesson in the party primaries. Fearing a repeat scenario in 2013, the president of the party avoided primaries and demanded consensus instead. However, achieving consensus in Mbankomo, as in other places in the country, was not an easy task. Finally, after several hours of waiting for all parties to return to the council premises in vain, I headed home, abandoning my YCPDM companions in the hope of learning about the outcome of the prolonged conclave the next day.

7.5 Investiture Saga in Mbankomo: Contrasting Opinions I

7.5.1 Councillor Zele

As I woke up the next day, my main thought was to find out the outcome of the conclave. Leaving home, I had just one person in mind, councillor Zele. I managed to catch up with him at dusk. Zele was someone I had encountered many times during my stay in Mbankomo. He had on previous occasions informed me that he was the chairman of the economic and social affairs committee of the outgoing council team and a close personal friend of the Mayor. I was very keen to know what the shape of the consensus list looked like.

He began by stating the obvious, that the meeting stretched beyond the time allotted and after intense negotiations both sides were still unable to arrive at a compromise. As a result the incumbent Mayor's list of which he was a member and that of the *hommes politiques* were forwarded that same night to the departmental committee in Ngoumou. At Ngoumou, the incumbent Mayor's list was rejected for being incomplete. This according to him was nothing short of a putsch against the Mayor orchestrated by the *hommes politiques,* in conjunction with the local members of the CC delegation. He also chastised the chairman's duplicity when he publicly asked everyone not to pay the requisite caution money, despite being aware that the fees for the opposition list had been paid. This further dented the latter's credibility in relation to statements he made in the council hall when it was suggested to him by the YCPDM president that he request the contending list leaders to select two people each prior to the conclave.

Asked how the plot unfolded, he said a lot of underhand tactics were employed by their adversaries in the dying minutes of the conclave. Thus, before it was decided that two lists should be forwarded to the departmental committee, both sides almost reached consensus, but discussion broke down over who would head such a list. As a result, it was decided to forward both lists to the departmental committee. However, on examining the Mayor's list, it turned out to be incomplete because some documents were missing, while that of the *hommes politiques* was complete. At this juncture, they couldn't do much, considering that the deadline was fast approaching and the time available to them was insufficient to compile a new dossier. Further, in what he described as 'grotesque sarcasm,' the *hommes politiques* offered to take four names off their list and replace it with people from the incumbent Mayor's, something which they could not accept. Days after the deadline for submission of documents to ELECAM had passed, the missing documents were discovered on the grounds of a secondary school in Yaoundé several kilometres from where they were deposited.

From what I could see, 'incomplete files' was the main argument presented by the CC departmental delegation in the Mefou and Akono Division to disqualify alleged undesirable lists. To a visibly angry Zele, such actions were not only an affront to the militants at the base, but went against the wishes of the national chairman. Further, he added, when aggrieved people wanted to express their frustrations, they were asked to respect party discipline. According to him, the actions of party big wigs caused enormous consternation in Mbankomo, because people were furious at the putsch against the incumbent Mayor. Though I did not see any sign of it, he said the population, spearheaded by local motorbike taxi riders, were very angry about the whole thing and wanted to protest, but he personally went down to calm them. Asked why this mattered so much to the motorbike taxis, he said they had got wind that the new council team was planning to impose taxes on them and were not happy about it.

Echoing one of the YCPDM militants I spoke to on the night of the conclave, Councillor Zele said "it is clear that corrupt elements in the party have once more succeeded."[203] He also seemed visibly frustrated because, as he put it, "people don't want to help the head of state to achieve his 'Greater Realisation' plans for this country, in fact these people don't want to see progress in this community."[204] According to him, the incumbent Mayor was a very progressive man and this was reflected in the 'representative' list he put together, which included all segments of the population of Mbankomo. This list contained nineteen new people, most of them at the behest of the local population. This was in line with the Mayor's belief that the presence of people from other parts of the country who have settled in Mbankomo on a permanent basis should not be ignored. Rather, it should be seen as contributing to the diversity and development of the municipality. It therefore seemed that the Mayor's attempt to challenge the local variant of 'autochthony' was met with stiff resistance by the *hommes politiques*, who felt threatened by the idea of 'foreigners' sitting on the council.

According to Zele, the selection of municipal councillors on the basis of tribe was not only counterproductive, but anti-developmental. The list put up by the other side contained only indigenous (Ewondo) people, which in his view was absurd because Mbankomo was no longer a village and should not be considered as such. It was high time, he fumed, that people woke up to the reality that this place has developed and is expanding ever further. In fact, he went on, we have over 500 non-indigenes living in this town, and they can't just be side-lined on the pretext of promoting tribal equilibrium. We can't act as if they do not exist; in many ways they contribute to the development of this town and

---

[203] Personal communication 07/18/2013.
[204] Personal communication 07/18/2013.

that has to be taken into account. Further, the list that went through consisted mostly of members of the elite and their protégées who have not mastered local realities and do not know the problems of the villages. In fact, they don't live in the areas they supposedly represent. Most of them live in Yaoundé and people only know they exist during election campaigns, when they come back and displace local people.

Asked why he thinks they mounted a putsch against his mentor, he said it simply boils down to jealousy for, according to him, people are envious of the remarkable work *ce jeune homme* or this young man (referring to the Mayor whom he said was in his mid-late 40s) has done in such a short space of time. He further argued that these *hommes politiques* were afraid of the Mayor who he described as a 'rising star' because of his great achievements in the community. They are envious that his good deeds might catch the eyes of the head of state, and are worried that he has the potential to outshine them in his eyes. Who knows, he might end up being appointed as a Minister, or even better Secretary General at the Presidency, just like two previous sons of this town.[205]

I then asked him to elaborate on the Mayors 'good deeds,' because I had wandered around the area and not seen any project that was attributable to him, but for the fact that he approved and almost immediately cancelled an initiative by a councillor and some local people to collect a token sum from a bi-weekly roadside market. He dismissed the money collection as a sham and insisted that the Mayor had established fruitful contacts in Switzerland, the USA, France, etc. These contacts in his view had the potential of transforming the municipality by providing it with machines and other heavy equipment that would greatly help in infrastructural development and other projects. I said if that were the case, whoever was at the helm of the council can still use the equipment for the intended purposes. He acknowledged this point, but added that negotiations were still very much at their infancy and he

---

[205] The previous sons he is referring to are Professor Titus Edzoa and Jean Marie Atangana Mebara. Prof Edzoa was President Biya's onetime personal physician, Minister of Public Health and the Secretary General at the Presidency. However, when he resigned from his post and attempted to challenge Biya in the 1997 Presidential elections, he was promptly arrested, tried for embezzling public funds and sent to jail for over 15 years. He was released in February 2014. Mr Mebara was Minister of Higher Education, then Secretary General at the presidency, and later Minister of Foreign Affairs before, being sacked. He is facing corruption and embezzlement charges.

was not sure if the incoming team will be able to pursue them because of animosity against the Mayor and everything he represented.

7.6 Investiture Saga in Mbankomo: Contrasting Opinions: II

7.6.1 Mr Abesolo

A day after my discussion with councillor Zele, I met Mr Abesolo (pseudonym) who, like the former, was someone I regularly interacted with during fieldwork in Mbankomo. He was a member of the clean-up team (discussed below) and also among the initiators of the market collection scheme. He described himself as a CPDM militant whose position on local issues was more aligned with those of the *hommes politiques*. Our conversation centred on the talk of the town i.e. the rejection by the divisional CPDM-CC team of the list headed by the Mayor of Mbankomo. He was very scathing about the Mayor. He said the outcome of the investiture saga was not a surprise to him and he would not be shocked if the outgoing team was investigated by the authorities for corruption.

Contrary to what councillor Zele said about him going personally to the main square to calm down motorbike taxi riders agitating against the putsch by the *hommes politiques,* Abesolo accused the Mayor of rabble-rousing and attempting to instigate motorbike taxi riders to protest against the rejection of his list. He added that motorbike riders will support anyone who hires them provided they are well remunerated. Talking about motorbike riders brought to mind a recent speech by President Paul Biya to young people delivered annually on the eve of national youth day festivities celebrated every February 11. During that speech, the president urged Cameroonians not to look down on them, but to 'acknowledge their unquestionably useful social role' (PRC, 2013). In response, throngs of motorbike taxi riders stormed the streets of Yaoundé on 1st March 2013 in what was clearly a carefully choreographed march to the heavily fortified gates of the presidential mansion to thank the president for acknowledging them in his address.

Relations between state officials, municipal authorities and the police on the one hand and motorbike taxi riders, particularly those operating in urban areas, were often confrontational (Konings, 2006). Anger against the state reached its apex in 2008 during what was termed the 'food riots.' This was a bloody uprising that was spearheaded in part by motorbike taxi riders protesting against the rising cost of living brought about by a hike in fuel prices. The strike action eventually morphed into a violent revolt against plans by CPDM officials to remove the constitutional limits on the presidential term of office (Schneider, 2008 and New York Times, 2008). The constitutional amendment was eventually adopted, paving the way for president Biya, who at the time had been at the helm of state for twenty six years, to seek re-election indefinitely.

Interestingly, during the run-up to the Municipal and Legislative elections, CPDM officials, including senior Ministers and the Prime Minister, were reportedly warming up to an assembly of motorbike taxi riders at a ceremony in the capital Yaoundé, dubbed *Moto-citoyen*. The purpose of this event according to the organisers was to mobilise sensitive national groups about the impending elections (Le Messager, 2013). Others saw it as an attempt to placate a highly volatile group with the potential to create trouble for the state, as was the case in 2008. To Abesolo therefore, motorbike taxi riders are a hopeless bunch who haven't got much to lose, so that they can be manipulated by anybody. Having said that, he was quick to point out that allegations of a *soulèvement populaire* or popular movement in Mbankomo led by motorbike riders was simply false.

Back to the investiture saga, he said everyone from the DO to the ex-minister (who hosted several meetings prior to the arrival of the CC team) was not very fond of the Mayor and his team, but couldn't really do much to get rid of them until the opportune moment. He described the latter as a money-monger, who was reputed to have confiscated and sold privately owned plots of land. I heard rumours about land confiscations involving the Mayor, but my attempts to contact alleged victims proved futile; my attempts to meet the Mayor were like searching for a needle in a haystack.

Further, Abesolo described the Mayor as an 'absentee landlord' who only appears when important personalities are visiting town or during public events such as the installation of the DO. Accordingly, the Mayor abandoned the day-to-day management of the Council to some auxiliaries and other private hands. I must point out that throughout my fieldwork in Mbankomo (roughly four months), I only saw the Mayor in an official capacity during the installation of the DO and numerous attempts to arrange a meeting with him proved futile. I occasionally caught glimpses of him around town and on one occasion observed him (while standing on the porch of the council) transferring huge files of documents between two cars parked in front of the municipal ceremonial grounds, situated opposite the council premises. On that same occasion, I also observed him in his capacity as civil status registrar append his signature to some documents brought to him for legalisation on the boot of a parked Mercedes Benz car.

The Mayor, Abesolo went on, was working with a select team of individuals who were in his private pay. He had a personal assistant who was not a staff member of the council and was not accountable to anybody in the council. Moreover, he went on, the Mayor felt that delegating responsibility to his official deputies as required by law meant that people would see them at work instead of him. This was something he could not tolerate, for he wanted everyone to know that he was the only one in charge and didn't want anyone to uncover his alleged shady dealings.

As for the deputy Mayors, I once accompanied the second deputy and a team made up of a councillor, the sanitary officer, other council workers, and some ordinary people, whom I dubbed the 'hygiene team', on a tour of the town to enforce the municipality's weekly clean-up operations. From my observations, the hygiene team goes around the town every Tuesdays between 0800-1100 to ensure that residents and local business clean their surroundings and other public spaces. At the end of the process a municipal truck goes round to collect the heaps of garbage for disposal. During the hours allotted for these 'clean-up' exercises, local businesses in and around Mbankomo centre are required to close. Defaulters' business premises were often sealed-up, or equipment seized, and only released upon payment of a hefty fine of CFA 5000 FRS. The 'hygiene team' was led by the second deputy Mayor, whom Abesolo (also part of the team) unsurprisingly described as an experienced hand in management of municipal affairs. He also informed me that before this he was an official of the Yaoundé City Council.

According to Abesolo, the Mayor ran the council as his personal fiefdom, and literally side-lined everyone, including his first and second deputies. In his view, the first deputy Mayor was completely side-lined and she never showed up at the council. As a matter of fact, I only saw her at the Council on the day of the budget session (details in chapter VIII), which incidentally was the last council meeting before the 2013 municipal elections. As for the second deputy, Abesolo went on, he was always there as you (referring to me) might have noticed, but was completely side-lined and had to keep himself busy by supervising the weekly clean-up activities.

Back to the investiture saga, notably the list spearheaded by the *hommes politiques* and accusations that it overlooked the growing number of non-natives in the area. He said that was largely true, but there was a reason for it. Other than the Hausa-Fulani, none of the other communities (i.e. Anglophones and Bamilékés) are organised or have attained a critical mass that could enable them to gain representation at the council. Even if this was the case, it must get the approval of all the tribal groupings and not be carried out unilaterally. He then cited the example of Anglophones and cast doubt on the level of solidarity among them, wondering how they would fare if an opportunity for representation on the council was offered them. Their lacklustre showing during preparatory activities leading up to the installation of their headman (Mr Ahmadou), who was my host, goes a long way to showing how disunited they are. He went on to draw my attention to the fact that the person who read the speech (which I wrote following Mr Ahmadou's guidelines) on behalf of the Anglophone community was neither from the North West or the South West Regions, but from the Centre who happens to be a trusted confidante of my host and very fluent in the English language.

Abesolo didn't have kind words for the Bamiléké community either. The Bamilékés are often referred to as the Igbos of Cameroon, not least because of their astute business acumen. According to Abesolo, inasmuch as they are better organised, their modus operandi, especially the tendency to aggressively acquire landed property in Mbankomo, is quite suspect.[206] Suspicions of the Bamilékés in Cameroon are legend, some of the stereotypes associated with them are not dissimilar to those often held about Jewish people. They are seen as "smart, industrious, successful, rich, and conspirational, manipulate the economy, and live in ghettos and worship strange spirits" (Gabriel, 1999, p. 191).

Such stereotypes are mostly employed to explain their spectacular and inexplicable economic successes; they may also stem from envy.

---

[206] For more details on the sometimes uneasy relationship between Bamilékés and their host communities, see Ndjio (2006). Crisis and Creativity: Exploring the Wealth of the African Neighbourhood.

According to Abesolo, the few of them in this area serve as conduits for others who seek only to acquire land. In fact, he went on, a lot of them possess property in this town, but do not reside here. The Mayor's inclusive list was therefore uncalled for as these people (Anglophones and Bamilékés), are not committed to Mbankomo, they (particularly Bamilékés) are self-interested and don't have the interest of the indigenes at heart. He added that if the so-called inclusive list was specifically aimed at accommodating the Hausa-Fulani, it would have made some sense, but most Anglophones are not well established in Mbankomo and there is no solidarity among them. The Bamilékés exhibit a similar propensity, the only difference being their insatiable thirst for landed property.

I reminded him that he once told me he was from the South Region and an outsider in Mbankomo. He agreed, but said that he had lived long enough in Mbankomo to be well-versed in local realities; also people from the South were ethnically closer to those from the Centre, which is why he feels at home in Mbankomo, and is married to a local woman. It was based on this wealth of experience that he advised the Mayor not to 'rattle the hornet's nest' by disrupting the tribal arrangements in place; but he paid no attention. He was certain that the Mayor's attempt to change arbitrarily the way things always have been done here that ruffled the feathers of *les hommes politiques* and probably other 'native' members of the divisional committee, thereby provoking the decision to get rid of him. In his view, were such a list to be put up in big cities like Yaoundé or Douala, where people from non-indigenous backgrounds constitute the majority in some areas, it might work, but not in Mbankomo. He cited an example in the Littoral Region where a Bamiléké woman (Francois Foning) was Mayor of Douala V council for over a decade; this was simply because the area was predominantly inhabited by fellow Bamilékés.

7.7 Conclusion

The controversy over investiture of candidates by the CPDM did not only rage in Mbankomo; it was a national phenomenon. As a result, the CC headquarters in Yaoundé was inundated with petitions by militants of the party. For example, the outgoing Mayor of Mboma subdivision in the Centre Region, who felt 'cheated' following the investiture saga, was reported to have camped outside the CC headquarters seeking the annulment of her rivals' list (Le Messager, 2013).

As noted earlier, the Supreme Court served as the final arbiter for political parties seeking redress following the rejection of lists by ELECAM. However, the court turned down almost all opposition petitions. There were a few exceptions even so, one of them headed by legal luminary-turned-politician and leader of the *Mouvement pour la Renaissance du Cameroun* (MRC), Pr. Maurice Kamto,[207] whose lists in the Centre, West and Littoral Regions were reinstated following a court ruling (Le Messager, 2013). Meanwhile, there was an unprecedented case, pitting CPDM vs. CPDM. Here the out-going Mayor of Mengang subdivision in the outskirts of Yaoundé begged the court to annul the decision of ELECAM to approve the list of her rival which was submitted by the CPDM-CC, because in her view the CC rejected it without foundation and later grafted some names from her list and added it to that of her rival. The peculiarity of this case prompted the Advocate General of the court to remark *cette juridiction ne doit pas servir de terrain de bataille entre les membres d'une même famille*, / this court is an inappropriate forum for members of the same family to publicly wash their dirty linen (Le Jour, 2013). There was a similar case opposing CPDM militants from the *Mayo-Tsanaga Nord* in the Far North Region and also one from the *Haut-Nyong* in the East Region (Le Messager, 2013).

In the end, fear of a possible *vote sanction* or protest vote from grassroots militants never materialised and the CPDM ended up with another *écrasante majorité* of 305 out of 373 councils in Cameroon, including Mbankomo and Bali Councils.

---

[207]He was amongst the lead counsels for Cameroon in the case against Nigeria over the Bakassi Peninsula, which Cameroon eventually won. He was later appointed junior minister at the ministry of justice and is famous for being amongst the rarest species of minster in Cameroon to have resigned from President Biya's government without ending up in the infamous Yaoundé Central prison at Kondengui or in exile.

Chapter VIII

Decentralisation and Community Participation: Analysis and Discussion

8.1 Introduction

The government of Cameroon presents decentralisation as a panacea to the country's developmental challenges. Following constitutional reforms in 1996 and their implementation in 2004, community participation was actively promoted in the drafting of Council Development Plans. This document in principle constituted a blueprint for developmental activities in local municipalities in Cameroon. Experiments with forms of local 'governance' in Francophone and Anglophone Cameroon date back to the colonial era with institutions like the *Conseils de Notables* and Native Authorities.

Following independence and reunification, the first local government reforms occurred in 1974; this law[208] outlined the functions and number of councillors per municipal area. Decades later, the present format of decentralisation and community participation was adopted amid economic crisis and political turmoil. In 2004, as we have seen, the law on the orientation of decentralisation[209] and the law on rules applicable to councils were promulgated.[210] These established the modus operandi of local municipalities as envisioned by the Cameroon state. For example Sections (15-22) of the rules applicable to councils outline the powers devolved upon local municipal authorities. Sections (23-57) describe the organs of the council and Sections (58-108) detail the regulations governing the positions of Mayor and deputy Mayors. These statutory provisions in principle transformed elected municipal councils from bodies with minimal responsibilities like issuing birth and marriage certificates into full-fledged agents of local development, with powers to carry out economic, health, social and cultural development.

---

[208] Law N° 74/23of 5th December 1974 on the organisation of councils.
[209] Law N° 2004/017 of 22nd July 2004 on the orientation of decentralization.
[210] Law N° 2004/018 of 22nd July 2004 to lay down rules applicable to councils.

In the 1990s, Cameroon like most sub-Saharan countries experienced serious political upheavals. Unlike the others, Cameroon did not descend into anarchy nor was the regime in place swept aside. The adoption of decentralisation as a strategy to promote local democracy and ensure economic development was more out of political expediency than a genuine desire for fundamental political reform. On a positive note, the functions of municipal councils depart markedly from what obtained during the monolithic era; they also constitute the first point of contact with government for many citizens. This chapter therefore explores decentralisation and community participation in Cameroon and contrasts it with elsewhere in the Global South. It draws on the case studies of Bali and Mbankomo councils to highlight the permutations inherent in practical implementation of decentralisation policy. Finally, I analyse how both municipal institutions have been impacted by the changes that have taken place in local government in Cameroon since 2004.

8.2 Background

In chapter III, I noted a number of scenarios advanced to justify the longevity of the Cameroonian regime. I also noted how, during the tripartite conference that was held between 1991 and 1993 to discuss constitutional reform, the government controlled the agenda and outcome of the debate. However, the constitutional talks ran aground because Francophones sought a measure of decentralisation within the unitary state, while Anglophones demanded a return to the pre-1972 federal structure.

Some political parties also weighed into the constitutional debate, for example, the National Union for Democracy and Progress party proposed "an ambitious scheme for elected and sovereign local councils and elected mayors" (Takougang & Krieger, 1998, p. 185). On the other hand, the SDF party proposed a draft constitution whereby: (a) Local Government Councils shall constitute the focal points of development in the Federated State and (b) each Local Government Area shall be governed by Councillors elected by universal suffrage, through direct and secret ballot.[211] Despite these rather lofty constitutional

---

[211] Social Democratic Front (SDF). Proposed Constitution for Cameroon. Bamenda, December 16, 1994: Article 231(3).

propositions from the political opposition, the governing CPDM party had other ideas. This was manifested in Law No. 96-06 of 18 January 1996 to amend the Constitution of 2 June 1972. Article 1 (2) of this law stated that Cameroon is a decentralised unitary state. Besides the National Assembly, the statute also made provisions for the following new institutions:

1). Constitutional Council: According to Article 46, this council "shall have jurisdiction in matters pertaining to the Constitution. It shall rule on the constitutionality of laws. It shall be the organ regulating the functioning of the [state] institutions." The constitutional council is still awaited.

2). The Senate: According to Article 20 (1), the senate "shall represent the regional and local authorities." It shall be composed of one hundred senators representing ten per region. Of the ten senators outlined in Article 20 (2), seven are "elected by indirect universal suffrage on a regional basis and three are appointed by the President of the Republic." This constitutional provision laid dormant until 2013 when a pioneer senate was set up amid controversy over the legitimacy of the Electoral College chosen to vote senators. According to these statutes, senators are elected by members of Regional Councils. However, because the latter do not exist, municipal councillors were drafted in to perform this role. The mandate of these municipal councillors who were elected for five years in 2007 had by 2013 long expired, but was extended by presidential decree. Plans by the government to get the senate elected by councillors whose mandate was sustained by presidential decree caused outrage among the opposition.

In response to the decree[212] convening senatorial elections, the National Chairman of the main opposition SDF party called upon his militants to sharpen their machetes and be prepared to use them to prevent the elections from taking place. *Le 7 mars 2013, le chairman opère un revirement à 180° en demandant à toutes les instances régionales de son parti de préparer les sénatoriales. La nouvelle fait l'effet d'une bombe. Ce d'autant que c'est au sortir d'un « concile » avec le directeur du cabinet civil de la présidence de la République et ses proches collaborateurs* / On March 7, 2013, the chairman performed a 180° turnaround and called on all regional organs of his party to prepare for the senatorial elections. This spectacular reversal

---

[212] Decree 2013/056 on 27 February 2013

was a bombshell, specifically because it was announced following a 'conclave' he held with the Director of the Civil Cabinet at the Presidency of the Republic and his close aids (Le Messager, 2013).

3). Regional and Local Authorities: Article 55 (1), of the constitution states that "Regional and local authorities of the Republic shall comprise Regions and Councils." Whereas Councils have been in existence since independence, Regional Councils as per Article 57 (1) do not exist. Like Municipal Councils, where the powers of the 'representatives of the state' supersede that of elected councillors, Article 58 (1) states that: "A delegate, appointed by the President of the Republic, shall represent the State in the Region. In this capacity, he shall be responsible for national interests, administrative control, ensuring compliance with laws and regulations, as well as maintaining law and order." Under Article 59 (1), the President of the Republic can suspend the Regional Council because of activities contrary to the constitution as well as undermining state security and territorial integrity.

The 1996 constitution was slightly modified in 2008 to remove the limitation placed on the number of terms a president can run for office (Article 6 (2)).[213] Participation and community participation have gained a lot of currency in recent times because they were seen by donors and national governments as the best outlet for ordinary people to play active roles in the management of local affairs.

8.3 Participation

[T]he very notion of participation implies a contradiction since all state participative development is based on a compromise between the state's goals and the citizens' aspirations (Abram 1998, 6).

Participation, community participation, citizen participation, the people's voice, bottom-up development etc., can be looked at from many angles. Participation by a community can either be individual or collective, it can equally be through formal or informal channels, and generally involves "voicing demands, making choices, and being involved in projects" (Fiszbein, 1997, p. 1034). Participation according

---

[213] According to the 1996 constitution the presidential mandate initially ran for a period of seven years renewable once, but following changes in 2008 the president can run for office indefinitely.

to the UNDP denotes a situation where "people are closely involved in the economic, social, cultural, and political processes that affect their lives" (UNDP, 1993, p. 21). Participation in this context can be seen as a development strategy whereby ordinary people get the opportunity to make decisions over issues to do with their livelihoods. Community participation in development also involves transparency and accountability, respect for human rights and a greater role for local organisations (Atchrimi, 2014).

According to Ake, (1996, p. 8): "Democratic participation is about being involved in making decisions about our *res publica*," but in most African states political participation usually revolves around and peaks at election periods. In other countries participation may also involve direct action by individuals, interest groups and lobby groups. According to Devas and Grant (2003, 308), "participation is about the ways in which [people] exercise influence and control over the decisions that affect them." In Africa generally, popular oversight and control of officials (elected or appointed) is very uncommon and, wherever such rules apply, proper enforcement is always wanting. However, direct action by citizens is gaining ground on the continent, which at times may not be to the liking of the elite, who usually try to obstruct the participatory process (Calderón & Szmukler, 2004).

Actions (or in some instances inaction) by the elite have over the years engendered widespread disaffection in the masses. In Cameroon and Africa generally, political elites are notorious for appearing during election periods to distribute gifts and bribes in the guise of electioneering and then expect people to vote for them in return. Upon attaining their objectives, politicians vanish, only to reappear at the approach of the next election cycle. This feeds the contention that, besides the act of voting, what generally obtains in African politics (Cameroon being no exception) is "the traditional model of local government in which representatives are elected to make decisions on behalf of citizens with little or no input from those citizens between elections" (Calderón & Szmukler, 2004, p. 309).

Popular participation therefore involves individuals or groups. Individual participation could be in the form of voting or other forms of political activism, including campaigning and protests. However, both categories could fall under group actions. Group participation could be via community organisations, political parties, NGOs and other civic organisations (Calderón & Szmukler, 2004). It is not without challenges; for example, in a situation where "participatory development takes place through rural communities acting as decentralized decision-making bodies endowed with considerable allocation responsibilities, there is a serious risk that the available resources will be spread thinly over many people and projects" (Abraham & Platteau, 2004, p. 219). However, in some instances, the fear might not be of thinly spread resources, but rather communities might have different ideas about how to utilise the resources placed at their disposal. For example, following reforms of the forestry sector in Cameroon in 1994, local communities were entitled to 10% of tax generated from forest revenues. However, people in some communities perceived the tax stipend as "compensation for generations of exclusion" (Ribot & Oyono, 2005, p. 213) and as a result indulged in gratuitous exuberances.

Despite the shortcomings of the participation approach, it is favoured by governments and donors. This is because available 'financial resources' from donors serve as a catalyst for agencies to 'spread them widely' on development projects, with the ultimate goal of reaching as many village communities as possible. Likewise, an abundance of cash to spend on 'participatory projects' is often eagerly anticipated by recipient governments who, together with donors, 'rush' to implement development through schemes such as the PNDP in Cameroon. Moreover, donor enthusiasm for participatory schemes often generate high expectations of 'rapid and visible results' and thus "persuade constituencies or supporters [back home] that the new strategy works well" (Abraham & Platteau, 2004, p. 212). I now examine community participation as I experienced it during a study-abroad trip in the Adamawa Region of Cameroon.

8.4 Community Participation in Cameroon

The current largely donor-driven decentralisation projects in Africa are based on several interlinked master narratives: the democracy and grass-roots narrative, the accountability narrative and the governance narrative (Bierschenk and de Sardan 2003, 145).

Beginning in the 1990s, the idea of "decentralizing governance from capital cities to regions, towns and villages [was seen as] the best means of promoting participation and efficiency" (UNDP, 1993, p. 66). In principle, "decentralization is often hailed for moving government closer to citizens and providing opportunities for participation in decision-making" (Wong & Guggenheim, 2005, p. 253). Because decentralisation is often synonymous with 'deepening democracy', municipal councils are presented as suitable arenas for deliberation and dialogue, specifically because of their proximity to local people (Calderón & Szmukler, 2004). However, successful decentralisation depends on a variety of conditions, including "establishment of mechanisms to promote broad civic participation and more responsive and accountable local governments" (Wong & Guggenheim, 2005, p. 253).

Considering that participation was somehow 'rediscovered' as a viable approach to local development in Cameroon in 2004, it was deemed necessary for stakeholders to be familiarised with the techniques involved in the participatory process. This necessitated the creation of structures to channel resources for the implementation of development programs. In line with this objective the PNDP was set up.[214] The objective of the PNDP was to empower decentralised local councils in Cameroon and provide the means for them to carryout effective development projects within their localities (PNDP, 2009). The PNDP was therefore established as a partnership between donors and the government of Cameroon to promote civic participation in local development. The creation of the PNDP was followed by the promulgation of the law on the orientation of decentralisation[215] and the law on the rules applicable to councils.[216]

Against this backdrop in 2010, I took a semester from my Master's studies to carry out a research internship with PNDP in the Adamawa Region. My aim was to experience how community participation was implemented in Cameroon. During this exercise, I accompanied staff from PNDP Ngaoundere on a two-week field exercise in the towns of Meiganga, Ngaoui and Djohong in the Mbere Division. The objective was twofold: the first phase involved a series of meetings and seminars

---

[214] Prime Ministerial Decision N° 002/PM of 09 January 2004
[215] Law N° 2004/017 of 22 July 2004.
[216] Law N° 2004/018 of 22 July 2004.

in the town of Meiganga during which representatives from NGOs and community-based organisations (CBO) were trained in techniques of data collection using the participatory approach.

The second phase was to collect data in the towns of Ngaoui and Djohong. The ultimate goal for PNDP was to educate workers from local organisations and equip them with the tools to collect information for a prototype Council Development Plan (CDP). This was a test case for drafting CDPs in the Adamawa Region. On successful completion, the methods of this experimental exercise would be rolled out in other parts of the Region. The justification for involving NGOs and CBOs in drafting the prototype CDP was the perception by central governments and donors that "local organizations are by their nature closer to citizens, and thus, more capable of understanding and responding to them" (Alsop & Kurey, 2005, p. 4). In Cameroon, however, the involvement of local organisations was limited to collecting data from communities, drawing up plans and handing them to municipal authorities to be implemented in partnership with the PNDP.

At the end of the seminar in Meiganga, participants were split into two teams and dispatched to the towns of Ngaoui and Djohong respectively. I was part of the team that went to Ngaoui Subdivision. The fieldwork was conducted in two phases, (a) in the village of Garga Pella, and (b) in the small town of Ngaoui. This exercise took four days, two in each location. Our team consisted of seven people, including a senior staff person from PNDP Adamawa who served as supervisor. The entire exercise was coordinated by the Mayor of Ngaoui council. Prior to commencing data collection, the team to which I belonged was split into three groups[217] of two people, each assisted by facilitators from the community. In both locations, the population was divided into three categories, men, women and youths. Within these categories and

---

[217] Because of cultural sensitivities and the rather marginal role of women in such a predominantly Muslim and conservative milieu, there was no mixing of the crowds. Moreover, the aim of this study was to identify the problems as seen through the eyes of the different segments (youths, men & women) in the area. Hence, females were taken care of by the two women in our team, the old men by senior male members of our team, and the younger population by two youthful members of our team. Because most of the sessions were conducted in the local *Fufulde* language, my role was limited to (i) observing the sessions and (ii) assisting the teams with logistics. Nevertheless, I was actively involved in aspects that language did not constitute a barrier to, such as the collection of geo-referential data using GPS technology, as well as the outlining of the transect.

depending on the size of the area (village, town, city), population size and the variety of occupations and types of trades, the people were further splintered into smaller groups such as farmers, herders, traders, butchers, motorbike taxi riders, builders, mechanics etc. Each group brainstormed on a number of themes including healthcare, education, social services and infrastructure.

These core themes were further broken down into sub-themes. For example, education was split into primary, secondary, tertiary, and vocational. The problems inherent in each sub-theme was then pored over by the groups in greater detail and members were encouraged to provide possible solutions to how to go about tackling them. For example, in Garga Pella, which was quite a remote area, the problems in the education sector included dilapidated buildings, inadequate staff and a lack of accommodation for teachers. The endogenous solutions proposed included repairing the roofs with local materials i.e. thatch, recruiting teachers through the parent's teachers association (PTA) and construction of a house for teachers using local materials. For solving problems, people suggested the PTA and government support. The same method was used to diagnose the other issues faced by the village, as seen through the eyes of men, women and young people. At the end of the exercise, the NGOs and CBOs compiled data from themes discussed with the population, put them into a single document, in this case a prototype CDP, before handing it over to the Mayors of Ngaoiu and Djohong councils.

In 2013, while conducting fieldwork, I obtained copies of the CPDs for Mbankomo and Bali Councils from the PNDP. Interestingly, the methods used in drawing up the CDP for both councils were not different to what I experienced in Ngaoundere in 2010. Nevertheless, it is worth highlighting certain aspects of both documents. First, data collection, processing, and analysis was carried out by two NGO's or Local Support Organizations (LSO). In Bali, the LSO was the Sustainable Integrated Balanced Development Foundation (SIBADEF), and in Mbankomo the *Cercle des Promoteurs du Développement Durable (CPDD)*. The final documents were presented to the authorities of both municipalities, in January 2011 for Bali council and June 2011 for Mbankomo council. Unlike the prototype CDP, which took roughly a month to produce, drawing up the CDPs for Mbankomo and Bali councils took roughly 6 months each.

The CDP also contained a strategic investment plan for both councils, which was designed to run for a period of three years. Thus, the Triennial Investment Plan for Bali Council was estimated at CFA 30,698,630,784 francs and was meant to cover the investment needs of a subdivision of 85,058[218] people. That for Mbankomo amounted to CFA 12, 333, 831, 400 francs, and was also meant to run for three years. These triennial plans were further scaled down to Annual Investment Plans (AIP) amounting to CFA 210,250,748 francs for Bali and CFA 112,181,000 francs for Mbankomo. The Mayors of both councils were responsible for determining projects to be executed annually. Finally, the review mechanism of the CDP and the assessment procedures of the AIP recommended the following:

> *The council development plan will be reviewed at the end of each year. A Strength, Weaknesses, Opportunities and Threats (SWOT) analysis approach will be used during the review. This will give room for effective review as well as ensure that strategies are being put in place to overcome future challenges. Projects planned in the previous year but not implemented will be re-planned alongside the operational plan for the next year.*

Unlike in Cameroon where community participation is limited to citizens providing raw data for the drafting of CDPs to NGOs, CBOs, LSOs etc., the cases examined below go much further and could be argued to be viable examples of 'effective decentralisation' because they exemplify "downwardly accountable, or representative authorities with meaningful discretionary powers" (Ribot, 2003, p. 159). These cases provide ample examples of active community participation involving ordinary people drafting municipal budgets, a Mayor personally going out to the community to discuss budget priorities, and another Mayor having powers to appoint officials within a district.

8.5 Decentralisation and Community Participation: Experiences from the Global South

Like most places in the global South, Latin America went through a long period when local government institutions merely performed

---

[218] Bali Council Monographic Study, August 2005.

ceremonial functions and had virtually no financial autonomy nor decision-making powers. However, things changed in the 1980s. Previously, Colombia had roughly 900 local municipalities that were led by appointed Mayors and locally elected municipal councillors. By the late 1980s the country introduced constitutional reforms granting more resources and greater decision-making powers to municipal authorities. The latter became responsible for provision of services such as education, healthcare, water supply, and sanitation.

In the municipality of Valledupar, "the mayor established a Press and Information Office that disseminated government programs through a 30-minute daily radio program" (Fiszbein, 1997, p. 1030). From 1992, the Mayor also had powers to appoint officials in the 14 *corregimientos* or townships in Valledupar without consulting central authorities. Such extraordinary power transfers to a local municipal official made Colombia an exemplar of democratic decentralisation of resources, tasks and decision making powers (Manor 1995). The transformative effects of decentralisation reforms had impressive results in Colombia; other successful cases include examples from Brazil, Bolivia, India, and Uganda.

The Brazilian port city of Porto Alegre has earned worldwide acclaim for its grassroots planning scheme known as 'the participatory budgeting'. This was introduced by the *Partido dos Trabalhadores* (PT) or Workers' Party in 1989. Upon assuming power, the PT introduced an experimental process whereby community groups were integrated into the process of drawing up municipal budgets. According to Heller (2001, p. 140); "the key innovation [was] the creation of district and countrywide budget councils consisting of delegates elected in open assemblies at neighbourhood and district levels." However, because of the difficulties some ordinary citizens encountered in grasping the technical aspects of the budgeting process, the municipality elected to limit the role of participants to determining priorities for spending rather than how resources would be allocated in detail. This led to a situation where "district councils in some cities were open to the public and in others they were formed by delegates from neighbourhood associations" (Abers, 1996, p. 44).

Next door in Bolivia, the Popular Participation (PP) law promulgated in April 1994 opened avenues for participation and representation by remote indigenous communities that were previously marginalised at the local municipal level. The PP law established new relations between the authorities and the people, and also enabled local actors to play prominent roles in municipal affairs. The PP law prescribed the repartitioning of fiscal revenues according to population density, so as to ensure equity in the distribution of available resources between cities and rural areas. Consequently, "municipal governments assumed responsibility for the planning and execution of programs intended to promote individual betterment at the local level" (Calderón & Szmukler, 2004, p. 301).

In India, the election that ushered the Communist Party of India-Marxist (CPM) into power in Kerala state in 1996 was followed by the introduction of a People's Campaign for Decentralised Planning. According to Heller (2001, p. 139), this campaign represented "the boldest and most comprehensive decentralisation initiative yet to be undertaken in India." The participatory campaign in Kerala was quite elaborate and multi-layered. Its practical implementation kicked off at the ward-level where general assemblies were presided over by local government or Panchayat officials. In the first stage, ordinary people defined and outlined development priorities and elected members to sit on the committee charged with drafting the local development report.

The second stage involved the appointment by the Panchayat of a special taskforce consisting of elected officials, communist party activists and local government officials to formulate projects from grassroots proposals. The main function of these groups was to bridge the gap between direct citizen participation and local government action. Meanwhile, another intermediate layer of actors, notably women's self-help groups, were also very active in the taskforces and technical review committees. Other local actors included NGOs, albeit those sympathetic to the ruling communist party, but whose actions nevertheless boosted the overall representativeness of elected Panchayats and ensured efficient service delivery to beneficiary communities.

Another interesting case from India is the State of Odisha. Previously the state budgeting process was out of bounds for most ordinary people and there were no opportunities for civil society organisations to present the views of grassroots people to the state administration. Further, because legislators did not possess adequate capacity and skills to master the budgeting process, the whole exercise was left in the hands of the executive. However, things changed in 2003 following the formation of the Centre Youth and Social Organisation (CYSO), later renamed the Odisha Budget and Accountability Centre (OBAC). This organisation was involved in building training schemes for budget literacy and the use of the budget as a device to monitor development programmes in the state. OBAC disseminated large amounts of analytical information in a simplified format to government officials and legislative members, to help them understand the budget allocation system and it also provided feedback on the state budget to local communities. This was mostly carried out through community radio programmes and small group discussions. Community aspirations were also compiled in district 'Charters of Demand' which were presented for approval to state pre-budget discussion sessions and finally to the state government for consideration in its final budget allocations (Mishra, 2014).

In Uganda, constitutional reforms in 1995 were followed by passing the Local Government Act of 1997. This transferred significant amounts of responsibility to the 45 District councils and 903 sub-county municipal authorities (van de Walle, 2003). This law succeeded in creating a system of participatory decision-making and provided "multiple opportunities for citizens, including the poor, to participate in public meetings and elections, from the village level up to the district" (Devas & Grant, 2003, p. 312). A key aspect of popular participation in Uganda is the system of annual budget conferences. These meetings were held at village as well as district levels and were designed to give opportunities for local people to put forward ideas about project priorities for the coming year. Some shortcomings of this project included the fact that meetings did not occur frequently and also the dwindling number of participants at budget events. However, in "Entebbe, the mayor undertook a major 'budget outreach' exercise each year, visiting villages to discuss priorities with residents, accompanied by municipal officials, councillors and civil society organisations" (ibid, 213).

Still in Uganda, and within the framework of a pilot governance programme known as Mwananchi, ten organisations were given grants by the UK Department of International Development (DFID) to implement innovative good governance and accountability-focused projects in six districts. Coordinated by the ODI, the projects included a community-based civil courts system, i.e. 'Bataka court' Village Budget Clubs, and Child Education Monitors. This project was a good example of donors, communities and civil society acting together to address local problems. However, the project faced some challenges, including a lack of mechanisms to enforce Bataka court decisions, resistance by some duty bearers to provide information to the Village Budget Clubs and the fact that some child monitors became victims of their own success by becoming envied at school by other pupils and even some teachers (Ssebunya, 2014). However, the project succeeded in empowering parents and pupils to demand accountability from service providers and increased overall citizen participation in civil litigation matters.

These examples have shown how community participation operates in countries that introduced local government reforms around the same period as Cameroon. The status of municipal councils in Cameroon is a significant departure from what obtained previously, specifically since the country now boasts Mayors elected via popular universal suffrage rather than appointed municipal administrators. However, a major setback for grassroots autonomy in Cameroon is the fact that municipal councils in major urban areas are grouped into city councils, where elected Mayors are lorded over by appointed Government Delegates vested with powers to manage council projects and financial resources. Moreover, city councils and municipal councils are also subjected to stringent oversight by the SDOs who are also known as 'representatives of the state'.

In Cameroon, election campaigns and the act of voting are the only observable exercises where active community participation actually occurs, if indeed such activities could be categorised as community participation. The credibility of the electoral process as demonstrated in previous chapters has over the years been the subject of much controversy if not acrimony. Consequently, the viability of elections as a genuine outlet for community participation is therefore in doubt. To confound things further, consultation (be it at the local or national level) that occurs between electoral cycles is practically non-existent. Instead it is entirely up to Mayors to pick and choose which projects to implement from the CDPs, which in a sense is exactly what they were elected to do. But again, elections in Cameroon, like elsewhere in Africa "are often contested on the basis of personalities and or ethnicities rather than on clear programmes or manifestos" (Devas & Grant, 2003,

p. 307) and the few ideas that are often splashed around appear more like vote-buying techniques than concrete policy ideas or proposals.

Elected Mayors have practically no manifestos, and investment plans from the CDPs are usually implemented in a haphazard manner, if at all. Worse, they may be subject to personal, tribal or other biases, or worse still depend on funding directly from the central government or auxiliary structures such as the PNDP; the inevitable question therefore is what kind of decentralisation are we really talking about? Further, granting opportunities for Mayors to decide on priority projects in municipalities makes them appear quite powerful. However, they count on the powers and interventions by the 'representatives of the state' who are appointed by the head of state, Paul Biya.[219] I next examine issues related to budgets and administrative accounts, public procurements, and income generation in Mbankomo and Bali councils.

8.6 Municipal Authorities and Public Procurement in Cameroon

In Cameroon, a public contract is defined as any written agreement drafted in accordance with the provisions of the public contracts code. According to the terms of this agreement, a contractor, supplier or service provider gives an undertaking to the state, a decentralized authority, a public institution, a public sector company or a parastatal to carry out works or to supply goods or services for a fee, Article 5 (1).[220] Other provisions of the text include Article 7 (1): Public contracts are awarded following competitive tenders from potential contractors.[221] Further, Article 7 (2) states that public contracts may also be awarded under exceptional circumstances via a procedure known as *gré à gré* i.e. by mutual agreement.[222] However, the sum of money involved under this procedure must not exceed CFA 5 million francs.

According to Article 71 (1) of the rules applicable to councils, the Mayor shall be responsible for directing council projects, ensuring the implementation of development programmes financed by the council or carried out in conjunction with the council. Further, the Mayor shall also

---

[219] For details on the origins and evolution of these authorities see Elong 2013; Bayart 2009; Takougang & Krieger, 1998; Johnson 1970 and Rubin 1971.

[220] Decree N°2004/275 of 24 September 2004.

[221] Decree N°2004/275 of 24 September 2004.

[222] Decree N°2004/275 of 24 September 2004.

take measures concerning the municipal road network, invite tenders, conclude leases and award contracts for council works.[223] However, a cabinet reshuffle[224] in December 2011 witnessed the creation of a Minister Delegate at the Presidency in charge of Public Contracts. A subsequent decree[225] reorganised the functioning of the public contracts commission, placing it under this ministry, effectively dissolving tender commissions at the level of municipal councils and stripping Mayors of the authority to award contracts in their municipalities.

A key reason cited for the elimination of municipal tender boards was *dysfonctionnements dans les procédures de passation de marches* (Cameroon Tribune, 2013). These shortcomings often ranged from abandoned projects to corruption and red-tape. It was hoped that, with the centralisation of these commissions at the divisional level, public contracts would be awarded swiftly, corrupt practices would be extinguished and monitoring of projects would be much more efficient. However, the reasoning behind the state's decision to dissolve municipal tender boards nationwide opens a 'can of worms.' For example Mezam Division is made up of seven subdivisions with each having a municipal council; this includes Bamenda which was recently upgraded to the status of a City Council and split into Bamenda I, II and III. It is therefore puzzling why the authorities deemed it much more efficient to move the tender boards from a decentralised to a centralised structure, considering that this only increased bureaucratic complexity and created a mammoth task for the divisional commissions. This certainly qualifies as a subject for future research. Meanwhile, before this drastic step by the government, local councils, as seen in the following example from Bali, enjoyed the privilege of awarding contracts for projects within their municipalities.

8.6.1 Delegated Credit for Rural Roads Maintenance in Bali

Cameroon began what is known in official circles as a *transfert des compétences* or skills transfer in 2010, whereby government ministerial departments allocate resources or credits to municipal councils to enable them to carry out activities falling within the jurisdiction of specific ministerial departments. These ranged from education and healthcare to

---

[223] Law N° 2004/018 of 22nd July 2004.
[224] Decree N° 2011/408 of 9 December 2011.
[225] Decree N° 2012/075 of 8 March 2012.

infrastructure. According to government figures, this process has enabled the rehabilitation of 2,214 classrooms and the construction, equipment and renovation of 351 health centres across the country (Cameroon Tribune, 2013). These projects are executed following public tenders; but the procedures for awarding contracts in Cameroon can be quite complex and often involve the disbursement of considerable financial resources before starting the project. As the following example shows, part of the money allocated for the rehabilitation of rural roads in Bali was actually swallowed up by attendance fees for people invited to examine tenders and other miscellaneous expenses.

In 2005, the Mayor of Bali Council and the Ministry of Public Works signed an accord[226] for the maintenance of four priority roads within the municipality. The roads included: Bawock-Pinyin (Nkonfune) road (13.70km), Ntanfoang-Mbufung-Guzang road (12.30km), Bali-Bossa-Bome road (11.90km) and Njenka-Ngwandikang (7.15km).[227] The contract was awarded to a local construction company, Merenge Constructions (pseudonym). According to the Mayor of Bali:

The total amount of the contract was CFA 9,618.324 francs, but due to all manner of taxes and other administrative bottlenecks, the actual credit that was made public was around CFA 7 million francs. Unfortunately the money was not paid to me or to the treasurer of the council. Instead, the government placed it as a bond at the public treasury and instructed whoever is awarded the contract after passing through the council tender board to purchase the bond from the treasury. I therefore had to spend close to CFA 1 million francs to summon a tender board. The purpose of these meetings was to select a contractor who then had to go and purchase a bond from the treasury before carrying out the roadworks. Because of red-tape, the money arrived at the Bamenda treasury in late November and, according to the finance law of Cameroon, if you don't struggle to get that money out of the treasury before the end of November, you might lose it. So out of fear of losing the entire sum we hastily approved a bid by one contractor. Taking advantage of the rather vulnerable position we found ourselves in, he (the contractor) proposed to use his connections to get the money out of the treasury, but would only give the council around CFA 4million

---

[226] Agreement N° 0439/CP of 16 September 2005.

[227] Correspondence addressed to the Minister of Public Works Cameroon by the Mayor of Bali Council, dated 9th May 2006.

francs. So from CFA 9 million francs Bali council lost over half the amount. What kind of decentralisation is this?[228]

In a report to the Minister of Public Works, the Mayor provided a detailed breakdown of how the money was spent. It began with the agreement signed with Merenge Co. Ltd, which required it to advance the sum of CFA 4,865.945 francs to the council. However, instead of the required amount, Merenge coughed up the sum of CFA 4,750.000 francs instead. As if not living up to its commitments were not enough, other expenses slowly crept into the list of requirements. First, in addition to the unspecified taxes mentioned above, an additional Value Added Tax (VAT), also an unspecified amount, was charged on the vouchers drawn from the public treasury.[229] As detailed below, the rest of the items in the Mayor's report were classified under broad headings that were in some cases broken down into smaller themes.

Under rubric (A) titled 'Tender Expenses,' CFA 1,075.000 francs were paid to tender board members for four sittings and CFA 125.000 francs were used for the production of tender files in English and French. Rubric (B) was captioned 'Mobilisation, Sensitisation and Training of Road Maintenance Committee and Animators.' The expenses here included unveiling the programme in Bali, reception of the Minister and the purchase of light tools, amounting to CFA 639,000 francs. Rubric (C) was captioned 'Credit Distribution to Road maintenance Committees for payment of manual labour intensive work.' The sum of CFA 1,400.000 francs was distributed to committees in the four areas where road maintenance was to be carried out. Rubric (D) was captioned 'Caterpillar repairs of high degradation.' This had one section (Bawock-Pinyin road) out of the four sections and amounted to CFA 500,000 francs. Rubric (E) was captioned 'Management of rain gates from May to September 2006.' Here the sum of CFA 200,000 francs was distributed to individuals in the four areas to manage two rain gates for a period of five months. Rubric (F) was captioned 'Supervision or follow-up expenses' and amounted to CFA 729,150. Finally rubric (G) was for the production of work schedules by technicians from the Ministry of Public Works, this amounted to CFA 200,000 francs. The

---

[228] Interview conducted in Bali on 03/01/2014.

[229] Correspondence addressed to the Minister of Public Works Cameroon by the Mayor of Bali Council, dated 9th May 2006.

total sum of these expenditures was CFA 4,743,150 francs out of an available credit of CFA 4,750,000 francs.[230]

Meanwhile, Bali Council also had to make a contribution of 30% of the total decentralised credit of CFA 7,869,539 francs which amounted to CFA 2,460,895 francs. The Mayor's report also detailed how this latter amount was spent; but the CFA 2,870,000 francs contributed by the council turned out to be slightly above the 30% required by law. In the end, the Mayor expressed deep dissatisfaction with what he called the experimental phase of the management of decentralised credit to municipal councils, which in his view was steeped in bureaucratic red tape and mired by corrupt practices.

The shortcomings encountered during the transfer of credits for road maintenance and other activities to local municipalities prompted the government to reform the public procurements sector. This witnessed the creation of a specialised ministry in charge of public contracts placed under the presidency and the dissolution of municipal tender boards in favour of divisional tender commissions. I wonder if this was an appropriate solution for the shortcomings in the public procurement sector in Cameroon. Was it not better to streamline the bureaucratic red-tape so as to facilitate disbursement of credits directly to local municipalities? Or, as the Mayor of Bali Council suggested, was it not better to transfer such credits directly into council bank accounts?[231]

Further, was it not appropriate to strengthen the accountability of local municipalities by promoting mechanisms that ensure proper checks and balances, backed by regular auditing of council operations and lengthy jail terms for those found guilty of malpractice? Or was the government never keen on implementing decentralisation in the first place, but constrained by circumstances; and later sensed an opportunity in the shortcomings of a broken system to retake powers it reluctantly handed down to local municipalities? Future research may show how this ostensibly new system of awarding contracts through divisional commissions has eliminated the shortcomings of its predecessor and has rendered the process free of corruption and other administrative

---

[230] Correspondence addressed to the Minister of Public Works Cameroon by the Mayor of Bali Council, dated 9th May 2006.

[231] Correspondence addressed to the Minister of Public Works Cameroon by the Mayor of Bali Council, dated 9th May 2006.

bottlenecks. The next section examines the use of the term 'local authority' in Bali, analysing the controversy it generated over plans by municipal authorities to upgrade the roads infrastructure within the town.

8.6.2 Local Authority in Bali: A Contradiction in Terms

Apparently, government red tape was not the only issue affecting road construction in Bali. Local complexities also sometimes constituted stumbling blocks to development initiatives. In 2002-3, corruption and red-tape were certainly a formidable ingredient that the elites of Bali and neighbouring Batibo had to deal with in their efforts to ensure that the stretch of road that forms the Lagos to Mombasa line of the Trans-Africa Highway Network was not diverted to pass through neighbouring Mbengwi subdivision. According to Page, Evans and Mercer (2010, p. 363), local elites "collected money to pay officials in Yaoundé in order to guarantee that the relevant papers moved through the system, that the contractor was paid promptly, and the work completed." This project was funded by the African Development Bank and contracted to the China International Water and Electricity Corporation (CWE). The CWE road construction project in Bali was subject to great controversy, particularly over the issue of local authority. Did the term local authority in this instance refer to the elite? The traditional authorities? Or to elected municipal authorities?

The story goes that during this road construction project, CWE had undertaken to pay royalties to the local authorities, i.e. Bali Council, on behalf of the population, for the exploitation of quarries, laterite, and disturbances of a general nature. In a situation reminiscent of the indemnities paid to Bali following the 1952 conflict with neighbouring communities, the local authorities in 2002-3 faced the dilemma of how to quantify the level of compensation to be paid to individuals for what one informant termed 'the inconveniences suffered' during this project. The difficulties involved in devising an appropriate mechanism for distributing said royalties was such that, instead of requesting cash, the council authorities asked CWE, as a side-line to constructing this highway, to rehabilitate and tar approximately 11km of roads in Bali town. The company returned a couple of days later to inform the municipal authorities that the cost of constructing 11km would be far more than the monetary compensation it was expected to pay. After further negotiations, both sides agreed on half the distance, approximately 5.5km.

Following this understanding between the authorities of Bali Council and CWE, the latter embarked on the preparatory phases of construction by grading and compacting the earmarked stretches of road in Bali town. The company began tarring some segments, starting with the stretch leading to the main government hospital in Bali which was seen as a priority for obvious reasons. It then moved to a very hilly area (Boh-Etoma), which had been a thorn in the side of many in Bali for generations. Suddenly the construction was halted without completing all the earmarked roads and CWE began hurriedly carting away its equipment overnight. The rest of the story is recounted by an eyewitness, who was then deputy Mayor in charge of road works at Bali Council.

> *I mobilised the population and we blocked the caterpillars and other heavy equipment. However, I was embarrassed that some personalities (whose name I will not mention), calling themselves local authorities, brought in gendarmes and ordered them to arrest me first and shoot at anybody who attempted to block CWE from leaving Bali. The actions of these individuals confirmed the fears of many that they had taken money from CWE. If somebody who pretends to be a Bali man and a deputy Mayor is mobilising the population to block a company in order to compel it to fulfil its obligations and you not only defend the company but go as far as threaten to use violence to dislodge people claiming their rights, it means your hands are soiled. This is why I will not mention names, but all I can say is that the so-called local authorities are the elites of Bali who were prepared to use force to stop the population from blocking CWE equipment. In the end they prevailed and CWE carried away its equipment without completing the 5.5km and without any explanation.[232]*

In the above clash between the elite and the masses, the former backed by the threat of force triumphed. They were former and current state officials and affiliates who promptly and effectively deployed the mechanisms of coercion to cow the population into submission. According to some informants, CWE could not have breached the agreement without the complicity of some member of the elite who

---

[232] Interview conducted in Bali on 03/01/2014.

most likely took money from the company and gave them the green light to leave. It could also be that these were some of the people mentioned by Page, Evans and Mercer (2010), who saw an opportunity to recoup the money they used to oil the corrupt state mechinery in Yaoundé to get the construction process off the ground in the first place, and hence were in no mood to compromise on the opportunity for a 'return on their investment.'

According to Fokwang (2003, p. 118): "Almost every contentious issue in Bali could be explained in terms of party politics. Apparently the 'demons' were CPDM militants, while the 'saints' were the SDF."[233] This dichotomy was certainly at play over the issue of royalties from CWE. At the time of the incident, the SDF party was in control of Bali Council and, according to the former Mayor, was being harassed by CPDM elites to give up the council, so that development projects can come to Bali. Yet, while a development project initiated by the SDF party was under way, it was the same elite (under the banner of local authority), the majority of whom belonged to the CPDM, that allegedly torpedoed plans to beautify the town with paved roads, according to the agreement between Bali Council authorities and CWE. According to the former Mayor of Bali, "the word local authority had an overtone which gave us the impression that some elites claimed to CWE that they were the local authorities and by dint of that gave them the clearance to leave. How such actions bring development to Bali, I wonder…"[234]

8.7 Mbankomo: Revenue Collection in Disarray

Controversy over local development did not only brew in Bali. In Mbankomo a group of individuals, including councillors and other council staff, took the initiative to generate revenue for the council from a bi-weekly roadside market. However, their plans was abruptly halted because they apparently did not have the required mandate to do so. As mentioned earlier, elected Mayors, under section 71 of the Rules Applicable to Councils,[235] can authorise expenditure and prescribe

---

[233] Fokwang J. T. D (2003) Chiefs and democratic transition in Africa: an ethnographic study in the chiefdoms of Tshivhase and Bali. Master's Thesis, University of Pretoria.

[234] Interview conducted in Bali on 03/01/2014.

[235] Law N° 2004/018 of 22nd July 2004.

revenue collection. Section 71 (1) also grants them powers to delegate functions to deputy Mayors and if need be to councillors. In Bali the newly elected Mayor following the September 2013 municipal elections assigned specific responsibilities to each of his four deputies. These included, water supply (first deputy), education (second deputy), revenue and recovery (third deputy), and human resources/personnel (fourth deputy).

In Mbankomo, [see above for this story] the third deputy Mayor was responsible for supervising a weekly hygiene and sanitation activity during which a team of people dubbed the 'hygiene team' went round every Tuesday from dawn to 11:00am to enforce the council's directive for citizens and local business owners to clean their surroundings. At some point, they[236] came up with an initiative to generate revenue for the Council from a bi-weekly roadside market. They sought and obtained the authorisation of the Mayor, who later called it off. Curiously, Mbankomo town has a market with roofing and individual stalls for vending; this facility was built by the council to serve as the main market for the town. The expectation was that it would be occupied by the vendors who ply their wares at the bi-weekly road-side market every Wednesday and Saturday, and also others who occupy different spots around the town deemed illegal by the council. Other than a handful of vendors who sporadically occupy a few rows, the market was deserted.

Councillor Amugu (pseudonym), a member of the hygiene team, informed me that he took the initiative to approach the Mayor and got his consent to carry out the revenue collection scheme on the understanding that the money would be paid into council coffers. This he thought could serve as money to fuel the council truck that goes round every Tuesday to collect refuse generated by the clean-up activities. However, after successfully collecting the money on the first day, some people began questioning why the dedicated council staff were not carrying out the exercise instead.

The scheme's mode of operation was that each vendor was required to pay CFA 100 francs per market day. Asked why they took it on themselves to do what is supposed to be the council's job, considering that the municipality had people whose responsibility was to collect

---

[236] All of them were members of the 'hygiene team,' but for the second deputy Mayor.

revenue, Amugu said that the initiative came out of a realisation that none of the official revenue collectors seemed bothered about a potentially significant source of revenue for the municipality, so they took it upon themselves to carry out the scheme. On the first day they raised close to CFA 30,000 francs. I asked if they issued receipts and was informed that they intended doing that on subsequent occasions but it never occurred because the scheme was discontinued by the Mayor.

I also asked councillor Zele about the activities of the 'hygiene team' and their unsuccessful attempt to collect money on behalf of the Council. He had a rather unflattering opinion about it. He acknowledge that the idea was put forward by councillor Amugu in a council session, but it didn't get the approval of the assembled councillors. They somehow convinced the Mayor to approve the scheme. Councillor Zele felt it was not proper to collect money from vendors at the roadside because they were located in an open and hazardous space, exposed to the elements and without sanitary or toilet facilities. I put it to him that there is a market right outside his house which was not being used. He agreed, but quickly added that the appropriate sanitary facilities required for the proper functioning of the market were not yet in place, but the council was working on it and as soon as everything was ready they would invite the authorities to inaugurate the market officially.

As chairman of the social affairs committee of Mbankomo council, he was not happy to learn that the Mayor had given his go-ahead to the members of the 'hygiene team.' Councillor Zele starkly contradicted the information I received from councillor Amugu about the number of times they went out to collect the market levy. According to Zele, they went three times and as they attempted to conduct the fourth exercise, market women marched to his house expressing their disapproval. He immediately rang the Mayor to report the incident and the latter ordered an immediate halt to the collection exercise. To Councillor Zele, the 'hygiene team' were a dubious bunch who, despite the tacit approval of the Mayor, did not have the rightful authority to carry out revenue collection without being accompanied by someone from the finance department or the council treasury. He also wondered where they kept the money they collected, because there was no evidence in the council that they had actually paid any money into its coffers. In the course of piecing together the details of this story, I spoke to the *Percepteur Municipale* or treasurer, the *Comptables Matières* or Accountant, and the

Agent Financiere or Finance Officer, but no-one knew anything about the money that was collected by the 'hygiene team,' even though they insisted that the money was paid to the council. It was difficult to get to the bottom of the story and, as I have said, I never succeeded in talking to the Mayor.

8.8 Discussion and Conclusion

I rounded up my fieldwork in both municipalities by attending two very important meetings. The first took place on 13 September 2013 in Mbankomo town hall. This was the last council meeting of the year and was convened to examine the Mayor's administrative accounts. It also took place on the eve of the September 30 municipal/legislative elections. This was the first time for me to see all councillors gathered together in one setting. By law Mbankomo council is supposed to have 25 councillors; but on this occasion 23 councillors were expected and 21 were effectively present. Two councillor were unavoidably absent and in conformity with Section 32 (2) of the rules applicable to councils,[237] they 'gave legalised proxies to their peers to vote for them.' Another councillor was deceased, and the final absentee was the former Mayor who fled to France fearing arrest because of his alleged implication in a financial scandal that saw the trial and conviction of the Director General of the state-run National Petroleum Storage facility or SCDP,[238] a native of Mbankomo.

This meeting was the first opportunity to reunite the outgoing council team, following the investiture process in Mbankomo. It commenced with the new Secretary General of the council welcoming everyone present and outlining the purpose of the meeting which was to examine the Mayor's administrative account. She then handed over the floor to the outgoing Mayor who presented a statistical summary of the administrative account. Not surprisingly, he drifted a bit from the main item on the agenda by stating that "whatever happened during the investiture is now history, and now is the time for party militants to put all their differences aside and work for the success of the party in the upcoming elections."[239] This came in the wake of the bruising

---

[237] Law N° 2004/018 of 22nd July 2004
[238] Société Camerounaise des Dépôts Pétrolière.
[239] Statement by the outgoing Mayor of Mbankomo Council on 13/09/2013.

'investiture saga' when his attempt to seek re-election was thwarted by a formidable array of CPDM officials. These included retired former ministers and current government officials including a cabinet minister(s).

Following the Mayor's statement, the floor was handed over to the SDO who began by lauding the excellent collaboration between the Mayor and all local administrative authorities. He also noted that Mbankomo had always recorded brilliant scores for the CPDM in elections in his time as *Préfet* of the Mefou and Akono Division, and he was sure it would be the same in the upcoming elections. Regarding the 'investiture saga', he commended the Mayor's 'exemplary' spirit of reconciliation and his positive attitude towards the upcoming elections. Finally he called on the outgoing councillors not to turn their backs on the council when their mandates expired. Rather, they should continue to play active roles in development activities in their respective areas.

In sum, the meeting proceeded with a rather smooth examination of the budget. Other than a hiccup about a CFA 5 million francs subvention granted by the Ministry of the Environment for the planting of trees in Mbankomo, which was omitted from the administrative accounts 'by mistake', the rest of the meeting went smoothly and the Mayor's administrative account was approved by acclamation.

The second meeting I attended took place at Bali Council on 18 December 2013 and the agenda was to examine the Council budget for 2014. Events kicked off in dramatic fashion as the newly elected Mayor was taken ill and had to be rushed to hospital, but was sent home and asked to rest. On the day he was elected at the Bali Multipurpose Hall, the Mayor described himself as 'man of action and few words.' This action-man mantra led him to go to the office very early in the morning, sometimes without eating breakfast. Commenting on this health scare, the SDO, while performing his functions as 'representative of the state', advised that the Mayor be told to always eat before leaving home in the mornings, so as to avoid a repeat in future. The consequence of this 'crisis' was that the rest of the budget session was chaired first by the Second deputy Mayor and later by the First deputy who had accompanied the Mayor to the hospital and returned when he was discharged and sent home.

For most councils in Cameroon, local income-generating capacity is weak and susceptible to corrupt practices, so that the temptation to rely on state subventions is quite high and for good reason. Sections 22-27 of the law on the orientation of decentralisation[240] details the various mechanisms through which the state finances local municipalities. These measures include 'tax transfers or ceded revenue' or both; there is also a Common Decentralisation Fund which is financed by funds drawn from the annual state budget. With such a vast array of state subventions at their disposal, the incentive for local municipalities to develop alternative sources of finances is quite low. Moreover, these measures might have been designed by the central authorities in Yaoundé to keep a close eye on the finances of local municipalities. However, as the law of unintended consequences goes, such measures might be good for central control but bad for grassroots autonomy, because they engender a dependency culture whose narcotic power can be quite addictive. Going by the discussions during the budget session in Bali, it appeared that the council budget had over-relied on state subventions. As a result, the SDO recommended that the council revise the budget, seek ways to curb expenditures and also to improve local income-generating capacity rather than relying too much on state subsidies.

Meanwhile, in a move that was designed to boost the revenue-generating and collection capacities of local municipalities, the PNDP entered into partnership and provided every council in Cameroon with two key staff members, a Finance officer and a Development officer. Their function was to develop and strengthen the income-generating capacity of local municipalities. It appeared they had not done their job in this instance or maybe there were simply no significant revenue sources in Bali for the council to be less reliant on state subventions. In any case, following the SDO's remarks, the acting chair of the budget session and second deputy Mayor called upon the staff members concerned to take note and take immediate action.

The next highlight was the formation of committees, including the Finance, Projects, Health and Sanitation, Education and Cultural affairs, Communications and External Relations, Socio-Economic and Agricultural affairs committees. Following the election of the Mayor a few weeks earlier, councillors were requested to submit CV's and indicate which committee they felt competent to be part of. The budget session therefore served as an opportunity to nominate councillors to

---

[240] Law N° 2004/017 of 22nd July 2004.

the various committees, based on their professional backgrounds and skills.

Another highlight of this meeting which generated some heat was the transfer of management of the Bali water project from the community to the council controlled by the governing CPDM party. During this meeting councillors were asked to vote to approve this *fait accompli*. Despite all 35 Councillors belonging to the CPDM party, many expressed shock and indignation at this act. Some also expressed fears that it might be a prelude to handing over the water back to the government. They vowed to defend it with their blood if such a move was ever contemplated.

Handing the water over to government here refers to giving it to the successor of SNEC, CAMWATER, which the Mayor had been in contact with for help/advice on how to revamp the water project.[241] Some councillors I spoke to recalled that it was a similar move by the community water management body to solicit help from the government in the 1980s for the expansion of the water network that ended up being surreptitiously handed over to SNEC without compensation. They therefore vowed that if the Mayor was anticipating such a move, he should be prepared to face the wrath of the 'Bali man.'

The outgoing manager of the water project, who also doubles as councillor, defended the decision to hand over the water to the council on the grounds that they were merely respecting 'a presidential decree.' According to excerpts of the speech that was read at the handing over ceremony which took place on 24 May 2013,[242] the decision was arrived at following Sections 4, and 33 of the law on the orientation of decentralisation.[243] However, Section 4 is quite vague and merely alludes to the administrative and financial autonomy granted to municipalities for the management of regional and local interests. Likewise Section 33 only states that "local public services of regional and local authorities may be run under council supervisions as concessions or leases."[244]

---

[241] Reference: 142/CW/DG/DT/SDPL/NIS/13. Correspondence from CAMWATER to Bali Council, on 29 April 2013.

[242] Official Handing-over Speech of Bali Community Water Commission by John Ndansi Fomuso (President General of BANDECA), TO Raymond Dinga Gwanyalla (Lord Mayor of Bali Council) 24th May 2013.

[243] Law N° 2004/017 of 22nd July 2004.

[244] Law N° 2004/017 of 22nd July 2004.

There is no obligation per se for the managers of the community water project to hand it over to the municipal authorities, as argued in the handing over speech and also during the Bali Council budget session. According to some informants, the real reasons behind the transfer to the council was manifold. The first issue was management gaffs, notably a lax attitude towards non-payment of water bills by consumers which led to the accumulation of unpaid bills amounting to over CFA 1 million francs. By the time I left Bali (in February 2014), defaulters were being threatened with legal action if they did not pay up. The second popular reason for the 'water crisis' in Bali was structural flaws in the design and construction of an alternative spring water source that it was hoped would use sand filtration to purify water instead of chemicals and also use the power of gravity to pump water to the storage tanks instead of electrical power. Had these innovations been successful, there would have been effective cost savings for the water project. However, both ran into trouble, only adding to the woes of the water management committee.

As noted in chapter IV, the community successfully managed the water project from its creation up until 1984 when SNEC took over and again after it was sent packing in 1994. Only in recent times did the 'water crisis' escalate, most likely due to increased demand because of a growing population and rapid urbanisation. Critics contended that the management chose to transfer the water project to the council under false pretences i.e. without admitting its failures, because it calculated that it was much easier for the council to muster financial resources from government. These views were prophetic, since information from Bali indicated that the government had indeed made some funding available to the council for a 'permanent solution' to the water crisis in Bali. Fears about the rationale for handing over the water project to the council were allayed by the injection of cash by the government to salvage the 'water crisis. The quest for a 'permanent solution' to the Bali water crisis could be an interesting topic for future research.

Chapter IX

Conclusion:
Political Project and Policy Boomerang

This study has examined how constitutional changes that were enacted in Cameroon in 1996 to promote decentralisation and community participation in local development have played out on the ground since 2004. In principle, decentralisation entails devolving decision-making powers and responsibilities down the politico-administrative hierarchy to institutions that are in touch with the everyday realities of ordinary citizens. In practice, however, decisions are often made by officials who are not abreast with the realities on the ground and are far "removed from the society they are charged with governing" (Scott 1998, 76).

The basis of decentralisation in Cameroon was the 1996 constitution which, according to (Geschiere, 2009, p. 51), "is permeated by the spirit of decentralization, albeit a special Cameroonian version". I argue that this 'Cameroonian version' involves a conception of decentralisation policy that accords ordinary people hardly any voice at all. I also suggest that the form of community participation outlined by the state and supported by some donors falls within the realm of cheap sloganeering and elaborate theatrics that convey a message whose practical implementation leaves much to be desired.

In my view, meaningful decentralisation must devolve authority for decision making very close to the location of maximum impact which, in the case of Cameroon, is the municipal council. Whereas official discourse claim that this has been done, the reality is that the power to take decisions has been left largely in the hands of government officials and other 'experts' who are portrayed as dealing with nothing more than technical issues. As a result, aspects of decentralisation that often appear prominently in policy dossiers and official discourses, i.e. the everyday experiences of ordinary people, tend to be marginal in practice. This study broached what I consider to be at the core of decentralisation as a democratic concept, and how the process has impacted the lives of ordinary Cameroonians in general, and in the two local municipalities where I conducted fieldwork, Bali and Mbankomo.

The core finding of my research was that decentralisation in Cameroon, like many complex issues, cannot be reduced to the argument that the policy reforms were meaningless cosmetic changes. Likewise, it is also a simplification to firmly claim that the policy changes have brought about real devolution of power to municipal councils and have promoted active community participation in local development. This contrast is inextricably linked to the historical, political and socio-economic development of Cameroon. As I observed in chapter one, unravelling this complex web of events required expertise in different academic domains, so I approached my study from an interdisciplinary perspective. My research methods enabled me to analyse how local issues impact and are impacted upon by national discourses and debates. I also explored how the advent of multiparty politics impacted the relationship between the leadership (traditional and political), and the citizens/subjects of Cameroon. My results testify to the flexibility of my approach.

In the course of dissecting the democratic process in Cameroon, it emerged that what was termed *démocratie avancée* was merely a smokescreen for a personality cult around the president and the coterie of bureaucrats answerable to him. The elite were opposed to any meaningful democratic advancement because it was perceived as "a threat to 'authentic' African culture and a challenge to secular values of respect to the chief (the authoritarian head of state)" (Monga, 1996, p. 72). This leads me to the conclusion that democratic reform in Cameroon was a strategy for political survival that enabled the regime of President Paul Biya to weather the 'wind of change' storm that swept across the African continent in the 1990s. The outcome was the "inauguration of an administrative-style multi-party system, [without] political liberalism, let alone a shift to democracy" (Mbembe, 2001, p. 143).

Historical patterns were crucial for analysing the issues I engaged with throughout this study. In chapter two, I examined the history of Cameroon from a German protectorate through British and French mandates to independence and reunification. It was clear that the form of governance implemented in both territories by the colonialists significantly shaped the form of state that emerged at independence. The British policy of indirect rule in the Southern Cameroons manifested itself on the ground in the form of Native Authorities. In the Bamenda

Grassfields, Native Authorities were headed by chiefs who, according to Awasom, (2003, p. 103), were "near-deities and containers of ancestral spirits". However, reverence for traditional rulers in the Grassfields was shattered at the time of the advent of multiparty politics in the 1990s, specifically because of their staunch support for an unpopular regime.

Critics of indirect rule describe it as a form of "mediated decentralised despotism" (Mamdani, 1996, p. 17), largely because the system entrenched the leadership of hereditary, and by implication unelected and unaccountable, monarchies. However, many Native Authorities in the Southern Cameroons were arenas of decentralised management involving a high degree of grassroots participation in local development. This spirit of self-reliance imbued a do-it-yourself attitude in Anglophones, which in many respects was at odds with what obtained in French Cameroon, where local institutions such as the *Conseils de Notables* were cosmetic and served largely as window dressing. The situation was compounded by the segmentary nature of some communities in French Cameroon which not only eased colonial penetration but fostered divide and rule, further splintering any semblance of local cohesion. It is important to note that Britain also carried out similar policies in some areas of the Southern Cameroons.

Another key tenet of French colonialism was the attempt to transform Africans into Frenchmen. This policy deliberately undermined traditional institutions. In some cases it involved dismissal of established chiefs in favour of handpicked lackeys, while in others the creation of artificial chiefdoms. These practices destabilised the social fabric and ensured that the loyalties of artificial chiefs, local headmen and henchmen rested with colonial officials. The consequences of this policy were that it stunted local development initiatives and left many in French Cameroon to rely on the colonialists rather than the community for inspiration. Generally, long exposure to centralised control created a dependency culture in Francophone Cameroon, where the state was seen as the main if not the only vehicle for development. Because the forms of state that emerged in Anglophone and Francophone Cameroon were a function of their respective colonial pasts, there was bound to be friction when both territories merged in 1961.

Francophone Cameroon was the larger of the two territories in land area and population. Conscious of this asymmetry and its long-term ramifications, Anglophones sought to obtain firm safeguards for their heritage of grassroots autonomy during the constitutional talks held in Fumban. However, the negotiating position of the delegation headed by Foncha was weakened by British betrayal when the Southern Cameroonians voted against Britain's wish for the territory to join the Nigerian Federation. This severely undermined the bargaining position of the Anglophone negotiators vis-à-vis their Francophone counterparts, who were headed by Ahidjo and backed by an armada of French advisors. The outcome of the Fumban Constitutional Conference was a centralised federation that vested the president with enormous powers to appoint and dismiss elected officials, and to make unilateral changes to the constitution.

Chapter three assessed why the economic crisis and political upheavals that affected sub-Saharan African countries in the 1980s and 1990s swept away many autocratic leaders there, but not in Cameroon. The 'democratic wind of change' came after a peaceful political transition from President Ahidjo to President Biya in 1982, and after the former's futile attempt to 'recuperate the state' via a putsch in 1984. At face value, this seemed to be a fairly straightforward power struggle; but scratching beneath the surface revealed a tale that cut deep into the core of the leadership enigma (some say dilemma) in Cameroon. This historical cleavage at the helm of the state also partly explains why the present leadership is wary of change and has devised overt and covert mechanisms to ensure its long-term survival. But how did it get to this point?

The lead-up to independence in Francophone Cameroon was marked by jostling for power on the part of an elite that was dominated by Southern politicians. During these political manoeuvres no one foresaw that a relatively obscure Northern politician would emerge as leader of the country. However this ignored behind the scenes machinations by French authorities which, as elsewhere in Francophone Africa, sought to protect their vital interests in Cameroon (Keese 2007 and Renou 2002). Ahidjo eventually emerged as the most suitable client to perform this role; but, following two decades at the helm of Cameroon, he appeared no longer to enjoy favour in Paris, and according to some conspiracy theories, was tricked by his French doctors into renouncing power on the grounds of ill-health in 1982. Southern politicians hailed Biya's succession as restitution by the French of their rightful place in the political sun.

After successfully shaking off threats to his rule, Biya embarked on consolidating power and surrounded himself predominantly with his fellow ethnics. The elite then indulged in gratuitous prebendary politics and squandered state resources with reckless abandon. These actions coincided with the outbreak of economic crisis and the resulting advocacy by the Bretton Woods institutions of the notion that "market forces represent the most efficient way of securing the optimal allocation of resources" (Mbembe, 2001, p. 78). However, allocation of resources under the SAP was haphazard and largely skewed in favour of fellow ethnics whose political support was crucial during the volatile 1990s. Dithering on economic reforms by the state exacerbated the crisis.

Inspired in part by the 'democratic wind of change' that swept across the continent in the 1990s, Cameroonians demanded the end of one-party rule because for many it symbolised political inertia, economic mismanagement and social stagnation. The masses also demanded a 'sovereign' national conference to discuss constitutional reform. However, fearing that conceding to this demand was tantamount to political suicide, as happened elsewhere on the continent, Paul Biya defiantly rejected the demand for a national conference by proclaiming '*le Cameroun c'est le Cameroun*' (Monga, 1996). Cameroun's exceptionalism took tangible form when the regime transformed the constitutional debate into a smokescreen and organised the first in a series of sham elections in 1992, leading Nyamnjoh (1999, p. 114) to observe "that democracy is not necessarily having as president the person the majority wants."

Meanwhile, the opposition was largely responsible for its own misfortune, given that it remained divided during electoral consultations, thereby severely undermining its chances of ousting Biya democratically. It may have dawned on the collective of opposition parties that ousting Biya through the ballot box was near impossible, but the allure of devouring the 'national pie' was much more feasible; hence joining the feast became so tempting that much of the opposition resolved "to substitute the ruling bellies, and not the wellbeing of everyone" (Nyamnjoh, 1999, p. 114).

Another crucial element that played-out during the volatile 1990s was demands by Anglophones for a return to the status quo ante, i.e. the two-state federation that had been dissolved by Ahidjo in 1972. Nostalgia for the legacy of grassroots autonomy enjoyed by

Anglophones and the fact that people from the North West had voted overwhelmingly to join French Cameroon in 1961 largely explains why Bamenda was the centre of opposition politics in the 1990s. Anglophones spearheaded the formation of the Social Democratic Front (SDF) party in 1990, a move which contributed to forcing the government to liberalise the political landscape and sounded the death-knell of political monopoly. The end of political monopoly did not mean democracy, however; being an astute politician, President Biya declared: "I brought you to democracy and liberty . . . You now have liberty. Make good use of it" (Mbembe, 2001, p. 105).

According to President Biya therefore, political liberalisation in the 1990s was a generous gift to the people by a benevolent leader. Biya may have kept his word on 'liberty', but 'democracy' remained merely a semblance. Despite taking centre stage in the 1996 constitution, devolution of powers to municipal councils and elected mayors was delayed by the government until 2004. Upon implementation, the laws on the orientation of decentralisation and the rules applicable to councils bestowed enormous powers and prerogatives on 'representatives of the state'. In principle, the policy constituted a significant milestone in the enhancement of local governance in Cameroon. However, by placing appointed bureaucrats over and above elected officials, these laws effectively nullified the policy's raison d'être, stifled independent action by local authorities, and defeated the rationale for devolving powers to municipal councils. In spite of this, decentralisation and community participation were projected as the panacea for Cameroon's developmental challenges. However, self-reliant or community development had long been engrained in the Southern Cameroons, where Native Authorities had constituted arenas for grassroots participation in local development. As discussed in chapter four, the Bali Community Water scheme was an example of a grassroots development project under the aegis of a decentralised local authority. This case contrasts starkly with the largely top-down system Biya put in place in 2004, whereby municipal councils are funded by the state, are subjected to the dictates of 'representatives of the state', and are accountable to no one other than the head of state.

People in Bali turned to the state for assistance when a need to expand the water scheme arose in the late 1980s; they did so because their project was located within a sovereign state which had ostensible obligations towards its citizens. However, the paternalistic state viewed it as an opportunity to assert control over an important local resource, effectively placing it on a collision course with the inhabitants of Bali. Refurbishing and handing over the community water system to SNEC was controversial because the people had sought assistance from the state not because they had failed to manage the water resource properly, but because it had become necessary to modernise the water installations, which only the state had the wherewithal to do.

Moreover, SNEC was a striking example of a bleeding parastatal company that the government had failed to privatise during structural adjustment because it served as a juicy vehicle for ethnic patronage (Page 2002). Mismanagement at SNEC epitomised decay at the helm of the state; it also gave rise to inefficiency at the local level, as was the case in Bali. At the time, the government's credibility and moral authority were seriously dented, partly because of perceived failings in tackling the economic crisis and its socio-economic impact. This prompted the population of Bali to expel SNEC in 1994 and to repossess the water installations. The moral of this tale is that the population of Bali challenged the state and got away with it.

Chapter five demonstrated how the promulgation in 2004 of the law on decentralisation and that on the rules applicable to councils, albeit after a long and unexplained delay, empowered the authorities of Bali Council to commission a monographic survey aimed at documenting developmental potential in the municipality. This initiative by the Mayor of Bali was arguably in line with the spirit of self-reliance that had long been ingrained in the mind-set of people in the Grassfields in general and Bali in particular. But this study degenerated into violence and land conflict in Bali subdivision. The findings of the survey demystified long-held views about Bawock village, exposed its actual size as a minuscule neighbourhood in Bali, and shattered its residents' dream of gaining an 'independent jurisdiction'.

Their ambition had not been entirely unreasonable, given that, as Bayart observed (2009, p. ixxxv), "pressure to create new administrative units lies behind a great deal of social mobility in sub-Saharan Africa". But when they realised that their long-held dream of an 'independent jurisdiction' plus related 'benefits and privileges' in Bali was doomed, the traditional authorities of Bawock orchestrated a plot to sabotage implementation of the monographic survey by playing the innocent victim and oppressed minority. The goal was to reignite a simmering historical cleavage over land and boundaries with Bali Nyonga. This issue mutated into a political conflict because the Mayor of Bali was from the opposition SDF party and some elite members from Bawock, including the chief, belonged to the governing CPDM. Paradoxically, municipal councillors and members of the SDF from Bawock also vehemently opposed the findings of this survey; they promptly set aside loyalty to the party in favour of loyalty to the tribe. The outcome was a violent struggle for land and the disqualification of the SDF party's candidates list for the 2007 municipal elections which, in turn, paved the way for the CPDM to gain control of Bali Council. This episode mobilised the CPDM elite and erstwhile foes from all sides (Bali Nyonga, Bawock and Bossa) to set aside inter-community squabbles and unite to oust the SDF party from Bali Council.

In early 2004, the government, in conjunction with donors, created, funded and charged the PNDP with the task of promoting Council Development Plans (CDP) to serve as reference documents for developmental activities in local municipalities. Curiously, the CDP drawn up for Bali not only mirrored the findings of the monographic survey, but in some instances lifted information from it word for word. By overlooking and appropriating the findings of the monographic survey, the government demonstrated its disregard for a bottom-up initiative, thereby questioning the rationale behind its decentralisation agenda. This episode also raises the question of why did the state not support and encourage replication of the Bali plan elsewhere in the country. Was it simply a lack of capacity, as often claimed by state officials? If so, why not involve NGOs, civil society and or International Non-Governmental Organisations (INGOs) to work directly with councils, as had been the case with the working relationship between Bali Council and Helvetas? Was it simply a case of a paternalistic state seeking to consolidate central control and spoon-feed citizens with an exclusive vision and approach to local development, as the example of the PNDP and the CDPs demonstrated?

In view of socio-political realities on the ground, therefore, chapter six elaborated on the profound mutations that occurred in the political landscape of Cameroon following the end of the monolithic era in the 1990s. I observed that these changes occurred on many fronts, including electoral campaigning. Likewise, pluralism transformed the electoral arena into a battleground where political actors often deployed unconventional tactics and 'irrational' methods to secure electoral success. As a result, the government developed sophisticated rigging machinery, involving the use of state officials, government bureaucrats, party cadres and traditional authorities. These actors worked at various levels to ensure electoral success and maintain political control.

In North West Cameroon, the CPDM co-opted traditional chiefs into its ranks in the hope of turning the growing tide of support for the opposition. The government's strategy to win back support from disillusioned citizens in this part of the country was to hitch a ride on the reverence their subjects had for traditional chiefs. This created tension between chiefs, the majority of them aligned to an unpopular CPDM government, and many ordinary citizens/subjects who sympathised with the opposition. However, the government's strategy backfired and the outcome was massive electoral defeat for the CPDM party in the 1996 elections in the North West. This episode not only dented rapport between chiefs and subjects, but significantly depleted the formers' moral authority and the aura of their personalities, something many have struggled to reverse over the years since these elections. Ganyonga III of Bali contested the 1996 municipal elections on the CPDM ticket and was humiliated at the polls by the opposition SDF party. The SDF ran Bali Council until 2007, when the CPDM gained control by disqualifying the opposition rather than by a show of electoral support.

The 2013 municipal elections presented the CPDM and SDF with the opportunity for a re-match on a more equal footing. Both parties sought to maximise their chances of electoral success, leading to a fight to the death for the control of Bali Council and re-enactment of the electoral contest that had not taken place in 2007. Prior to the electoral battle, the *Fon* of Bali attempted to revive his electoral fortunes but was muzzled by the CPDM party hierarchy. Ganyonga III was eventually appointed senator, and in line with the view that "individuals must give the president total support if they wish to maintain, climb to or come by high office and the favours that go with it" (Nyamnjoh, 1999, p. 106), he campaigned vigorously for the CPDM in the municipal elections. He also sought to coerce the population to elect the CPDM list for Bali Council, arguing that failure to do so would be tantamount to rejecting his senatorial appointment and could lead to its revocation. Leaving nothing to chance, he ordered the feared ancestral cult Voma to impress the need for a CPDM victory on his subjects. The municipal elections also witnessed the introduction of a biometric voting system in Cameroon but, despite its much-vaunted infallibility, polling was marred by episodes of electoral fraud similar to malpractices previously ascribed to the sophisticated rigging apparatus already in place, thereby confirming the adage that 'old habits die hard'.

Chapter seven continued with electoral politics, this time in Mbankomo, where the CPDM sought to enforce party discipline on grassroots militants. In Bali the CPDM and SDF were enmeshed in pre-electoral imbroglio involving accusations of occultism. Events in Mbankomo were completely different from this. The pre-election bickering in Mbankomo occurred within the CPDM, and was over the incumbent Mayor's expressed wish to seek re-election for a second term in office. But his ambitions were vigorously opposed by a section of the CPDM elite dubbed *hommes politiques,* who employed skulduggery to oust him. This episode documented how the CPDM party's political strategy was replete with duplicity: on the one hand, it showed up the party as an organisation that will stop at nothing to gain electoral success at the national and local levels; on the other hand, it portrayed a movement that courts controversy in its modus operandi and ruthlessly enforces party discipline. This dichotomy was manifested as carrots and sticks, with the former employed to placate grassroots militants in order to win votes, and the latter to ram down party, and on occasion personal, dictates on the masses.

Interference by the CPDM party's barons dates back to the monolithic era and, despite official denials, was widespread during the 2013 municipal/legislative elections. Enforcing party discipline in the selection of candidates was justified on the grounds that the CPDM was seeking to promote the emergence of honest and dynamic men, women and youths capable of conveying to the grassroots the president's vision of transforming Cameroon into an emerging economy by the year 2035. Candidates selected by the grassroots were often dispatched with utter contempt by party bosses, as in Mbankomo, leading many observers to wonder how Cameroon might meet this goal given that meritocracy and competence were clearly being sacrificed at the altar of mediocrity and cronyism. Further, selecting CPDM militants to convey the president's vision for the country was seen as tantamount to politicising development for the party's gain and seeking to make cheap capital out of unrealistic political rhetoric.

Likewise, the decision to select candidates through investiture rather than primaries was often viewed as a smokescreen to avoid a repeat of the events of 2007. Selection of CPDM candidates via primaries on this occasion was in stark contrast to what obtained in the past, whereby people seeking public office were simply endorsed by acclamation. The absence of popular consultation within the CPDM meant that candidates for public office were often oblivious of the true extent of their (un)popularity. Further, the rash and somewhat abrasive attitude of most elected officials, coupled with strong backing from the party machine, gave many observers the impression that the officials regarded themselves as invincible.

This was compounded by the fact that most members of the party elite only appeared during electoral campaigns, made fantastic promises, offered gifts and bribes, got elected and then disappeared, only to repeat the cycle at the approach of another election. Their sense of impunity blinded many in the party elite to the level of resentment among grassroots CPDM militants. The disillusionment this generated had resulted in the humiliation of a large number of party barons who had sought endorsement during party primaries in 2007, but were voted out of contention at the grassroots. This greatly embarrassed CPDM officials who were not accustomed to defeat of any kind, let alone from within. But, of course, in a show of elite solidarity, many of these barons had simply been reinstated by the party hierarchy.

Many grassroots militants were enraged by the actions of the CPDM and some vowed revenge at the earliest opportunity. The 2013 municipal/legislative elections therefore presented the perfect opportunity for retribution, but the party opted for consensus lists instead of competitive primaries. As in many parts of the country, achieving consensus in Mbankomo was difficult if not impossible. Given that the party had the final say over the eligibility of a prospective candidate, its decisions were contested in some cases and detested in others. As a result, some militants who felt cheated vowed openly to punish the CPDM by voting for the opposition in the elections. This was accompanied by wild speculation about the potential for mass desertion by voters, which raised the spectre of massive electoral defeat for the CPDM. However, the results of the polls put paid to all these prognostications and confirmed the CPDM's dominant position in Cameroon.

It appears that the CPDM is the 'natural' party of government in Cameroon by book, hook or crook, and that the core of its governance strategy is 'community participation'. Chapter eight therefore examined the concept of participation and reflected on similar cases of decentralisation and community participation in the Global South. Most of the cases examined contrast starkly with what obtains in Cameroon, and lay bare the shortcomings of the Cameroonian model. In many instances local councils constitute institutional arenas where decentralisation undergoes practical implementation, and community participation impacts the day-to-day activities of local municipalities. As these cases show, financial autonomy and self-sufficiency of local government, and its ability and discretion to dispense public procurement contracts constitute essential ingredients for effective decentralisation.

Many observers have lauded the fact that local councils in Cameroon were granted powers to award contracts for public works within municipalities; this was viewed as a significant step forward in enhancing grassroots autonomy and promoting community development. But this prerogative was rapidly withdrawn by presidential decree following the creation of the Ministry of Public Contracts in 2012. Henceforth, the award of public tenders became the preserve of divisional delegations of this ministerial department which, unlike other ministries in the country, was placed directly under the authority of the president.

Depriving local councils of the prerogative to award public contracts in favour of divisional commissions not only removed a key component of grassroots autonomy from the councils, but raised questions about which authority was competent to allocate public tenders within municipal areas. Municipal officials I encountered during fieldwork argued that it was wrong for government to withdraw this prerogative because council areas on which earmarked project(s) have a direct bearing are best placed to impress upon prospective contractors the need for the job to be carried out diligently. The concern was that conferring such responsibilities on a detached body composed of civil servants and bureaucrats who, despite being 'experts' in the domain, may not be aware of the realities on the ground outside the files presented to them for adjudication, was tantamount to 'abridged practices' (Scott

1998). Moreover divisional public contracts commissions were given the mammoth task of allocating tenders for contracts emanating from not only local councils but also other public and para-public institutions in specific administrative divisions. The new dispensation therefore raised questions about the efficacy of this new layer of bureaucracy, the risks of influence peddling, and the propagation of corrupt practices, all of which the reform was designed to stem. It remains to be seen how this reform will impact public procurement in Cameroon.

In analysing these events I employed an interdisciplinary approach to portray the big picture of decentralisation in Cameroon. In fact, I demonstrated throughout this study how the social movements in the 1990s and the power struggles that ensued caused the elite to develop strategies to maintain power, and how the masses were impacted by the tumultuous events. I also argued that decentralisation and community participation in Cameroon was a strategy for political survival that enabled the elite to retain political control to the present. But this is not the full picture. My anthropological perspective complemented the political science one, by demonstrating how the new policy initiatives fit into a local-level story that started long before the initiatives were taken, and how people's response to new policy is shaped not by the policy alone but also by the local-level story. My contribution is therefore situated in my attempt to bridge the rigours of academic boundaries and to bring the political science and anthropological perspectives together, enabling me to unveil a comprehensive picture of decentralisation and community participation in Cameroon. This assessment contrasts starkly with the official rhetoric that presents decentralisation as a genuine opportunity for grassroots autonomy, and municipal councils as credible forums for community participation in local development.

My conclusions follows the lead of most critical scholarship on the state of decentralisation in Cameroon and the mode of governance in place. Authors including but not limited to Fombad (2012) Geschiere (2009), Mbembe (2001), Nyamnjoh (1999), Mentan (1998), have deconstructed decentralisation and community participation in Cameroon unequivocally. These authors examined decentralisation from a macro (national) and micro (local) levels. Some of them are political scientists, and they display a tendency to critique the policies of decentralisation on the basis of their understanding of national politics in Cameroon and other African countries and they skim the surface of the local. Other authors are anthropologists, who understandably go into greater depth about the local; but they tend to keep their discussions of local and national politics separate, often dealing with them in different publications. Some of these publications are about the 'big' issues – the president, the CPDM, opposition parties, social movements and protests, others about 'small' issues chiefs, witchcraft, local identities and claims about autochthony, land conflicts and so on.

I have made an effort to bring these together to show, for instance, how national policy changes enter fields of local politics which have a long history, and that the meaning of the changing policies to people on the ground comes not only from the intentions of those who devise them (the president and his party elite) but also from the manner in which the new policies intersect and interact with local political dynamics. I have sought to demonstrate this point quite succinctly on a number of instances throughout this study; these include the water scheme in Bali and the land disputes between Bali Nyonga and its neighbours.

Finally, what the democratisation and decentralisation of the 1990s and 2000s means to people in Bali (and therefore how they react to them) turns on the way in which these top-down initiatives intersect with long-standing local politics. This point of convergence also partly explains why political developments in Cameroon is considered by some to be an enigma and by others a nightmare. This dichotomy is based on the fact that from independence there was a noticeable and persistent boomerang in the implementation of public policy in Cameroon. Decentralisation was no exception; instead it confirms the rule.

Bibliography

Abers, R., 1996. From Ideas to Practice: The Partido dos Trabalhadores and Participatory Governance in Brazil. *Latin American Perspectives, Vol. 23, No. 4, The "Urban Question" in Latin America,* pp. 35-53.

Abraham, A. & Platteau, J.-P., 2004. Participatory Development: Where Culture Creeps In. In: *Culture and Public Action.* Stanford: Stanford University Press, pp. 210-233.

Abram, S., 1998. Introduction: Anthropological perspectives on local development. In: *Anthropological perspectives on local development: Knowledge and sentiments in conflict.* London: Taylor & Francis, pp. 1-17.

Achankeng, F., 2014. *British Southern Cameroons; Nationalism and Conflict in Postcolonial Africa.* Victoria : Friesen Press.

Africa Confidential, 2014. *Nigeria; Ekiti, the shape of things to come..* [Online]
Available at: http://www.africa-confidential.com/article/id/5679/Ekiti,_the_shape_of_things_to_come
[Accessed 19 07 2014].

Ake, C., 1996. *Is Africa Democratizing?.* CASS Monograph No 5 ed. Lagos: Malthouse Press Limited.

Akoko, R. M., 2004. Roll-Back: Democratization and Social Fragmentation in Cameroon. *Nordic Journal of African Studies 13(1),* p. 1–12.

Alexander, C., 2010. The Third Sector. In: *The Human Economy A Citizens Guide.* Cambridge: Polity Press, pp. 213-224.

Alsop, R. & Kurey, B., 2005. *Local Organizations in Decentralized Development: Their Functions and Performance in India.* Washington, DC: The World Bank.

Amanor, K. S., 2008. Sustainable Development, Corporate Accumulation and Community Expropriation: Land and Natural Resources in West Africa. In: *Land & Sustainable Development in Africa .* London: Zed Books, pp. 127-158.

Amanor, K. & Ubink, J., 2008. Contesting Land and Custom in Ghana: Introduction. In: *Contesting Land and Custom in Ghana: State, Chief and the Citizen.* Leiden : Leiden University Press, pp. 1-26.

Amin, A. A., 2011. The Government's Social Policy and National Integration. In: *Regional Balance and National Integration in Cameroon: Lessons Learned and the Uncertain Future.* Bamenda: Langaa RPCIG, pp. 91-97.

Amungwa, F. A., 2011. The Evolution of Conflicts Related to Natural Resource Management in Cameroon. *Journal of Human Ecology 35(1),* pp. 53-60.

Anyang-Nyong'o, P., 1995. Discourses on Democracy in Africa. In: *Democratisation in Africa; Problems and Prospects.* Dakar: CODESRIA, pp. 29-42.

Anyangwe, C., 2013. Manumission from black-on-black colonialism; Sovereign statehood for the British Southern Cameroons. In: *Bondage of Boundaries and Identity Politics in Postcolonial Africa; The 'Northern Problem' and Ethno-Futures.* Pretoria: Africa Institute of South Africa, pp. 163-184.

Argenti, N., 2007. *The Intestines of the State: Youth, Violence, and Belated Histories in the Cameroon Grassfields.* Chicago & London: The University of Chicago Press.

Atchrimi, T., 2014. Community development and participation in Togo: the case of AGAIB Plateaux. *Field Actions Science Reports (FACTS),* pp. 97-102.

AusAID, 2001. *Decentralisation and Development Cooperation,* Canberra: Asia Research Centre Murdoch University.

Austen, R. A. & Derrick, J., 1999. *Middlemen of the Cameroons Rivers; The Duala and their Hinterland, c. 1600–c. 1960.* Cambridge: Cambridge University Press.

Auty, R. M., 1988. Internal Constraints on Prudent Oil Windfall Deployment for Resource-based Industrialisation: Nigeria and Cameroon. *Geoforum Vol. 19,1':0.2,* pp. 147-160.

Awasom, N. F., 2003. The vicissitudes of twentieth-century Mankon *fons* in Cameroon's changing social order. In: *The dynamics of power and the rule of law; Essays on Africa and beyond,in honour of Emile Adriaan B. van Rouveroy van Nieuwaal.* Leiden: LIT Verlag / African Studies Centre,, pp. 101-120.

Awung, W. J. & Atanga, M., 2011. Economic Crisis and Multiparty Politics in Cameroon. *Cameroon Journal on Democracy and Human Rights. Vol. 5 No 1,* pp. 94-127.

Bayart, J.-F., 2009. *The State in Africa; Politics of the Belley.* Second Edition ed. Cambridge: Polity Press.

Bejeng, S. P., 1985. *The Passing of a Great Leader; Galega II of Bali Nyonga (1906-1985).* Bamenda: Nooremac Press.

Bernard, H. R., 2006. *Research Methods in Anthropology Qualitative and Quantitative Approaches.* Fourth Edition ed. Oxford: AltaMira Press.

Berry, S., 2001. *Chiefs Know their Boundaries: Essays on Property, Power, and the Past in Asante 1896-1996.* Cape Town: David Phillip Publishers (Pty) Ltd..

Berry, S., 2008. Ancestral Property: Land politics and the deeds of ancestors' in Ghana and Cote d'Ivoire. In: *Contesting Land and Custom in Ghana; State, Chief and the Citizen.* Leiden: Leiden University Press, pp. 27-53.

Bierschenk, T. & Olivier de Sardan, J.-P., 2003. Powers in the Village: Rural Benin Between Democratisation and Decentralisation. *Africa 73 (2), ,* pp. 145-173.

Bierschenk, T., 2004. *The local appropriation of democracy; An analysis of the municipal elections in Parakou Republic of Benin, 2002/03,* Mainz: Institut für Ethnologie und Afrikastudien, Johannes Gutenberg-Universität,.

Biya, P., 1987. *Communal Liberalism.* London: Macmillan Publishers.

Bratton, M. & van de Walle, N., 1994. Neopatrimonial Regimes and Political Transitions in Africa. *World Politics Vol. 46, No. 4,* pp. 453-489.

Bryden, J. M., 2010. Local Development. In: *The Human Economy.* Cambridge: Polity, pp. 248-260.

Calderón, F. & Szmukler, A., 2004. Political Culture and Development. In: *Culture and Public Action.* Stanford: Stanford University Press, pp. 281-306.

Cameroon Tribune, 2013. *Cameroun: Le Challenge de la Décentralisation.* [Online]
Available at: http://www.cameroon-info.net/stories/0,51273,@,cameroun-le-challenge-de-la-decentralisation.html
[Accessed 20 01 2015].

251

CameroonPostline.com, 2013. *Biya has signed a pact with Bali people – Senator Ganyonga.*. [Online]
Available at:
http://cameroonpostline.com/Conthttp://www.cameroonpostline.com/biyahassignedapactwithbalipeople/
[Accessed 10 07 2014].

CERD, 2008. *International Convention on the Elimination of all forms of Racial Discrimination. Reports submitted by states parties under article 9 of the Convention.*. [Online]
Available at:
https://www.ecoi.net/file_upload/470_1263138712_cerd-c-cmr-19.pdf
[Accessed 12 03 2015].

Chabal, P. & Daloz, J.-P., 1999. *Africa Works; Disorder as Political Instrument.* London: Villiers Publications.

Chazan, N., 1992. Africa's Democratic Challenge. *World Policy Journal Vol. 9, No 2,* pp. 279-307.

Cheka, C., 2007. The State of the Process of Decentralisation in Cameroon. *CODESRIA Africa Development,* XXXII(2), p. 181–196.

Cheka, C., 2008. Traditional Authority at the Crossroads of Governance in Republican Cameroon. *CODESRIA Africa Development,* XXXIII(2), p. 67–89.

Chem-Langhee, B., 1983. The Origin of the Southern Cameroons House of Chiefs. *The International Journal of African Historical Studies, Vol. 16, No. 4,* pp. 653-673.

Chiabi, E. M., 2011. Redressing Regional Imbalance in Cameroon: The Lessons from The Past. In: *Regional Balance and National Integration in Cameroon: Lessons Learned and Uncertain Future.* Bamenda: Langaa RPCIG, pp. 41-58.

Chilver, E. M., 1964. A Bamilike Community in Bali Nyonga; A Note on the Bawock. *African Studies,* 23(3-4), pp. 121-128.

Chilver, E. M. & Kaberry, P. M., 1970. Chronology of the Bamenda Grassfields. *The Journal of African History,* 11(2), pp. 249-257.

Clapham, C., 1993. Democratisation in Africa: Obstacles and Prospects. *Third World Quarterly Vol. 14, No. 3,* pp. 423-438.

Conyers, D., 2000. "Decentralisation: A conceptual analysis (Part 1)." Local Government Perspectives:,. *News and Views on Local Government in Sub-Saharan Africa, Vol. 7, No. 3,* pp. 7–9, 13..

Cooper, F., 2008. Possibility and Constraint: African Independence in Historical Perspective. *The Journal of African History:*, 49(02), pp. 167 - 196.

Crook, R. C. & Manor, J., 1998. *Democracy and Decentralisation in South Asia and West Africa; Participation, Accountability and Performance.* Cambridge: Cambridge University Press.

Crowder, M., 1964. Indirect Rule: French and British Style. *Africa: Journal of the International African Institute, Vol. 34, No. 3*, pp. 197-205.

Crowley-Henry, M., 2009. Ethnography: Visions and Versions. In: *Approaches to Qualitative Research: Theory & Its Practical Application. A Guide for Dissertation Students.* Cork-Ireland: Oak Tree Press, pp. 37-63.

Dafinger, A. & Pelican, M., 2006. Sharing or Dividing the Land? Land Rights and Farmer-Herder Relations in Burkina Faso and Northwest Cameroon. *Canadian Journal of African Studies / Revue Canadienne des Études Africaines, 40, No. 1 ,* pp. 127-151.

DeLancey, M. D., Mbuh, R. N. & DeLancey, W. M., 2010. *Historical Dictionary of the Republic of Cameroon.* Fourth Edition ed. Lanham, Maryland • Toronto • Plymouth, UK: The Scarecrow Press, Inc..

Delancy, M. W., 1989. *Cameroon; Dependence & Independence.* Colorado: Westview Press Inc.

Devas, N. & Grant, U., 2003. Local Government Decision-Making--- Citizen Participation and Local Accountability: Some Evidence from Kenya and Uganda. *Public Administration and Development,* Volume 23, p. 307–316.

Diduk, S., 1989. Women's Agricultural Production and Political Action in the Cameroon Grassfields. *Africa: Journal of the International African Institute Vol. 59, No. 3 ,* pp. 338-355.

Diduk, S., 1992. The Paradoxes of Changing Land Tenure in Kedjom Chiefdoms, Northwest Province, Cameroon. *Paideuma,Bd. 38,* pp. 195-217.

Diprose, R. & Ukiwo, U., 2008. *Decentralisation & Conflict Management in Indonesia & Nigeria,* Oxford: Centre for Research on Inequality, Human Security and Ethnicity (CRISE) University of Oxford.

Doh, E. F., 2008. *Africa's Political Wastelands: The Bastardization of Cameroon.* Bamenda: Langaa RPCIG.

Eaton, K., Kaiser, K. & Smoke, P., 2010. *The Political Economy of Decentralization Reforms; Implications for Aid Effectiveness,* Washington, D.C.: The World Bank.

Egbe, S., 2002. Forest Tenure & Access to Forest Resources in Cameroon. In: *The Dynamics of Resource Tenure in West Africa.* London: IIED, pp. 61-71.

Elong, E. E., 2013. The Anglophone problem and the secession option in Cameroon. In: *Bondage of Boundaries and Identity Politics in Postcolonial Africa; The 'Northern Problem' and Ethno-Futures.* Pretoria: Africa Institute of South Africa, pp. 148-162.

Engard, R. K., 1988 . Myth and Political Economy in Bafut (Cameroon): The Structural History of an African Kingdom. *Paideuma,Bd. 34 ,* pp. 49-89.

Erbe, N. et al., 2009. Negotiating and Mediating Peace in Africa. *Pepperdine Dispute Resolution Law Journal Volume 9 Issue 3 Article 2,* pp. 1-38.

Erdmann, G. & Engel, U., 2006. *Neopatrimonialism Revisited Beyond a Catch-All Concept,* Hamburg: GIGA German Institute of Global and Area Studies.

Escobar, A., 1995. *Encountering Development; The Making and Unmaking of the Third World.* Princeton: Princeton University Press.

Evans, P. & Appleton, B., 1993. *Community Management Today The Role of Communities in the Management of Improved Water Supply Systems,* Delft, The Netherlands: IRC International Water and Sanitation Centre .

Eyoh, D., 1998. Conflicting Narratives of Anglophone Protest and the Politics of Identity in Cameroon. *Journal of Contemporary African Studies. Vol 16, 2,* pp. 249-276.

Eyoh, D., 1998. Through the Prism of a Local Tragedy: Political Liberalisation, Regionalism and Elite Struggles for Power in Cameroon. *Africa Vol. 68 Issue 3,* pp. 338-359.

Eyoh, D. & Stren, R., 2007. Decentralization and Urban Development in West Africa, an Introduction. In: *Decentralization and the Politics of Urban Development In West Africa.* Washington DC: Woodrow Wilson International Center for Scholars, pp. 1-22.

Eyongetah, T. & Brian, R., 1974. *A History of the Cameroon.* London: Longman.

Fanon, F., 1963. *The Wretched of the Earth.* New York: Grove Press.

Fardon, R., 1983. Chronology of Pre-Colonial Chamba History. *Frobenius Institute,* Paideuma, Bd.(29), pp. 67-92.

Ferguson, J., 1994. *The Anti Politics Machine; "Development", Depoliticization and Bureaucratic Power in Lesotho.*. Minneapolis: University of Minnesota Press.

Fisiy, Ç. F., 1992. *Power and Privilege in the Administration of Law: Land Law Reforms and Social Differentiation in Cameroon.* Leiden: African Studies Centre.

Fisiy, C. F., 1995. Chieftaincy in the Modern State: An Institution at the Crossroads of Democratic Change. *Paideuma,* Bd(41), pp. 49-62.

Fisiy, C. & Goheen, M., 1998. Power and the Quest for Recognition: Neotraditional Titles Among the New Elite in Nso', Cameroon.. *Africa, Vol. 68 Issue 3,* p. 383. 400.

Fiszbein, A., 1997. The Emergence of Local Capacity: Lessons From Colombia. *World Development, Vol. 25, No. 7,* pp. 1029-1043.

Fochang, B., 2011. Old Wine in New Wineskin? Social Change and Traditional Religion in Bali Nyonga. In: *Society and Change in Bali Nyonga; Critical Perspectives.* Bamenda: Langaa RPCIG, pp. 23-35.

Fohtung, M. G., Njie, P. K. & Chilver, E. M., 1992. Self-Portrait of a Cameroonian. *Paideuma,* Bd(38), pp. 219-248.

Fokwang, J., 2009. *Mediating Legitimacy; Chieftancy and Democratisation in Two African Chiefdoms.* Bamenda: Langaa RPCIG.

Fokwang, J., 2011. Introduction: Society and Culture in Early 21st Century Bali. In: J. Fokwang & K. Langmia, eds. *Society and Change in Bali Nyonga; Critical Perspectives.* Bamenda: Langaa RPCIG, pp. 1-20.

Fombad, C. M., 2012. *Cameroon Introductory Notes,* Pretoria: University of Pretoria .

Fonchingong, C. C. & Tanga, P. T., 2007. Crossing Rural-Urban Spaces The "Takumbeng" and Activism in Cameroon's Democratic Crusade. *Cahiers d'Études Africaines,* Vol. 47(185), pp. 117-143.

Forje, J. W., 2008. Developing Viable Independent Institutions for political and Economic Development in Cameroon. *Cameroon journal on Democracy and Human Rights; CJDHR Vol2, No.2,* pp. 31-43.

Fowler, I. & Zeitlyn , D., 1957. Introduction: the Grassfields and the Tikar. *African Studies,* 16(2), pp. 108-113.

Funteh, M. B., 2008. Conflict Prevention and Peace Making in Cameroon: The Case for Indigenous Strategies in the Grassfields Region. *Global South. South-South Exchange Programme for Research on the History of Development,* pp. 17-23.

Gabriel, J. M., 1999. Cameroon's Neopatrimonial dilemma. *Journal of Contemporary African Studies ,* 17(2), pp. 173-196.

Geary, C. M., 1988. Art and Political Process in the Kingdoms of Bali-Nyonga and Bamum (Cameroon Grassfields). *Canadian Journal of African Studies / Revue Canadienne des Études Africaines,* 22(1), pp. 11-41.

Geschiere, P., 1992. 'Kinship, Witchcraft and "the Market": Hybrid Patterns in Cameroonian Societies. In: *Contesting Markets: Analyses of Ideology, Discourse and Practice.* Edinburgh: Edinburgh University Press, pp. 159-79.

Geschiere, P., 1993. Chiefs and colonial rule in Cameroon: inventing chieftaincy, French and British Style. *Africa, ,* Volume 63, pp. 151-175.

Geschiere, P., 1997. *The Modernity of Witchcraft; Politics and the Occult in Post-Colonial Africa.* Charlottesville: University of Virginia .

Geschiere, P., 2009. *The Perils of Belonging; Autochthony, Citizenship, and Exclusion in Africa and Europe.* Chicago and London: University of Chicago Press.

Geschiere, P. & Gugler, J., 1998. The Urban-Rural Connection: Changing Issues of Belonging and Identification.. *Africa 68 (3),* pp. 309-319.

Gluckman, M., 1940. Analysis of a Social Situation in Modern Zululand. *Bantu Studies,* 14(1), pp. 1-30.

Gonne, B., 2010. Karal Land: Family cultural patrimony or a commercialised product on the Diamare Plain?. In: *The Struggle Over Land in Africa: Conflicts, Politics & Change.* Cape Town: HSRC Press, pp. 71-82.

Gordon, D., 1997. On Promoting Democracy in Africa: The International Dimension . In: *Democracy in Africa: The Hard Road Ahead.* Boulder: Lynne Rienner Publishers Inc., pp. 153-163.

Graham, C., 1997. Democracy, Adjustment, and Poverty Reduction in Africa: Conflicting Objectives?. In: *Democracy in Africa: The Hard Road Ahead*. Boulder: Lynne Rienner Publishers Inc., pp. 83-103.

Greene, R., 2000. *The 48 Laws of Power*. London: Profile Books Limited.

Grindle, M. S., 2007. *Going Local; Decentralization, Democratization, and the Promise of Good Governance*. Princeton: Princeton University Press.

Gros, J.-G., 1998. Introduction: Understanding Decentralisation . In: *Democratization in Late Twentieth-Century Africa*. Westport: Greenwood Press, pp. 1-20.

Hann, C. & Hart, K., 2011. *Economic Anthropology*. Cambridge: Polity Press.

Hansen, K. F., 2010 . Inside Electoral Democracy: Gift-Giving and Flaunting in Political Campaigning in Cameroon. *Journal of Asian and African Studies 45*, pp. 432-445.

Harriss, J., 2002. *Depoliticizing Development; The World Bank and Social Capital*. London: Anthem Press.

Harriss, J., Stokke, K. & Törnquist, O., 2004. Introduction; The New Local Politics of Democratisation. In: *Politicising Democracy*. Hampshire: Palgrave Macmillan, pp. 1-28.

Hart, K., 1982. *The political Economy of West African Agriculture*. Cambridge: Cambridge University Press.

Hart, K., Laville, J.-L. & Cattani, A., 2010. Building the Human Economy Together. In: K. Hart, J. Laville & A. D. Cattani, eds. *The Human Economy: A Citizens Guide*. Cambridge: Polity, pp. 1-17.

Heller, P., 1996. Social Capital as a Product of Class Mobilization and State Intervention: Industrial Workers in Karela India. *World Development, vol 24, no6*, pp. 1055-71.

Heller, P., 2001 . Moving the State: The Politics of Democratic Decentralization in Kerala, South Africa, and Porto Alegre. *Politics Society Vol 29, No 1*, pp. 131 - 163.

Higgott, R., 2000. Contested Globalization: The Changing Context and Normative Challenges. *Cambridge University Press*, pp. 131-153.

Huggins, C., 2010. Shades of Grey: Post-conflict land policy reforn in the Great Lakes Region. In: *The Struggle Over Land in Africa; Conflicts, Politics & Change*. Cape Town: HSRC Press, pp. 37-51.

Hughes, D. T., 1969. Democracy in a Traditional Society: Two Hypotheses on Role. *American Anthropologist, New Series, Vol. 71, No. 1*, pp. 36-45.

Hyden, G., 2006. *Between State and Community; Challenges to Redesigning Governance in Africa.* Indiana, University of Florida, Gainesville, pp. 1-28.

Ianni, V., 2014. New forms of democratic local governance: The case of the Citizen's Committee for Decentralise Cooperation ot the City of Rome. *Field Actions Science Reports (FACTS),* pp. 27-33.

Javelle, A.-G., 2013. *Focus on Land in Africa. Brief: Land Registration in Cameroon.* [Online]
Available at:
http://www.focusonland.com/fola/en/countries/brief-land-registration-in-cameroon/
[Accessed 15 01 2015].

Javelle, A.-G., 2013. *Focus on land in Africa: Brief; Cameroon: Experiences with Transferring Forest Rights.* [Online]
Available at: http://www.focusonland.com/silo/files/cameroon-experiences-with-transferring-forest-rights.pdf
[Accessed 26 03 2015].

Jeffreys, M. D. W., 1957. The Bali of Bamenda. *African studies,* 16(2), pp. 108-113.

Johnson, W. R., 1970. *The Cameroon Federation: Political Integration in a Fragmentary Society.* Princeton: Princeton University Press.

Jua, N. & Konings, P., 2004. Occupation of Public Space Anglophone Nationalism in Cameroon. *Cahiers d'études africaines 175,* pp. 609-633.

Jua, N., 2005. The Mortuary Sphere, Privilege and the Politics of Belonging in Contemporary Cameroon. *Africa 75 (3),* pp. 325-355.

Jua, N., 2011. Contested Meanings: Rulers, Subjects and National Integration in Post-Colonial Cameroon. In: *Regional Balance and National Integration in Cameroon: Lessons Learned and Uncertain Future.* Bamenda: Langaa RPCIG, pp. 99-118.

Kaberry, P. M., 1962. Retainers and Royal Households in the Cameroons Grassfields. *Cahiers d'Études Africaines,* 3(10), pp. 282-298.

Kaberry, P. M., 2004. *Women of the Grassfields; A study of the economic position of women in Bamenda, British Cameroons.* London & New York: Routledge.

Kaberry, P. M. & Chilver, . E. M., 1961. An Outline of the Traditional Political System of Bali-Nyonga, Southern Cameroons. *Africa: Journal of the International African Institute,,* 31(4), pp. 355-371.

Kaiser, K., 2006. *Decentralization Reforms.* [Online] Available at: http://siteresources.worldbank.org/INTPSIA/Resources/490023-1120845825946/3622-06_Ch06.pdf [Accessed 06 11 2010].

Keese, A., 2007. First Lessons in Neo-Colonialism: The Personalisation of Relations between African Politicians and French Officials in sub-Saharan Africa, 1956–66. *The Journal of Imperial and Commonwealth History,* 35(4), p. 593–613.

Konings, P. & Nyamnjoh, F. B., 2003. *Negotiating an Anglophone Identity; A Study of the Politics of Recognition and Representation in Cameroon.* Leiden,: Koninklijke Brill NV.

Konings, P., 2003. Chieftaincy and privatisation in Anglophone. In: *The dynamics of power and the rule of law; Essays on Africa and beyond,in honour of Emile Adriaan B. van Rouveroy van Nieuwaal.* Leiden: LIT Verlag / African Studies Centre,, pp. 79-99.

Konings, P., 2006. 'Bendskin' drivers in Douala's New Bell neighbourhood: Masters of the road and the city. In: *Crisis and Creativity: Exploring the Wealth of the African Neighbourhood.* Leiden: Brill Academic Publishers,, pp. 46-65.

Konings, P., van Dijk, R. & Foeken, D., 2006. The African neighbourhood: An introduction. In: *Crisis and Creativity.* Leiden: Brill Academic Publishers, pp. 1-21.

La Nouvelle, 2013. *Septentrion: Cavaye perd définitivement le Nord.* [Online] Available at: http://www.cameroon-info.net/stories/0,43384,@,septentrion-cavaye-perd-definitivement-le-nord.html [Accessed 12 11 2014].

L'Actu, 2013. *Listes électorales: Le Sous-préfet d'EboIowa II opte pour des inscriptions forcées dans les villages.* [Online] Available at: http://www.cameroon-info.net/stories/0,40206,@,listes-electorales-le-sous-prefet-d-eboiowa-ii-opte-pour-des-inscriptions-forcee.html [Accessed 19 05 2014].

Le Jour, 2013. *Cameroun - Contentieux préélectoral des Municipales: Le Rdpc contre le Rdpc.* [Online]
Available at: http://www.cameroon-info.net/stories/0,50455,@,cameroun-contentieux-preelectoral-des-municipales-le-rdpc-contre-le-rdpc.html
[Accessed 1 11 2014].

Le Messager, 2013. *Cameroun - Contentieux des législatives: Maurice Kamto mis en compétition dans le Mfoundi... Elecam sommé de réhabiliter les listes du MRC dans le cadre des législatives.* [Online]
Available at: http://www.cameroon-info.net/stories/0,50179,@,cameroun-contentieux-des-legislatives-maurice-kamto-mis-en-competition-dans-le-m.html
[Accessed 11 10 2014].

Le Messager, 2013. *Cameroun - Genre et composantes sociologiques: Un casse tête pour les juges de la Cour suprême.* [Online]
Available at: http://www.cameroon-info.net/stories/0,50178,@,cameroun-genre-et-composantes-sociologiques-un-casse-tete-pour-les-juges-de-la-c.html
[Accessed 12 06 2014].

Le Messager, 2013. *Cameroun - Législatives-Municipales 2013: Les yeux doux du gouvernement aux motos-taxis.* [Online]
Available at: http://www.cameroon-info.net/stories/0,50338,@,cameroun-legislatives-municipales-2013-les-yeux-doux-du-gouvernement-aux-motos-t.html
[Accessed 1 11 2014].

Le Messager, 2013. *Cameroun - Mefou et Akono: Le volcan en perpétuelle ébullition crache désormais le feu.* [Online]
Available at: http://www.cameroon-info.net/stories/0,50339,@,cameroun-mefou-et-akono-le-volcan-en-perpetuelle-ebullition-crache-desormais-le-.html
[Accessed 10 05 2014].

Le Messager, 2013. *Cameroun. Investitures: Grégoire Owona fait pleurer une maire Rdpc.* [Online]
Available at:
http://www.cameroonvoice.com/news/news.rcv?id=11690
[Accessed 30 10 2014].

Le Messager, 2013. *Cameroun. Le Rdpc investit un candidat condamné pour vol....* [Online]

Available at:
http://www.cameroonvoice.com/news/news.rcv?id=11931
[Accessed 1 12 2014].

Le Messager, 2013. *Gratuité des CNI…: La grande ruée dans les commissariats de Douala.* [Online]
Available at: http://cameroon-info.net/stories/0,40139,@,gratuite-des-cni-la-grande-ruee-dans-les-commissariats-de-douala.html
[Accessed 12 10 2014].

Le Messager, 2013. *Investiture au Sdf : Les disqualifiés protestent chez Fru Ndi.* [Online]
Available at:
http://www.cameroonvoice.com/news/news.rcv?id=11698
[Accessed 15 07 2014].

Le Messager, 2013. *Législatives et municipales: Des militants du RDPC corrompent pour se faire élire.* [Online]
Available at: http://www.cameroon-info.net/stories/0,52027,@,cameroun-legislatives-et-municipales-des-militants-du-rdpc-corrompent-pour-se-fa.html
[Accessed 15 11 2014].

Le Messager, 2013. *Sénatoriales - Accords politiques: Le deal RDPC-SDF est-il réversible?.* [Online]
Available at: http://www.cameroon-info.net/stories/0,44555,@,senatoriales-accords-politiques-le-deal-rdpc-sdf-est-il-reversible.html
[Accessed 15 01 2015].

Le Vine, V. T., 1964. *The Cameroons from Mandate to Independence.* California: University of California Press.

Luckham, R. & White, G., 1996. Democratisation in the South; Introduction. In: *Democratisation in the South.* Manchester: Manchester University Press, pp. 1-10.

Lund, C., 2008. *Local Politics and the Dynamics of Property in Africa.* Cambridge: Cambridge University Press.

Machiavelli, N., 1515. *The Prince.* Florence: Constitution Society (Translated by W.K. Marriott).

Mamdani, M., 1995. Democratic Theory and Democratic Struggles. In: *Democratisation Process in Africa; Problems and Prospects .* Dakar: CODESRIA, pp. 43-62.

Mamdani, M., 1996. *Citizen and Subject: Contemporary Africa and the Legacy of Late Colonialism.* Princeton: Princeton University Press.

Manor, J., 1995. Democratic Decentralization in Africa and Asia. *IDS Bulletin 26 2,* p. 81–88.

Mawhood, P., 1983. Decentralisation: the concept and practice . In: *Local Government in the Third World; Experience of Decentralisation in Tropical Africa 2nd ed..* Chichester: John Wiley & Sons, pp. 1-23.

Mbah, E. M., 2009. Disruptive colonial boundaries and attempts to resolve land/boundary disputes in the Grasslands of Bamenda, Cameroon. *African Journal on Conflict Resolution Volume 9,* , pp. 11-32.

Mbah, E. M., 2013. Globalisation and Rural Land Conflict in North-West Cameroon:A Historical Perspective. In: *The Political Economy of Development and Underdevelopment in Africa.* New York: Routledge, pp. 74-92.

Mbembe, A., 2001. *On the Postcolony.* Berkeley and Los Angeles: University of California Press.

Mbuagbo, O. T. & Akoko, R. M., 2004. "Motions of Support" and Ethno-Regional Politics in Cameroon. *Journal of Third World Studies, Vol. XXI, No. 1,* pp. 241-258.

Mbuy, T. H., 2011. Assessing the Impact of Tribalism and Regionalism on the Development of Cameroon. In: *Regional Balance and National Integration in Cameroon: Lessons Learned and the Uncertain Future.* Bamenda: Langaa RPCIG, pp. 177-194.

Medad, C., 2010. 'Indigenous' land claims in Kenya: A case study of Chebyuk, Mount Elgon District. In: *The Struggle over land in Africa: Conflicts, Politics & Change.* Cape Town: HSRC Press, pp. 19-36.

Mentan, T., 1998. Cameroon: A Flawed Transition to Democracy. In: *Democratization in Late Twentieth-Century Africa.* Westport: Greenwood Press, pp. 41- 58.

Mentan, T., 2011. The Political Economy of Regional Imbalances and National "Unintegration" In Cameroon. In: *Regional Balance and National Integration in Cameroon: Lessons Learned and Uncertain Future.* Bamenda: Langaa RPCIG, pp. 19-39.

Miakatra, L. S., 2014. Community participation and water supply in deprived areas of Madagascar. *Field Actions Science Reports (FACTS). The Journal of Field Actions, Veolia Institute Paris.,* pp. 75-79.

Ministry of Justice, 2007. *Report by the Ministry of Justice on Human Rights in Cameroon in 2007;,* Yaounde : Ministry of Justice, .

Mishra, P. R., 2014. Citizens Participation in the budget making process of the State of Odisha (India): Opportunities, Learnings And Challenges. *Field Actions Science Reports (FACTS)*, pp. 61-65.

Mkandawire, T., 2013. *Neopatrimonialism and the Political Economy of Economic Performance in Africa: Critical Reflections*, Stockholm: Institutet för Framtidsstudier/Institute for Futures Studies.

Mkandawire, T., 1997. *Crisis management and the making of 'choiceless democracies' in Africa*. Cambridge, MA, s.n., pp. 1-21.

Mkandawire, T. & Soludo, C. C., 1999. *Our Continent Our Future; african perspectives on structural adjustment*. Dakar: CODESRIA.

Monga, C., 1996. *The Anthropology of Anger Civil Society and Democracy in Africa*. Boulder: Lynne Rienner Publishers, Inc..

Mope Simo, J., 2002. Customary Land Tenure Regimes in North Western Cameroon. In: *The Dynamics of Resource Tenure in West Africa*. London: IIED, pp. 37-47.

Mope Simo, J. A., 2011. Land Disputes and the Impact on Disintegration In Contemporary Western Grassfields: Case Study of The Ndop Plain Chiefdoms. In: *Regional Balance and National Integration in Cameroon: Lesson Learned and the Uncertain Future*. Bamenda: Langaa RPCIG, pp. 399-426.

Mope Simo, J. A., 2011. *Land grabbing, governance and social peace-building issues in Cameroon: Case study of the roles of elites in land deals and commoditisation in the North West Region*. Sussex, Land Deals Politics Initiative (LDPI) in collaboration with the Journal of Peasant Studies and hosted by the Future Agricultures Consortium at the Institute of Development Studies, University of Sussex.

Munro, G. & Hart, K., 2000. 'The Highland Problem': State and Community in Local Development. *The Arkleton Centre for Rural Development Research, University of Aberdeen, Aberdeen, Scotland*, pp. 5-43.

Mutations, 2011. *Présidentielle 2011: Paul Biya décrète la gratuité de la carte d'identité*. [Online]
Available at: http://www.cameroon-info.net/stories/0,28752,@,presidentielle-2011-paul-biya-decrete-la-gratuite-de-la-carte-d-identite.html
[Accessed 2 11 2014].

Mwenda, A. M. & Tangri, R., 2005. Patronage Politics, Donor Reforms, and Regime Consolidation in Uganda. *African Affairs 104/416,* pp. 449-467.

Nchari, A. N., Ngaba, E. N. & Amouye, N., 1997. *Community Water Management Experiences in Cameroon,* Delft, The Netherlands: IRC International Water and Sanitation Centre.

Ndedi, A. A., 2008. *In the Name of Demicracy; Dynamics of Elections in Cameroon.* Pretoria: University of Pretoria Printers.

Ndjio, B., 2006. Intimate strangers: Neighbourhood, autochthony and the politics of belonging. In: *Crisis and Creativity: Exploring the Wealth of the African Neighbourhood.* Leiden: Brill Academic Publishers, pp. 66-88.

Njeuma, M. Z. & Awasom, N. F., 1990. The Fulani and the Political Economy of Bamenda Grasslands, 1940-1960. *Paideuma, Bd. 36, Afrika-Studien II ,* pp. 217-233.

Njoh, A. J., 2003. *Planning in Contemporasry Africa; The State town Planning and Society in Cameroon.* Hampshire: Ashgate Publishing Limited.

Njoh, A. J., 2006. *Tradition, Culture and Development in Africa: Historical Lessons for Modern Development Planning.* Hampshire: Ashgate.

Njoh, A. J., 2011. Municipal councils, international NGOs and citizen participation in public infrastructure development in rural settlements in Cameroon. *Habitat International 35,* pp. 101-110.

Nkwi, P. N., 1997. Rethinking the role of elites in rural development: A case study from Cameroon. *Journal of Contemporary African Studies,* , 15(1), pp. 67-86.

Nkwi, P. N. & Nyamnjoh, F. B., 2011. Introduction: Cameroon Regional Balance Policy and National Integration: Food for an Uncertain Future. In: *Regional Balance and National Integration in Cameroon: Lessesons Learned and the Uncertain Future.* Bamenda: Langaa RPCIG, pp. 3-18.

Nkwi, P. N. & Socpa, A., 2011. Ethnicity and Party Politics in Cameroon: The Politics of Divide and Rule. In: *Regional Balance and National Integration in Cameroon: Lessons Learned and the Uncertain Future.* Bamenda: Langaa RPCIG, pp. 247-268.

Nolte, I., 2003. Negotiating party politics and traditional authority: Obafemi Awolowo in Ijebu-Remo, Nigeria, 1949–1955. In: *The dynamics of power and the rule of law: Essays on Africa and beyond, in honour of Emile Adriaan B. van Rouveroy van Nieuwaal.* Leiden: LIT Verlag / African Studies Centre, pp. 51-68.

Nurani, L. M., 2008. Critical Review of Ethnographic Approach. *Jurnal Sosioteknologi Edisi 14 Tahun 7,* , pp. 441-447.

Nyamdi, N. B., 1988. *The Bali Chamba of Cameroon; A Political History.* Paris: Editions Cape.

Nyamnjoh, F. B., 1999. Cameroon: A Country United by Ethnic Ambition and Difference. *African Affairs,* pp. 101-118.

Nyamnjoh, F. B., 2003. Might and right: Chieftaincy and democracy in Cameroon and Botswana. In: *The Dynamics of Power and the rule of law; Essays on Africa and beyond, in honour of Emile Adriaan B. van Rouveroy van Nieuwaal.* Leiden: LIT Verlag / African Studies Centre,, pp. 121-149.

Nyamnjoh, F. & Rowlands, M., 1988. Elite Associations and the Politics of Belonging in Cameroon. *Africa 68 (3),* pp. 320-337.

Nyang'oro, J. E., 1992. The Evolving Role of the African State Under Structural Adjustment. In: *Beyond Structural Adjustment in Africa: The Political Economy of Sustainable and Democratic Development.* New York: Praeger Publishers, pp. 12-27.

Nyang'oro, J. E. & Shaw, T. M., 1992. Introduction: African Development in the New International Division of Labour. In: *Beyond Structural Adjustment in Africa: The Political Economy of Sustainable and Democratic Development.* New York: Praeger Publishers, pp. 1-9.

ODI, 1995. *Structural Adjustment and Sustainable Development in Cameroon. Working Paper 83.,* London: Overseas Development Institute,.

Olivier de Sardan, J.-P., 2005. *Anthropology and Development: Understanding Contemporary Social Science.* London & New York: Zed Books.

Olowu, D., 2003. African Governance and Civil Service Reforms. In: *Beyond Structural Adjustment: The Institutional Context of African Development.* New York: Pelgrave Macmillan, pp. 101-130.

Ottaway, M., 1997. From Political Opening to Democratization . In: *Democracy in Africa: The Hard Road Ahead.* Boulder: Lynne Rienner Publishers Inc., pp. 1-13.

Oyono, P. R., Kouna, C. & Mala, W., 2005. Benefits of forests in Cameroon. Global structure, issues involving access and decision-making hiccoughs. *Forest Policy and Economics 7,* p. 357– 368.

Page, B., Evans, M. & Mercer, C., 2010. Revisiting the politics of belonging in Cameroon. *Africa 80 (3),* , pp. 345-370.

Page, B., 2002. *"Accumulation by dispossession: communities and water privatisation in Cameroon".* Oxford, PRINWASS, pp. 1-23.

Page, B., 2002. Urban Agriculture in Cameroon: an anti-politics machine in the making?. *Geoforum Vol 33,* pp. 41-54.

Page, B., 2003. Communities as the agents of commodification: The Kumbo Water Authority in Northwest Cameroon. *Geoforum ,* Volume 34, p. 483–498.

Palmer, C., 2001. Ethnography: A Research Method in Practice. *International Journal of Tourism Research.,* Volume 3, pp. 301-312.

Pellini, A., 2007. *Decentralisation Policy in Cambodia,* Tampere: Tampere University.

PNDP, 2009. *Second Phase of the PNDP,* Yaounde: PNDP National Coordination Unit.

PNDP, 2010. *Rappel sur le PNDP I et l'Orientation du du PNDP II,* Ngaoundere: Unpublished.

PRC, 2013. *President Paul BIYA calls on youths to uphold moral standards.* [Online]
Available at: https://www.prc.cm/en/news/speeches-of-the-president/17-president-paul-biya-calls-on-youths-to-uphold-moral-standards
[Accessed 21 11 2014].

Rambousek, W. H., 1982. Regional Planning in Cameroon: The Case of Planning without Facts. *Geoforum, Vol. 13, No.2,,* pp. 163-175.

RDPC-CPDM, 2013. *Circulaire N°03 /RDPC/PN DU 05 Juillet 2013..* [Online]
Available at: http://www.rdpcpdm.cm/en/content/circulaire-n%C2%B003-rdpcpn-du05-juillet-2013-le-pr%C3%A9sident-national
[Accessed 11 11 2014].

RDPC-CPDM, 2013. *Elections Législatives et Municipales du 30 Septembre 2013. Investiture des candidats du RDPC. Commissions Régionales de Supervision. Yaoundé, le 7 Juillet 2013.* [Online]
Available at: http://www.rdpcpdm.cm/content/elections-l%C3%A9gislatives-et-municipales-du-30-septembre-2013
[Accessed 11 11 2014].

RDPC-CPDM, 2013. *Note n° 0039/RDPC/SG/CAB du 1er août 2013.*.
[Online]
Available at:
http://www.rdpcpdm.cm/en/content/communiqu%C3%A9-de-presse-2
[Accessed 14 10 2014].

Renou, X., 2002. A New French Policy for Africa?. *Journal of Contemporary African Studies,* 20(1), pp. 5-27.

Ribot, J. C., 2003. Democratic Decentralization of Natural Resources: Institutional Choice and Discretionary Power Transfers in Sub-Saharan Africa. In: *Beyond Structural Adjustment: The Institutional Context of African development.* New York: Pelgrave Macmillan, pp. 159-182.

Ribot, J. C. & Oyono, P. R., 2005. The Politics of Decentralisation. In: *Towards a New Map of Africa.* London: Cromwell Press, pp. 205-216.

Robinson, M., 1996. Economic Reforms and the Transition to Democracy. In: *Democratisation in the South; a Jagged Wave.* Manchester: Manchester University Press, pp. 69-118.

Rodney, W., 1982. *How Europe Underdeveloped Africa.* Washington DC: Howard University Press.

Rodrik, D., 2006. 'Goodbye Washington Consensus, Hello Washington Confusion?'. *Journal of Economic Literature ,* pp. 339-352.

Rowlands, M. & Warnier, J.-P., 1988. Sorcery, Power and the Modern State in Cameroon. *Man, New Series, Vol. 23, No. 1,* pp. 118-132.

Rowlands, M. J., 1979. Local and Long distance trade and incipient state formation on the Bamenda Plateau in the late 19th Century. *Paideuma,Bd. 25,* pp. 1-19.

Rubin, N., 1971. *Cameroun: An African Federation.* London: Pall Mall Press.

Rubin, N. N., 1970 . Matrimonial Law among the Bali of West Cameroon: A Restatement. *Journal of African Law,* 14(2), pp. 69-97.

Sardar, A., Hakobyan, L., Tayyar, N. & Davtyan, T., 2014. Smart Policy Making: Citizens' Voice, Sustainable Choice. *Field Actions Science Reports (FACTS),* pp. 35-42.

Schilder, K., 2011. Regional Imbalance in Northern Cameroon. In: *Regional Balance and National Integration in Cameroon: Lessons Learned and the Uncertain Future.* Bamenda: Langaa RPCIG, pp. 319-345.

Schneider, M., 2008. *"We are Hungry!" A Summary Report of Food Riots, Government Responses, and States of Democracy in 2008*, Ithaca: Mindi Schneider.

Scott, J. C., 1998. *Seeing Like a State; How Certain Schemes to Improve Human Condition Have Failed*. New Haven and London: Yale University Press.

Sen, A., 1999. *Development as Freedom*. Oxford: Oxford University Press.

Sharp, J. S. & Spiegel, A. D., 1985. Vulnerability to Impoverishment in South African Rural Areas: The Erosion of Kinship and Neighbourhood as Social Resources. *Africa: Journal of the International African Institute*, 55(2), pp. 133-152.

Shaw, T. M., 1992. Revisionism in African Political Economy in the 1990s. In: *Beyond Structural Adjustment in Africa: The Political Economy of Sustainable and Democratic Development*. New York: Praeger Publishers, pp. 49-70.

Sithole, M. P., 2009. State Democracy Warming up to Culture: An Ambivalent Integration of Traditional Leadership into the South African Governance System 1994-2009. In: *South African Governance in Review. Anti-corruption, Local Government, Traditional Leadership*. Cape Town: HSRC Press, pp. 39-51.

Skalník, P., 2003. Nanumba versus Konkomba: An assessment of a troubled coexistence. In: *The dynamics of power and the rule of law: Essays on Africa and beyond, in honour of Emile Adriaan B. van Rouveroy van Nieuwaal*. Leiden: LIT Verlag / African Studies Centre, Leiden, pp. 69-78.

Songwe, O., 2011. At Arm's Length. *BBC, Focus on Africa Magazine; January- March 2011; Volume 22, No 1*, 30 01, pp. 14-15.

Southall, R., 2003. *Democracy in Africa: Moving Beyond a Difficult Legacy*. Cape Town: HSRC Publishers .

Ssebunya, A. K., 2014. Why local realities matter for Citizens' Voice and Accountability. Lessons from Mwananchi Uganda pilot projects. *Field Actions Science Reports (FACTS)*, pp. 89-95.

Stein, H., 2008. *Beyond the World Bank Agenda; An Institutional Approach to Development*. Chicago: The University of Chicago Press.

Suret-Canale, J., 1971. *French Colonialism in Tropical Africa 1900-1945*. London: Billing & Sons Limited.

Suryani, A., 2008. Comparing Case Study and Ethnography as Qualitative Research Approaches. *Jurnal Ilmu Komunikasi*, 5(1), pp. 117-127.

Takougang, J. & Krieger, M., 1998. *African State and Society in the 1990s; Cameroon's Political Crossroads*. Oxford: WestviewPress.

Taylor, M., 2010. Community Participation. In: *The Human Economy*. Cambridge: Polity Press, pp. 236-247.

The New York Times, 2008. *Anti-government rioting spreads in Cameroon*. [Online]
Available at:
http://www.nytimes.com/2008/02/27/world/africa/27iht-27cameroon.10504780.html?_r=2&
[Accessed 10 10 2014].

The World Bank, 1989. *Memorandum and Recommendation of the President of the International Bank for Reconstruction and Development to the executive directors on a on a proposed loan of USD $ 150 million equivalent to the Republic of Cameroon for a Structural Adjustment Program*, Washington DC: The World Bank.

The World Bank, 1989. *Sub-Saharan Africa: From Crisis to Sustainable Growth. A Long-term Perspective Study*. Washington, DC: The World Bank.

Torri, M. C. & Herrmann, T. M., 2011. *Bridges Between Tradition and Innovation in Ethnomedicine: Fostering Local Development Through Community Based Enterprises - in India*. London, New York: Springer Dordrecht Heidelberg.

UNDP, 1993. *Human Development Report 1993*, New York, Oxford: Oxford University Press.

van de Walle, N., 1989. Rice Politics in Cameroon: State Commitment, Capability, and Urban Bias. *The Journal of Modern African Studies, Vol. 27, No. 4*, pp. 579-599.

van de Walle, N., 1997. Economic Reform and the Consolidation of Democracy in Africa. In: *Democracy in Africa: The Hard Road Ahead*. Boulder: Lynne Rienner Publishers, Inc., pp. 14-37.

van de Walle, N., 2003. Introduction: The State and African Development. In: *Beyond Structural Adjustment: The Institutional Context of African Development*. New York: Pelgrave Macmillan, pp. 1-33.

Vubo, E. Y. & Ngwa, G. . A., 2001. Changing Intercommunity Relations and the Politics of Identity in the Northern Mezam Area, Cameroon. *Cahiers d'Études Africaines,* 41(161), pp. 163-190.

Wantchekon, L., 399–422. Clientilism and Voting Behaviour Evidence from a Field Experiment in Benin. *World Politics 55,* p. 2003 .

Ward, A. & Alden, C., 2010. Introduction: The struggle over land in Africa: Conflicts, politics and change. In: *The struggle over land in Africa: Conflicts, politics and change.* Capetown: HSRC Press, pp. 1-15.

Warnier, J.-P., 1993. The King as a Container in the Cameroon Grassfields. *Paideuma, Bd. 39 ,* pp. 303-319.

Warnier, J. P., 1980. Trade Guns in the Grassfields of Cameroon. *Paideuma, ,* Bd(26), pp. 79-92.

White, G., 1996. Civil Society, Democratisation and Development. In: *Democratisation in the South; a Jagged Wave.* Manchester: Manchester University Press, pp. 178-219.

Whitehead, T. L., 2004. What is Ethnography? Methodological, Ontological, and Epistemological Attributes. *The Cultural Systems Analysis Group (CuSAG) Department of Anthropology University of Maryland,* pp. 1-29.

Whitehead, T. L., 2005. Basic Classical Ethnographic Research Methods. *The Cultural Systems Analysis Group (CuSAG) Department of Anthropology University of Maryland,* pp. 1-28.

Wiseman, J. A., 1996. *The New Struggle for Democracy in Africa.* Aldershot Hants: Ashgate Publishing Limited.

Wong, S. & Guggenheim, S., 2005. Community-Driven Development: Decentralization's Accountability Challenge. In: *East Asia Decentralises: Making Local Government Work.* Washington DC: The World Bank, pp. 253-267.

Young, C., 1982. *Ideology and Development in Africa.* New Haven: Yale University Press,.

Young, T., 1993. Elections and Electoral Politics in Africa. *Africa Vol 63 No 3, ,* pp. 229-212.

www.ingramcontent.com/pod-product-compliance
Lightning Source LLC
Chambersburg PA
CBHW060030030426
42334CB00019B/2254